Advance Praise for *Value Leadership: Winning Competitive Advantage in the Information Age* **by Michael C. Harris**

Harris has crammed a lifetime of thought and research on the subjects of quality and leadership into one incredible volume. His treatment of metrics and measurements is the most complete and practical I have encountered.
   —Jack Zenger
      Retired Chairman of the Times Mirror Training Group
      Co-founder of Zenger Miller

Michael Harris has done a masterful job of linking today's and tomorrow's key business issues of leadership, value creation, the voice of the customer, and strategic planning into a comprehensive and usable model. His advocacy of a "control panel" approach to aligning a business, vertically and horizontally, to the customer is a new contribution to organizational pursuit of service quality.
   —Wayne C. Shannon
      Vice President, Quality Service Culture
      Dobbs International Services

Value Leadership can give managers and professionals, at any level, the "how-to" create significant customer value through leadership. Top managers can find out what they must do to create value and then send the book down to middle- and front-line managers as the book explains in easy terms, with plenty of examples, how to actually do it! If you never really understood "value" and how it makes products, services, and organizations world-class competitors—this book is for you.
   —Charles A. Aubrey, II
      Vice President
      Juran Institute

Value Leadership is a success oriented road map for leaders at all levels to achieve market prosperity as the velocity of information, communication, and business dynamics grows at an unparalleled rate. The book is a practical guide to the leadership changes required by the ongoing geometric growth in technology and its impact on our organizations and their ability to deliver value in both service and manufacturing. The emphasis on prioritizing what you measure is alone worth the read.
   —Joe Parkinson
      Chairman and CEO
      8×8, Inc.

I am particularly impressed by the depth and clarity of thought demonstrated throughout this work, and by how well these thoughts are turned into a step-by-step approach to the creation and execution of a winning formula. This book should be required reading for every executive concerned about winning through value.

—John P. Indrigo
Senior Vice President and General Manager
AMSC, Inc.

If you're serious about leading your organization into the Information Age, I strongly recommend that you read and heed *Value Leadership*. Mike Harris' writing style is user-friendly—his summarization of each chapter will service as a great reference.

—Peggy Jennings
Vice President
American Supplier Institute

Michael Harris presents an effective way to develop, implement, and maintain an organization to properly respond to economics and business shifts as the society makes the tough transition into the Information Age. The processes are thorough and user-friendly; they go to the heart of the organization.

—Spencer Hutchens, Jr.
President
Intertek Testing Services—Technical Services Division

With the almost infinite availability of information today, consumers are fully equipped to discern true value and value that will be king in the "Age of the Consumer." Michael Harris provides a practical roadmap for leaders in pursuit of value creation.

—Rob Davis
Senior Vice President & Chief Quality Officer
NCR

Value
Leadership

Winning Competitive Advantage
in the Information Age

Also available from ASQ Quality Press

A Review of Managing Quality and Primer for the Certified Quality Manager Exam
Thomas J. Cartin and Donald J. Jacoby

Goldratt's Theory of Constraints: A Systems Approach to Continuous Improvement
H. William Dettmer

Insights to Performance Excellence 1997: An Inside Look at the 1997 Baldrige Award Criteria
Mark L. Blazey

Leading the Way to Competitive Excellence: The Harris Mountaintop Case Study
William A. Levinson, editor

Understanding and Applying Value-Added Assessment: Eliminating Business Process Waste
William E. Trischler

Quality Quotes
Hélio Gomes

The Reward and Recognition Process in Total Quality Management
Stephen B. Knouse

Staffing the New Workplace: Selecting and Promoting for Quality Improvement
Ronald B. Morgan and Jack E. Smith

The Change Agents' Handbook: A Survival Guide for Quality Improvement Champions
David W. Hutton

Let's Work Smarter, Not Harder: How to Engage Your Entire Organization in the Execution of Change
Michael Caravatta

To request a complimentary catalog of ASQ Quality Press publications, call 800–248–1946.

Value Leadership

Winning Competitive Advantage in the Information Age

Michael C. Harris

ASQ Quality Press
Milwaukee, Wisconsin

Value Leadership: Winning Competitive Advantage in the Information Age
Michael Harris

Library of Congress Cataloging-in-Publication Data
Harris, Michael C., 1946–
   Value leadership : winning competitive advantage in the
information age / Michael C. Harris.
      p.   cm.
   Includes bibliographical references and index.
   ISBN 0-87389-378-6 (alk. paper)
   1. Information technology—Management.   2. Leadership.   I. Title.
HD30.2.H373   1998
658.4'038—dc21   97–27663
                                                                        CIP

Trademark Acknowledgment
"Post-it" is a trademark of the 3M Corporation.

10 9 8 7 6 5 4 3 2 1

ISBN 0-87389-378-6

Acquisitions Editor: Roger Holloway
Project Editor: Jeanne W. Bohn

ASQ Mission: To facilitate continuous improvement and increase customer satisfaction by identifying, communicating, and promoting the use of quality principles, concepts, and technologies; and thereby be recognized throughout the world as the leading authority on, and champion for, quality.

Attention: Schools and Corporations
ASQ Quality Press books, audiotapes, videotapes, and software are available at quantity discounts with bulk purchases for business, educational, or instructional use. For information, please contact ASQ Quality Press at 800-248-1946, or write to ASQ Quality Press, P.O. Box 3005, Milwaukee, WI 53201-3005.

For a free copy of the ASQ Quality Press Publications Catalog, including ASQ membership information, call 800-248-1946.

Printed in the United States of America

          Printed on acid-free paper

American Society for Quality

Quality Press
611 East Wisconsin Avenue
Milwaukee, Wisconsin 53202

Contents

Preface   *xiii*

Acknowledgments   *xxvii*

Chapter 1 INTEGRATED LEADERSHIP   1

High Value in the Information Age   2

The Driving Principles of Integrated Leadership   4

The Remaining Principles of Integrated Leadership   6

Expanding Role of Information   11

Value—The Key Metric   14

A Monumental Transition   17

Supporting Concepts of Integrated Leadership   19

Creating a New Vision   24

Key Points   24

Notes   25

Chapter 2 FOUNDATION PLANNING AND ORGANIZATIONAL ALIGNMENT   27

The Case for Foundation Planning   28

The Foundation and the Vision   28

Harley-Davidson—An Integrated Foundation   35

The Planning Process   35

Planning/Deployment Model   39

Vertical Alignment   41

Control Panel   44

The Challenges of the Leader   48

Key Points   49

Notes   50

Chapter 3 UNDERSTANDING CUSTOMERS   53

Creating Customer Delight   53

Customers as Partners   54

The Little Things Add Up   55

Working with the Value Formula   57

Expectation and Performance   64

Voice of the Customer/Quality Function
Deployment   68

Four Powerful Customer/Competitive Metrics   69

The Challenge   75

Key Points   75

Notes   76

Chapter 4 VALUE-ADDED PROCESS ALIGNMENT   79

Horizontal Alignment   79

Value-Added Process—The Means of Alignment   80

Customers—The Target of Alignment   82

The Customer Chain—The Linkage   83

Customer Requirements—The Metrics   88

Critical Process Specifications   93

Two Views of an Organization   94

Establishing and Tracking Performance to Meet
Customer Requirements   102

Key Points   109

Notes   110

Chapter 5 VALUE MANAGEMENT   111

Traditional Approaches to Cost   112

The Costs of Ineffectiveness and Inefficiency   115

Managing Effectiveness   117

*The Cost of Inefficiency—Two Supplemental Costing
Methods   118*

Identifying High COQ Opportunities   123

*Confirming Opportunities—A Short Primer
on Assessing the Cost of Quality   127*

Being the Low-Cost Provider   128

Highlighting Cost Metrics on the Control Panel   130

Key Points   133

Notes   133

Chapter 6 CONTINUOUS VALUE IMPROVEMENT   135

Improvement 101   136

The Foundation of Improvement Tools   139

Improvement—The Advanced Course   141

*Some Control Panel Indicators Identifying Improvement
Opportunities   145*

Won–Lost Reports   145

The Future   156

Key Points   157

Notes   158

Chapter 7 RESULTS THROUGH WORKING TOGETHER   159

*Scientific Management—The Basis
of the Industrial Age   160*

*Leadership and Teamwork—The Basis
of the Information Age   163*

Beyond Teams   169

Control Panel Application   172

Key Points   174

Notes   175

Chapter 8 YOU GET WHAT YOU MEASURE   177

The Performance Review System   178

Jobs   183

Jobs in Transition   190

The Search for Objective Measures   190

Job Metrics   191

Training   193

Connecting Control Panels   194

Key Points   195

Notes   196

Chapter 9 CONTROL PANEL THROUGH INTEGRATING METRICS   197

The Big Question Is What   198

The Basis of Current Control Panels   198

Moving Toward Tomorrow's Control Panel   199

A Few Examples of Changing Control Panels   200

Control Panel Concepts   208

Control Panel Issues   212

Using the Control Panel   214

A Perspective on Control Panels and Integrated Leadership   221

Key Points   222

Notes   223

Chapter 10 THE FUTURE 225

Perfect, Reusable, and Evolving Processes 226
The Essentials 228
The Transformation 230
The Cost of Nonadherence 230
A Journey of Value 231
Return to Taylor's Mental Revolution 232
Greater Understanding by the Individual
in the Information Age 234
The Individual Reacts 235
Key Points 236
Notes 237

Appendix A USING THE HOUSE OF QUALITY FOR CONTROL PANEL INFORMATION 239

Appendix B CURRENT ASSESSMENT TOOL, QUALITATIVE 247

Appendix C LESSONS FROM AUSTRALIA 255

Appendix D STUDYING LEADERSHIP 261

Bibliography 265
Index 269

Preface

HOW THIS BOOK WILL HELP YOU

This book is written for tomorrow's leaders; people who will make an impact on our organizations, institutions, and society and those who will help lead the tough transition into the Information Age. This includes anyone in a leadership position today, anyone who desires to be a leader in the future, and anyone who wants to make a positive difference by elevating themselves and others.

This book is about the leadership and systems required to produce and deliver high value in the twenty-first century. Almost everything a living creature does somehow relates to value. From the most basic need of survival to the extremes of self-actualization, the human being bases most decisions on value. It is the cost/benefit analysis that we continuously apply throughout our lives. The higher the benefit in relation to the cost, the higher the value. The study of value, then, is the study of the human species. This makes it fun, exciting, and mysterious.

The more we understand how others use value to make choices the more we can provide the products and services that they will demand. By adding value to others, we enrich both ourselves and our organizations.

The value of this book is immense; its price is small compared to the time and effort it takes you to acquire it and absorb its messages. In return for investing your two most valuable resources, your time and your mind, you receive a priceless treasure that will help you leave the lower value characteristics of the Industrial Age to gain the wealth creating potential of the Information Age. If you believe you are already there—*do not stop reading*—you may be in danger. If you want to assure you have the necessary knowledge, this book is for you. If you are not sure, there are assessment tools in the book that will help you. Even if you think you do not have to change or that you are already years ahead of your competition, you definitely want to see more of what the future holds and what you will be competing against.

The only good reason for not pursuing information on how value will be created in the Information Age is if you really do not care. If that is the case, you would not have read this far.

The format of the book is designed to accommodate your reading style. Some prefer to read a book from cover to cover; others primarily look for salient points that help fill in gaps in their current requirements. The person who wants to skim, find key places, and then delve into the material will be right at home, since each chapter has a bullet-point summary and is structured to easily jump in at any point. The person who reads everything in order will find a logical sequence but may see a little redundancy that helps the reader who jumps around. However, the thorough reader will appreciate this, as it both highlights the most important points and acts as a reinforcement later.

THE SEARCH

An Intriguing Question

Almost a decade and a half ago, retired Admiral Frank Collins[2] was scheduled to give a presentation for the management personnel of a large division of a major corporation. At the time, the author was the division's manager of strategic planning and we were in the middle of implementing some radical and profound plans. We had just been "reengineered" and "downsized" with the help of a large consulting firm.

One of the corporation's manufacturing divisions had recently experienced some problems in delivering acceptable products to the military. Since Admiral Collins had overseen the purchasing function of the Navy and had been a zealot in his pursuit of quality, he was hired to help.

In addition to strategic planning and activity value analysis, the corporation was also experiencing another popular phenomenon of that era, a hostile takeover attempt. The last thing the financial services division needed was a manufacturing quality guru coming around preaching Japanese theories, the cost of scrap and rework, and zero defects.

The meeting began promptly at 0800, as one would expect from an admiral. At the front and center of the room was a flipchart with the following question:

> How come we never have time to do things right the first time, but we always find time to fix them later on?
> —The Old Work Brigade

Figure P.1   Admiral Collins poses an intriguing question.

The question was fascinating. It must have an answer. No one in the room had an adequate response. The best answers provided were: "That's the way things are and have always been"; "It doesn't apply here"; "It's all part of the cost of business, and we pass those on to customers"; and "An admiral, or anyone from manufacturing, doesn't understand our business anyway."

The remarkable truth was that everyone present had the same dilemma as the old work brigade. Denial seemed to be a more pleasant answer than considering the alternatives.

It was not the futility of an answer that was so noticeable, but the fact that only a few really seemed to be concerned with the question. One might think there would have some cause for concern, since the reengineering, the hostile takeover, and the fact that the admiral's question could not be answered just might be related.

THE SEARCH BEGINS

A few months later, as I moved into the role of Chief Quality Officer (CQO), I began the pursuit of a solution to the admiral's question. To take some of the bite out of the phraseology, it was reworded to a proactive search for methods to "Do the right things right the first time every time." Yesterday's locomotive or today's airliner is a complex system, particularly if measured by the technology and knowledge level of the time it was created. However, both are miserably inadequate to carry passengers to a distant planet and return them safely. The leadership and organization models used for the past hundred years are just as inadequate to compete in the global markets of the future.

Most people in organizations today face the same dilemma as those in the old work brigade. They do not operate anywhere near an optimum level. The largest barrier is the incapability of their work processes to deliver value that is anywhere close to optimum.

What is lacking most is a linked approach to help define and achieve the chief purpose of the organization. In many cases, the majority of employees or members do not know the long-term purpose or goals of the organization. Additionally, many leaders do not know how to adequately harmonize processes, and very few have a system of metrics that allows a proactive instead of a more common reactive approach.

THE WINDS OF CHANGE

We are in transition from the Industrial Age to the Information Age.[3] Probably the most visible and profound sign is the massive global political upheaval that culminated with the fall of communism in the former Soviet Union. The changes seem to be characteristic of a pendulum that swings from some form of chaos, inward to a degree of order, and back to chaos again.

However, political change is driven by institutions that are, in turn, modified by the influence of smaller organizations, which is affected by desires and interaction of individuals. Thus, the global shift is the cumulative effect of a number of intense changes at the individual and small organizational level.

Although the change has been fueled by technology, it is not the driver. The driver is information, or more appropriately, the speed in the distribution and understanding of networked information.

The tremendous acceleration in the flow of information is the genesis of the new age. We have seen glimpses of the power of breakthrough global connectivity, but we have not yet arrived. We are still carrying too much baggage from the past, and we have not harnessed the force of connected information availability on a global basis.

The transition to the Information Age has huge implications on the relationship between individuals and organizations. One of the more emotional changes is the diminishment of the traditional career. This creates upheaval for both employees and management. One of the major issues that must be resolved is a carryover from the Industrial Age—the entitlements associated with improved organizational performance.

One term that fuels the emotion is *outsourcing*. Management sometimes optimistically views outsourcing as a better means to control costs by using a *just in time* approach to labor, while employees look at it as a threat to security and jobs. The truth probably lies somewhere in between. In free and competitive markets, the measurement of the value of labor and the value of creativity will be readily available to both management and labor. The economic principles of supply and demand will determine their market prices. Then, it will matter little how they are packaged and distributed. Some employers may be willing to pay more for predictability and stability and others may prefer to pay premiums during shortages of labor supply and less during more labor-abundance periods. In the longer run, the more efficient and effective methods will prevail. The same laws govern the panic associated with hostile takeovers, downsizing, reengineering, and general layoffs.

The universal law that determines return on investment is the value that it ultimately adds in the market. This is true of investment in one's self, in capital or in an idea. As the Information Age matures, the entrepreneur will continually emerge and drive most people to be more concerned with how they can add value instead of with what they can eke out of a system. Once information is more readily available on how value is added and the return it provides, many of the issues that evoke high emotions today will disappear.

SOME IMPORTANT CHARACTERISTICS OF THE INFORMATION AGE

Following are some emerging trends that will likely occur as the Information Age unfolds.

- The Information Age will radically change the structure of both private and public organizations as knowledge joins capital as a primary source of value. This movement will be global in scope.
- Individuals and organizations will increasingly gain access to the information and knowledge necessary to understand the measurement of value delivered in the goods and services they need and desire. This information will be available by provider.
- As the level of information and knowledge increases, competitive factors will demand that organizations be more efficient and effective. This will help drive out waste, rework, duplication, and unnecessary activity.
- Through greater understanding, the customer will become part of the value-adding process and will gain tremendous power. This power will place the customer more in a partnership role with providers so both parties are motivated to achieve high value added.
- As customers become more enlightened through their understanding of value creation, they will demand reform of the basic institutions that either increase value or stifle it. The most powerful reform may be in the political process itself and may demand a combined vision for the future.
- These trends, combined with organizational and institutional resistance to change and the huge opportunities created, will lead to a flourishing of entrepreneurs. Entrepreneurial associations and strategic partnerships may replace many large organizations and institutions in the delivery of value to society.
- The strongest driver of value is education, which is the fuel of the knowledge and creativity required in the Information Age. The focus on education will parallel a shift of fundamental values.
- As information becomes the primary creator of value in the global economy, tens of millions of employees will move from low value-added jobs to higher value-producing jobs. Great opportunity will be abundant, as unheralded value is created from information.

WHAT THIS BOOK IS ABOUT

In many respects this book pursues a methodology to not only help the old work brigade develop and perform its mission better than any other work brigade on the planet, but to assure that it continues that position into the twenty-first century by mastering the awesome changes of the Information Age.

Its bedrock principle is that *value is quickly becoming the most important measure of success in organizations*. This applies to organizations in all sectors of society. It is also built on the premise that most organizations do not primarily focus on value or that they are relatively inefficient and ineffective in its delivery. Those organizations that find better ways to deliver value in the short term will gain tremendous long-term advantage over those who delay the pursuit. Those who wait may be doomed.

The common themes in the book revolve around the concepts of value, leadership, integration, metrics, and control panel. *Value* is what customers receive, and high value should be the focus of every organization. The other elements are paramount in understanding, producing, and delivering high value.

MEETING THE CHALLENGE

As the characteristics of the Information Age unfold, organizations must adjust to be competitive and survive. Their major strategies should include the following:

- Since the Information Age will provide the customer with essentially unlimited choice through massive customization, high involvement and tremendous knowledge of the value of goods and services, organizations must have superior market information and knowledge.
- Organizations must understand their mission or role in the global production and servicing of value and set a vision or target of what they will accomplish. They must then design and build the organization that will accomplish the mission by continually aligning with its vision and with changing customer requirements.
- Organizations must fully understand their customers' current and future needs and requirements and the competitive forces that they encounter in the market. Organizations' understanding of customers must include the total use and support of the product and its services. Competitors' understanding must include their ability and strategy to meet or exceed customer requirements at the root need level and their delivery of value at every aspect of the current and potential use of goods and services.
- Organizations will need strategic alliances and partnerships with suppliers, customers, and, perhaps, even competitors to provide the value most markets will demand.
- The key to success is *integrated leadership*. This requires that the organization is led with a holistic approach that focuses on the interdependence of its communication and control processes. The organization must be maximized as a producer of value through the interconnectedness of its pieces. There is no room for waste.
- Integrated leadership is assured through
  ⇒ the selection and continuous development of sound leaders.
  ⇒ the selection and continuous development of competent employees.

⇒ the optimal use of teams and teamwork.
⇒ the use of continuous improvement principles applied to achieve maximization of value delivered.
⇒ effective use of metrics.
• The chief tool of integrated leadership is a *control panel* designed to understand and coordinate internal and external movement with successful results throughout the organization.

VALUE

Competitiveness exists among all organizations. In the past, the primary target of competition was physical resources; in the future, it will be information and the value that it adds. As value becomes better understood through advanced metrics, it becomes the focus of an organization and assumes its proper perspective as the leading indicator of financial performance. Today's profits are a result of yesterday's value and tomorrow's profits are driven by the value that is currently being delivered to customers.

Value is the perceived or calculated worth of a product, service, concept, or idea at a point in time. It is the reason people buy. They base their decision on what they believe they will receive in exchange for what they pay or forgo. Often value is very personal and cannot be explained with normative logic. One person's treasure is another person's junk, as the saying goes. On other occasions, value is predictable, logical, and almost linear. Superior value is achieved by being in the right place at the right time with the right solution at the right price. This is not accomplished by blind luck; it is the result of processes that are specifically designed to fulfill that end.

Value can be expressed mathematically as a benefit divided by the acquisition cost, making it the reciprocal of cost/benefit analysis. It can be used to measure the output of a process or combination of processes and can be determined for any state or form, whether tangible or intangible. Value can be added to or subtracted from any condition to provide something of either superior or inferior value. For example, a pizza has a particular value. However, its value will be influenced by its temperature, taste, availability, freshness, and other variables.

A cost/benefit analysis is a frequently used decision making tool to appraise the acquisition of major purchases, the undertaking of a project, or the viability of one option over others. Since value is the reciprocal of cost/benefit, it provides an ongoing methodology of assessment utilizing a quantifiable and proven means. Value also provides a comprehensive model by including the elements of quality, perception, inconvenience, and cost.

LEADERSHIP

The vast majority of today's leaders use Industrial Age methods to oversee their work force. Frederick Taylor's scientific management, which was formulated shortly after the beginning of the twentieth century, still permeates much of management theory and style.[4] The Industrial Age is driven by production costs and quotas; the Information Age is driven by high value-added solutions that meet and exceed customer requirements and needs. Simply stated, the past was producer driven; the future will be customer driven.

Leadership is the most basic ingredient of any successful organization or pursuit; however, it is woefully underdeveloped and underpracticed in most organizations. The human dynamics of leadership have been understood for centuries, while their application and supporting tools have continued to evolve.

The magnitude of the transformation from the Industrial Age to the Information Age will soon overwhelm the change from the Agrarian Age to the Industrial Age. Our leadership model must change. The new model must contain *continuous planning and organizational alignment*, both internally and externally. It must comprehensively *understand changing markets, customers, and competitive forces*. The new model must be capable of *continuous improvement in ever-decreasing cycle times* in the design, engineering, and operation of *critical and supporting processes*. Integrated leadership will also build and continually improve the *interconnected metrics and information systems* that support and link all internal and external aspects of the organization.

INTEGRATION

From an organizational standpoint, integration is shown by all the pieces working together effectively and efficiently to produce a desired result. Even the smallest organizations have problems with integration; marriages often falter, partnerships disintegrate, and businesses fail.

We now understand how some tremendously complex systems function and we can used this information to help unite our larger organizations. This knowledge is continually evolving and will help us move forward in the Information Age. For example, we can look to biology to provide one model for complex integration.

The human body contains billions of neurons that function as receptors, sensors, or relays that communicate with other neurons to process data to help us make decisions, either consciously or subconsciously. Today, we have the electronic hardware that can process more than 1,000 billion calculations in a single second. We are technically on the edge of being able to process the vast amount of information necessary to integrate our larger organizations to an unimaginable degree. An important question is, "How do we design, build, and integrate the *human and support systems* to be able to effectively utilize unprecedented amounts and speed of information?"

In addition to higher understanding of effective integration of single organizations, we have discovered methodologies to connect increasing numbers of diverse organizations. This ability probably began as primitive tribes formed alliances and later merged into nations. Today, we are connected through mass transportation systems, we launch space exploration missions, and we have fought global wars. These endeavors require enormous coordination and cooperation.

However, in spite of knowledge and understanding, most organizations are neither effectively nor efficiently integrated. This is primarily caused by the manner in which we structure organizations. We build most organizations on a hierarchical basis, where collective information flows to a centralized point where decisions are made and instructions flow back to various components of the organization for execution. There are two drawbacks to this approach. First, by routing excessive amounts of data and information to centralized points, much of it is inefficiently distributed. Second, it is a poor method for most decision making, for the reasons discussed next.

A hierarchical system may be adequate when operating in a stable external environment that is capable of prediction, where communication and information systems are manually processed and when competitors have similar limitations. However, as systems become more automated and information can be instantaneously processed, the rules change.

People who function in a hierarchical environment have a narrow perspective of the larger system. They are limited by defined boundaries. Those at the top generally look to more efficient ways of improving the current model instead of inventing newer models. The huge leap required to change demands serious modification of the fundamental organizational structure and the way individuals interact in addition to technological advances. Currently, the technology is ahead of the organizational issues.

The organizations who pursue higher and higher levels of integration will quickly outdistance those who seek the latest "flavor of the month" or management "fad." Unfortunately, the latest fad tends to undo or diminish the effect of the previous ones. This leads to disjoined activity and the need to reconcile old and new, which works against integration. One of the major keys to value improvement is integration and, like so many other things, the key to integration is leadership.

The power and importance of organizational cohesion became apparent in the mid-1980s as I toured a number of Japanese organizations in search for the few gems that could be used to gain significant competitive advantage. The major lesson learned was the Japanese did not have a "few techniques" to produce high quality, but they had an infrastructure that created and fostered integrated systems to provide world-class output.

The knowledge the Japanese had gained in producing superior products could not be easily observed and copied. Their corporations were too complex, vast, and interwoven into the larger society to comprehend in a two-week visit or to boil their success down to a few bullet points.

The information was not in the form one could bring back and implement in another organization. It has taken thousands of productivity and quality practitioners years to convert the wisdom accumulated from global best-in-class organizations into useful information, knowledge, and wisdom on adding high competitive value to goods and services.

METRICS

The term *metrics* is gaining in popularity as a term to describe a system of *measures* and *statistical analysis* used to mathematically comprehend the vast interconnectedness of the components of an enterprise in its pursuit of its mission. Metrics are used to provide a continuous measurement system that renders a high degree of assessment and understanding while monitoring both the drivers and distractors of success in the pursuit of goals. For our purpose, we will be primarily concerned with the metrics that drive and support value, which, in turn, drive long-term profits and success.[5]

Today, financial performance measures are considered the primary scorecard of most organizations. Many top management teams spend a high percentage of their time, particularly the last month of every quarter (last six weeks of a fiscal year), on the "numbers." Unfortunately, much of this time is wasted because:

- The forces that created the numbers occurred some time ago.
- Natural variation is never considered as an influential element.
- When things look grim, there is a tendency to borrow from the future to atone for the sins of the past, so the tough decisions can be postponed.
- When reality falls short of projections, the search is to find who to blame, not to study the vast network of cause-and-effect activity that produced the results.

What is missing in this financial control panel are the means of integrating the past with the future and harmonizing the organization with its larger environment. The needed set of metrics requires the analytical tools and technical systems of the Information Age. The comprehensive metrics of the future does not exclude or ignore traditional financial indicators, but they are placed in the proper perspective of being lagging measures.

CONTROL PANEL

The information networks used by tomorrow's leader will be unlike those in use today. The term that most frequently labels this type of information system is a *control panel*. The control panel tends to provide a continuous prioritization and alert system that allows the user to focus on the most important needs and emerging trends on a *continuous* basis. It is not the information available on demand or predetermined report-after-report systems of the Industrial Age. It is a self-managed, cybernetic-oriented approach that continually monitors performance, adjusts as it identifies opportunities, solves problems, eliminates waste and redundancy, and seeks improvement.

The control panel is a major leadership tool for the Information Age. It is the means of managing the massive amount of data available with the human dimensions that motivate customers, shareholders, employees, and customers. However, this tool must be designed and built with unity of information and human and organizational systems continuously in mind. It is not primarily an information system, it is an integration system. As such, it must continually grow and adapt.

The other critical pieces include powerful and high-quality automated and human production and creative systems and the means of continuous evolution and improvement. Since the foundation for practically all created value is the human mind, the linkage with the human system is the highest priority. As we move into the Information Age, human systems must always be at the forefront of integration. Human endeavor is part of the value-adding processes or the support of value-adding processes. The fundamental subprocesses that power the major critical processes are labeled as *jobs;* the robustness of jobs are both individual and team competency. The coordination that synergizes the individual and provides high value added output is called *teamwork.* The force that creates it all, establishes the vision, and assures the results is called *leadership.*

In reality, this book is about the leadership that is necessary to integrate information systems into the human systems of our organizations in order to create wealth from the abundance of knowledge and wisdom available in the Information Age. Using the old work brigade as an analogy, the secret is to do the right thing (add high value to markets), the right way (effectively and efficiently).

SOME ADDITIONAL HINTS

We are entering new territory; we have never had such proliferation of information. We must continually evolve and update our leadership models as we go. You will find a solid foundation and format to provide any organization with a blueprint for success in the following ten chapters.

The challenge in compiling this type of book is to address the countless variations of organizational models that currently exist and the unlimited ways they are applied to real-world situations. Every organization has a purpose for its existence and is on its journey to someplace. Every organization has strengths and every organization has vulnerabilities. Since every organization and every individual is unique, every organization must have unique solutions and the individuals and teams who will lead them must have the skills and competency required to integrate their systems and processes with the changing needs of customers and markets in order to produce high market value.

Your organization will already be doing many of the elements outlined in the chapters. You may be strong in understanding your customer, but not quite as strong in the consistent delivery of your service. Or, you may have a formal planning process, but your plans are not really current and different parts of your organization seem to be marching to different drummers. The key is balance, thoroughness, and integration of the pieces.

Although the major focus of the book is the integration of leadership using metrics through the creation and utilization of a control panel, it is essential that all of the principles be in place. Without a solid foundation, competent leadership, robust processes, organizational alignment and knowledge of markets, competitors and customers, metrics offer little help and a meaningful control panel cannot be built. Those areas where you have the pieces in place should be quickly scanned, so your time can be better spent building or coordinating areas where there is more work to be done.

No leader can change where they or their organization have been; they can only adjust their course for the future. An excellent way to use this book is as a course adjustment mechanism. Each principle has a few key elements that are outlined in the text and in the bullet point summary following each chapter. These elements are summarized in Appendix B in the form of a self-assessment chart. These key elements should be used as a guide to assess your organization's current level of performance by answering if it is currently being conducted and how effective it is. These responses will identify gaps and the gaps will indicate needed course corrections.

The assessment process should be a team effort. The leadership team of the organization should begin by assessing the entire organization, identify gaps, and begin modification and correction. After the top leadership team has assessed the higher level, other levels should be involved in more detailed assessment and implementation of the change.

Unfortunately, the top leadership level is not always the organization level that first identifies the need for change. If you are in middle management, you need to push higher level leadership to change as well as working with your team in assessing and correcting your level. If you are in lower positions in the organization or in a support role, you must continually push your leadership to change. At any level, you do not have much choice because, without change, there is little brightness for your organization and your role in the organization in the future.

The book is designed to help identify and assist in areas that require attention to achieve organizational balance and coordination. Those areas that are currently adding value and working should not be changed, but they should be connected to each other and to the new elements that are added. Every organization is unique and every control panel must be designed to help achieve the unique vision, mission, and goals of the organization. Use this book to identify areas for improvement and enhancement to add to the many valuable components that already exist.

Good luck in creating value as you improve your organization on your journey.

NOTES

1. Harley-Davidson, *1995 Annual Report*, Outside Back Cover.

2. Admiral Frank Collins later chaired the team that initially pursued a national recognition for quality that resulted in the formation of the Malcolm Baldrige National Quality Award.

3. The source for information on the transition from the Agriculture Revolution (First Wave) to the Industrial Age (Second Wave) to the Information Age (Third Wave) is Alvin Toffler, *The Third Wave* (New York: Bantam Books, 1981).

4. For discussion and references on Taylor and scientific management, see the first few sections of chapter 7.

5. An inspiration for much of the pursuit for better metrics and ways to effectively utilize them came from the following two articles. Robert S. Kaplan and David P. Norton, "The Balanced Scorecard-Measures That Drive Performance," *Harvard Business Review*, January–February 1992; and Robert S. Kaplan and David P. Norton, "Putting the Balanced Scorecard to Work," *Harvard Business Review*, September–October, 1993.

Acknowledgments

Thanks to my wife, Margaret, for her support throughout the writing and publication of *Value Leadership*.

I would like to express appreciation to the following for their assistance in reviewing this book and helping improve it.

Gene Lyons, principal, of Benefits Solution Company of Newport Beach, California, who looked at it from an executive's vantage point.

Art Peterson, president of PSG Consulting Services, Greenwood Village, Colorado, who is an expert in strategic planning and finance. In addition to his knowledge in these areas, he added the consultant's perspective.

Mark Crumly, manager of GTE, Ontario, California, who reviewed it from a middle manager and quality professional view.

A special thanks to the following for their assistance in helping me learn and evolve the concepts presented in *Value Leadership:* Cheryl Bates, Frank Collins, Brenda Dale, John Indrigo, Pat Sedelmaier, and Mary Richthammer in the United States; Virginia Johnson and Dick Love in Australia; and Paul Soper in the UK.

Chapter 1

INTEGRATED LEADERSHIP

> *Value is the most invincible and impalpable of ghosts,*
> *and comes and goes unthought of while the visible*
> *and dense matter remains as it was.*
>
> W. Stanley Jevons[1]

The cover story in the Money section of *USA Today* on September 10, 1996, stated the competitive difference of the Information Age: "Value-minded consumers call the shots."

Competition is coming from so many different angles that a company sitting fat and happy will get killed in this economy. . . . The rallying cry of American industry is to drive unnecessary costs out of the system and return them to consumers.[2]

For most of the twentieth century, price seemed to be the primary determinant on which people based their purchase decisions. In the last decade or two, much of the emphasis has been on quality. In reality, all decisions are based on value, which is driven by price, quality, and a few other factors.

The major reason we focus on one determinant over others is due to an insufficiency of basic knowledge about a product or service, or a lack of a reliable means of comparing one alternative against the other. In the emerging age, much greater knowledge will exist and all factors of value can be more fairly and easily determined. The more information that is available, the more value-based criteria will call the shots. Since information provides a means of comparing value, it becomes a value-adding resource and contributes to even greater value. This anomaly is a common characteristic of the Information Age.

HIGH VALUE IN THE INFORMATION AGE

Value is the chief criteria for product/service selection in open market systems, historically and probably long into the future. What is quickly changing in the Information Age is customer's ability to assess value, the producer's increasing speed and efficiency in producing value, and the strong role of information as a high value-adding component in goods and services.

When the knowledge of current value production is combined with the trends of the increasing impact of information on value, the following emerge as key characteristics of tomorrow's successful organization.

1. The organization must be designed on a solid foundation. It must know why it exists, what it plans to accomplish and how it will approach its objectives. (*foundation planning*)
2. The organization must be designed and built with the capability to carry out its plans and achieve its mission. (*vertical alignment*)
3. The organization must understand the changing needs and requirements of its customers, how value is determined by the market and have a high degree of knowledge of competitive market forces. (*customer/market driven*)
4. The organization must maximize the value it delivers by focusing on the customer as the chief recipient of value and aligning and streamlining its critical and supporting processes to produce and deliver high value. (*horizontal alignment*)
5. There must be a continuous improvement methodology that assures the organization remains a high value producer at a rate that exceeds competitive forces. (*value management*)
6. Effective leadership must be in place that assures competency, teamwork and the necessary integration and communication exist throughout the organization and its value producing relationship with suppliers and customers. (*leadership*)
7. The metrics and information systems must exist that assure the necessary knowledge is available to everyone to do their jobs and appropriate measures of success permeate all levels and aspects of the organization. (*control panel*)

The ideals that these seven factors define are the *principles of integrated leadership*. They are not shown in a particular order since they must all exist together and be connected throughout the organization. The first four are the basic building blocks of the value producing elements of an organization and the final three continually adjust the initial four and assure success.

These basic leadership principles have evolved over centuries and are well accepted, proven, and utilized around the globe. They are a compendium of management theory and practice ranging from early military leadership through the latest lean production and open book management

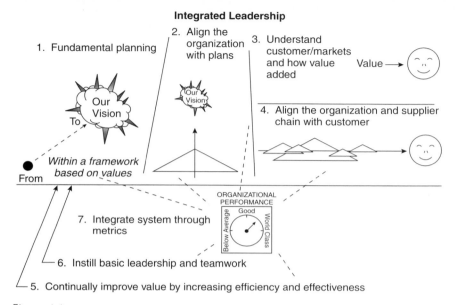

Fiqure 1.1 Integrated leadership links all aspects of an organization and is required to achieved high sustained customer value.

techniques of the past few years. They are based on the Malcolm Baldrige National Quality Award[3] (MBNQA or Baldrige Award) criteria.

The Baldrige Award is a quasi-organizational model that has undergone massive global study in a relatively short time. It was developed to recognize a very small number of organizations in the United States for performance excellence. The overwhelming strength of the Baldrige Award is its profundity in assessing the value-adding and wealth-creation application of an organization.

Where competitive effectiveness and efficiencies approach world-class levels, organizations can no longer afford to compete within their departments. Everyone, from suppliers to customers, must work together to improve results. Working together involves more than basic team concepts; it requires a system of communications integrated with plans, objectives, and metrics. Most importantly, the organization must consolidate all of its aspects into a meaningful set of metrics that leads to direct action. The concept is illustrated in Figure 1.1.

However, the challenge in designing, building, and maintaining an organization that delivers superior value in a fast-changing environment is not in merely understanding basic theory but in applying it in the real world. This chapter provides an overview of these principles along with definitions and supporting concepts, while the remaining nine chapters focus on techniques, practices, future considerations, and examples of their application.

THE DRIVING PRINCIPLES OF INTEGRATED LEADERSHIP

The key to success in most endeavors begins with the desire to excel. Once the desire is present, there are two factors above all others that determine the success of an organization. These are the non-negotiables; without them, success will always be very short-term. They are the *focus on customers/ markets* and *leadership*.

CUSTOMER/MARKET-DRIVEN

Organizations exist for one primary reason: to provide value to stakeholders. Stakeholders include customers, owners, employees, suppliers, and society. Long-term successful organizations provide value to all of these constituents, so everyone wins.

The primary determinant of wealth sharing is based on the paying customer receiving more value than they receive from other sources. In order to attain this result, the customer (or market of potential customers) must be the focus of the organization. A customer-driven organization cannot be a fair weather proposition; it must be paramount *all the time, every time, under every condition.*

The highest performance indicator that matters in the long-term success of an organization is the value it adds through its major processes. It is the only lasting guarantee of wealth creation, high economic value added, and profit. These are all outputs of being customer driven.

The operative word is *driven*. A *driver* is something that heavily influences or causes some result, or effect. It can be measured statistically using correlation techniques. Although every effect may have numerous causes that influence the result, there is usually one, or a few prevailing drivers.

The test of whether an organization is market driven or customer driven cannot be conducted when things are fine, nor can it be measured by words alone. It is only through conflict, like a poor financial return, a hostile takeover attempt, downturns in the economy, severe competition, and political upheaval at the top of the organization that what *drives* the organization can be determined. During these times, the actions and reactions of the organization show its *true drivers.*

Customer focus begins with understanding the changing customer and knowing and anticipating their changing needs, even in advance of the customer's knowledge. It requires continuous knowledge of competitive forces in the market at the basic needs fulfillment and feature levels. The term used to describe this critical knowledge is the *voice of the customer,* or VOC. Understanding the VOC is a constant theme, and is the primary topic of chapter 3.

The output of customer focus is value leadership, which is closely related to market leadership. Market leadership is the result, and value leadership is the means. Value leadership begins with an accurate and thorough understanding of the market, customers, and competitors. This is no easy task, since markets are often fuzzy, customers frequently do not know what they want and competitors change, become elusive or appear from non-traditional sources. The only reliable and meaningful indicator of value leadership comes in the market where it is measured against other providers. Those who best understand customers and the means of effectively and efficiently meeting their needs will be the winners of the value race and *become market leaders.*

EFFECTIVE LEADERSHIP

An organization can only create high long-term value added if it is designed and operated to do so. It is not accidental phenomena that drive wealth creating success. It is leadership.

Who is a leader? Everyone is a leader who is responsible for some role, work, output, or function. An individual who works alone is the leader of that operation. The individual who is in charge of that person is also a leader, and so on, up the organization. The person who is in charge of the overall organization is also a leader.

Leadership is taking the responsibility and performing or guiding the action necessary to plan for and achieve desired results. There are some basic competencies everyone needs in a leadership role. Some are common and are essential to the accomplishment of any role. Others are situational or vary with the scope of responsibility, the span of control, and the complexity of the work.

A primary role of a leader is to bring purpose, clarity, and direction to an organization. In a high performance organization, there is no one element that creates success. Combinations of factors drive high-level achievement of results. Leadership begins with the desire to achieve something and continues through its attainment. If the desire is wealth creation over a lengthy period, the objective or goal must be wealth creation for the long term.

Leaders always *know the target* and constantly keep it in mind. This is a variation of Stephen Covey's Habit Two of his seven habits of effective leadership:[4] "Begin with the end in mind." Only by knowing the target can one have a high degree of certainty in steering a course to it. This principle should be used for both the big picture strategy and tactics along the way. If the target, or end result, is value, the question is, "What creates value?" Integrated leadership endlessly searches for the answer and delivery to this question.

In the Information Age, leaders and teams need an integrated control panel that is capable of providing assessment and direction. Leaders need knowledge on optimum methods of deploying resources and closing identified gaps. Self-managed teams need this knowledge plus communication that is required to link with plans, direction, goals, and strategy. It is critical to provide the right blend and balance of information to everyone since an overload of information may be just as severe as an underload. This circuited system must promote learning, build a foundation for job performance appraisal and development of basic job competencies at the team level, and provide direction for continual job enhancement.

There are thousands of books and documents on leadership. The topic evokes many opinions and many different approaches and methodologies. Integrated leadership does not summarize theories or pretend that there is one superior approach to leadership. However, it does highlight the few basics that are frequently overlooked or misused, and provides some thoughts that will prove extremely valuable in building a world-class, high-performance organization. The theme of leadership is dominant throughout all chapters and is the primary emphasis of chapters 7 and 8.

Leadership is the one element that will seek the other six principles. It is the *encompassing* principle. It assures that the others are implemented and followed.

THE REMAINING PRINCIPLES OF INTEGRATED LEADERSHIP

The remaining five principles of integrated leadership are the means of implementation, or the actions that are necessary, to create high value.

DESIGNING THE FOUNDATION

Organizational success depends on the proper foundation. In the long term an organization maximizes wealth creation by having a purpose based on adding value to customers and all other stakeholders. This purpose should be formalized and communicated through a mission and a vision statement. These are the pieces of the foundation that connect to bedrock; everything else is based on them. These critical elements must be harmonized with each other.

Both common sense and experience show that planning is the key to most successes. In the West, cultures have evolved that place a high priority on action, with little relative regard for planning. This results in a mistaken belief that planning is a low-return endeavor. The opposite is true; proper and creative planning can be the highest value activity. Granted, planning can be overdone, but most organizations are on the short side by a substantial margin.

Plans that are improperly developed are not the central point of an organization, or are not managed for implementation and results create substantial waste. This leads to either abandonment or rework. Plans must be both developed for success and successfully implemented.

BUILDING THE ORGANIZATION (VERTICAL ALIGNMENT)

The planning process should include the means of deploying the plans throughout the organization, but frequently this step is overlooked or inadequate. Plans fail to achieve success for two major reasons: the plans themselves are unsound, or their implementation is flawed. If the plans are unsound, organizational alignment offers little help. On the other hand, if the plans are sound, the organization must be aligned with them to maximize their achievement. This is called *vertical alignment*.

A high value-producing organization designs efficiency and effectiveness throughout the planning process. When new or modified products and services are introduced, they work the way they were intended to because the organization is designed for success.

When these details are integrated and harmonious, the organization must align with them. This is accomplished through the deliberate effort of communications, operational planning, and the establishment of metrics that provide continuous tracking of all critical factors and the value they produce.

Most organizations conduct strategic planning, but many fail to integrate tactical operations with strategy. When the two are not synchronized during the planning phase, daily operations become dominant over longer-term strategy as the organization futilely attempts to achieve its goals.

Integration and harmonization are deployed throughout the organization by the clever use of metrics. In the increasingly competitive global environment, every person in an organization must fully understand their role and how it links to the whole. Vertical integration assures that the organization is built for the production of high value. Both foundation planning and vertical alignment are covered in chapter 2.

DESIGNING AND BUILDING VALUE-PRODUCING PROCESSES (HORIZONTAL ALIGNMENT)

Once the VOC is firmly established, the means of producing value that exceeds customer expectations and surpasses other competitors becomes the focus of the organization. Value is actualized through the critical processes of planning, designing, marketing, producing, selling, delivering, and supporting. These major processes are usually supported by other processes such as purchasing, recruiting, training, accounting, and legal. The importance of both the critical processes and the support processes depend on the type of business, the type of product or service, and the maturity of the organization.

The chain of value begins with the final target in mind. This may be specifications for a product or standards for services (all products have value-added services associated with them). These specifications or standards become quantified requirements that, in turn, become the target of value to customers.

With final quantified requirements established, each step along the process formulates requirements for internal and external suppliers. Each process owner knows the requirements of their customers and the capability of their process, and in turn works with their suppliers to meet customers' requirements.

Since all organizations are part of and dependent on connecting organizations and systems, performance must be coordinated with those organizations. Stated another way, there are great opportunities to enhance performance by improving connection points and becoming more skilled at what is handed off from one organization to another (whether internal or external). Identifying and capitalizing on these opportunities and the methodology for improvement are the major topics of partnership alliances within the supplier-customer value-added chain.

The pursuit of effectively coordinating processes and external organizations to create high value is called *horizontal alignment*. It assures that everyone is working on the *right thing*—adding value to customers.

Chapter 4 provides the base for aligning internal and external functions to produce high value-added products and services to meet the VOC and provide key output measures to link with the control panel.

IMPROVING VALUE

Value management brings life to the VOC and helps everyone do their job correctly. It creates a set of control panel gages that provide ongoing real-time indication of how well customer needs and perceptions are met.

Value is continuously managed and improved by using the Plan-Do-Check-Act (PDCA) cycle. Value management continually works on both sides of the equation to elevate the relationship by offering more at less proportionate cost. The psychological benefit of what is received is studied and improved, as well as the psychological costs of what is paid. The mental benefits of perceiving that a high value is received is, in and of itself, additional value. On the other hand, the feeling of being taken or "not getting the best deal" will negatively affect the actual value received.

One consistent element of value is time. Time works on both the benefit and cost sides, as well as influencing both reality and perception. Cycle time reduction is a combination of effective planning, customer and market knowledge, and the application of quality tools and techniques. On the other hand, cycle time improvement at the expense of quality may result in an overall reduction of value.

Chapter 5 looks at the high-level value chain for opportunities to gain both continuous and breakthrough improvements. Chapter 6 is closely linked, as it provides specific tools and techniques for improvement at all levels in both the cost and benefit sides of the value formula.

Many organizations have offered training in continuous improvement tools, but very few manage their improvement efforts through a centralized point. The linkage of value improvement activity with a control panel not only identifies top priority opportunities, but also coordinates and maximizes the results. The individual's linkage with the vision, mission, long-term plans, customers, and the value-adding conditions of the organization through metrics provides the individual with the tools they need to maximize results. In addition to high effectiveness and efficiency, meaningful metrics and access to needed job information greatly improve personal motivation and satisfaction.

CONTINUOUSLY UNDERSTANDING, MEASURING, AND MONITORING VALUE (CONTROL PANEL)

In the capital-intensive Industrial Age, ingenious tools were discovered and invented to manage and measure performance and success. Accounting and finance systems evolved, based on return on capital. These systems spread through entire organizations and provided management with a series of financial planning, budgeting, and control tools. Financial metrics were easily integrated through the application of double-entry bookkeeping. The financial control panel became dominated by a few standardized reports such as income statements, balance sheets, and cash flow analyses.

Using this accounting method, value added by an organization can be easily computed over any period of time by calculating profit against various denominators such as equity, assets, or sales. Market value added can be calculated by subtracting the initial owners' investment capital from current capitalization and adjusting for alternate investments and inflation.

The tools needed to manage in a knowledge-based economy are different from those used in the Industrial Age. The old tools alone are inadequate. The dashboard used to monitor an automobile driven from Los Angeles to Boston is totally insufficient to fly a spaceship from Earth to one of Jupiter's moons. Similarly, the dashboard of the Industrial Age cannot be converted to the control panel needed by the organizations that hope to succeed in the Information Age. Although today's solutions will not solve tomorrow's problems, tomorrow's problems will be solved by an evolution of today's solutions.

For the past fifty-plus years, financial metrics had been adequate for most organizations because they offer a review of performance as well as compliance with governmental regulations for tax and disclosure purposes. They were supplemented by "feel good"–type personnel or morale surveys that provide a "point in time" assessment of the employee force, and a variety of "customer satisfaction" surveys that furnish readings on customer opinions. These are insufficient in the Information Age to render the measures required to adjust processes to continually improve value.

In the past, an organization could have separate systems and metrics for different functions. The only linkage required was high-level financial figures, which were consolidated into an overall report. Staff departments were responsible for human resources, accounting, planning, communications, training, and, in some cases, even quality. Frequently, both operating and staff functions usually planned separately, linking only the highest level elements.

New competitive factors require integrated planning at the lowest levels to achieve value optimization. This is only possible with an evolved integrated system of metrics to provide the basis for planning.

A control panel coordinates the critical factors and goals of the organization with those of internal operations, customer information, market intelligence, and other external data sources to monitor and measure causal relationships. This balance allows the information of all aspects that drive and produce value to merge together into useful and actionable knowledge for the organization. In order to reach its destination, every organization needs it own unique control panel that is appropriate for its own purposes.

A comparison of control panels reveals the growth of the technology that supports the concept. For example, today's automobile has more computing power for gathering, displaying, and analyzing performance than all the onboard computing power of the manned flights to the moon.

Unlike the speed of technology growth, organizations are just now beginning to rediscover the power of the *war room* in directing future strategy to competitive markets. Long before the evolution of accounting, military strategists used the collection and analysis of a wide dimension of information to win battles and wars. Modern executives know that a wide variety of metrics are needed to win competitive battles and wars.

The basic principle that is driving this move toward a war room, or control panel approach, is *cause and effect.* Most financial measures used in modern organizations are the effect of strategy, tactics, and activities, and not the cause. Many of the most important measures used in financial reporting are results, or lagging indicators.

Measuring value added is becoming more popular with large corporations. An emerging trend is the measurement of economic value added, or EVA, which is supplementing return on equity (ROE) as an accepted standard. EVA attempts to determine the financial value that an organization produces over a period of time, which is above and beyond what the money equivalent of their net worth would have returned had they invested conservatively. Others evaluate EVA against inflation rates or their organization's hurdle rates with various adjustments.

Another popular method is market value added, or MVA. MVA is easier to calculate and more uniform, but constantly fluctuates with the market price of organization's publicly traded stock. It basically measures the cash invested into a business against the market capitalization at any point in time.

However, the search for value added will improve and become more meaningful and indicative of wealth creation as more driving metrics evolve. The current popular measures are lagging, and the search for their leading drivers is only in its infancy.

The principles of integrated leadership cannot be used as a checklist because they require both balance and unity. Since each is delicately interconnected to the others and depends on many variables to be fulfilled, they must be continually viewed together. This is accomplished through the development and use of a control panel, or the means of bringing integrated metrics together to assess and modify performance.

The control panel must be organization-specific, designed as the other elements emerge and continually fine-tuned to anticipate and accommodate change. Just as metrics add value to information by increasing understanding, a control panel adds value to metrics. The more it is tailored to a specific organization, the more valuable it becomes.

Chapter 9 offers other measures of value and outlines methodologies for establishing correlation linkages among critical lagging indicators and the leading sensors that drive them. It helps answer the question, "What are the most important measures of an organization, and how are they linked?" Every leader needs their own control panel, and those at the top need an integrated view of the entire organization.

EXPANDING ROLE OF INFORMATION

INFORMATION IS WHAT THE INFORMATION AGE IS ALL ABOUT

The term *information* covers a wide spectrum. Alvin Toffler, the futurist, struggles to find acceptable definitions of data, information, and knowledge. In *Powershift*, he established the following definitions for each and then used them interchangeably.

> *In general, in the pages ahead, data will mean more or less unconnected 'facts,' information will refer to data that have been fitted into categories and classification schemes or other patterns; and knowledge will mean information that has been further refined into more general statements. But to avoid tedious repetition, all three terms may sometimes be used interchangeably.*[5]

Figure 1.2 shows the flow from observation to wisdom. The model shows that observation provides data; that classification and analysis of data produces information; that explanation of information leads to understanding; that capability of prediction from understanding indicates knowledge; and with knowledge achieved, that the ability to prescribe denotes an attainment of wisdom.[6] In the illustration, understanding is shown as a necessary ingredient throughout the evolution from observation to wisdom.

Since the attainment of wisdom is probably rarely achieved in a linear flow from observation to final enlightenment, it is better shown in a circular movement that loops back or connects with other information flows.

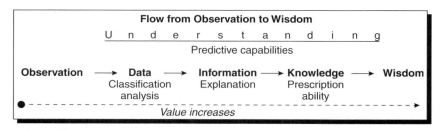

Fïgure 1.2   The attainment of wisdom comes from a valued-added flow.

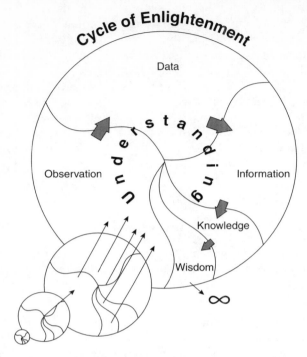

Figure 1.3 Ever-increasing attainment of enlightenment is the evolution and accumulation of cycles of learning processes from observation to wisdom.

Figure 1.3 shows that a cycle of enlightenment may reach a level of wisdom at one plain, but wisdom may be only a data point at another. In other words, profound wisdom at a certain point in time or place may have high value, but be essentially worthless at another. The accumulation of cycle after cycle of enlightenment leads to greater and greater enlightenment. The essence of the Information Age is the geometric expansion of these cycles in decreasing time frames. In a sense, all of the terms used to describe the cycle can generally be used interchangeably, since they evolve from one to another and then enter a new phase of evolution. The term most frequently used is *information*, unless an earlier state or an evolved state is referenced.

The flow from observation to wisdom is a natural evolution process that has taken us to our current state. We are entering the Information Age not because of the route information takes, but because of its increasing value that results from the growing volume of information, its availability, and the cycle-time reduction in its processing.

MOVING FROM THE INDUSTRIAL AGE
TO THE INFORMATION AGE

The Information Age is only possible because of the computer and its huge networking ability, including the Internet. Today, it is possible to input every business transaction into a database. Once data are in a database, they can be combined with other data (or information) and moved up the cycle of enlightenment.

The Information Age is truly a significant transition from the Industrial Age. Knowledge is extremely powerful and has high value-added character-istics. An example is the high technology movement that is revolutionizing the collection and processing of data. Value is being increased on both sides of the formula: the output per unit is quickly increasing while the price decreases.

Like the computer industry, the auto industry is entering the Informa-tion Age. This transformation has been labeled as the movement from mass production to *lean production*,[7] which has rendered mass production obso-lete in many industries. Lean production has expanded into lean distribu-tion by integrating production information systems with sales systems. The consolidation of these systems has greatly elevated the value received by customers.

Americans see the impact of the Information Age when they open their mailboxes, watch television, go shopping, or listen to the radio. They are the constant recipients of the output of precision marketing, or database marketing. Many industries and organizations are capitalizing on these gains by providing greater value to their customers. Others misuse this pow-erful tool and have diminished its value. Many have not yet discovered the immense capability of information and knowledge.

Toffler points out a characteristic of knowledge that is distinct from the drivers of the Industrial Age.[8] For example, a stamping machine that is set up with a die to produce widgets can only produce widgets. It cannot simul-taneously be used to produce window frames. On the other hand, an unlimited number of individuals can use the same knowledge at the same time, and they can use it to produce more knowledge.

Knowledge, like our numbering system, seems to have no finite limits. We can always add more knowledge to that which already exists. This propensity for increasing knowledge may also apply to the value usually associated with knowledge. In other words, unlike the finite value usually associated with goods and services, the value of knowledge appears to be much more elastic and may have extremely high upper bounds.

Knowledge and wisdom frequently change, since they are the result of the latest information, which changes based on latest observations, and so on. For example, the theories of what caused the extinction of the dinosaur, the age of the universe, or how to raise kids change frequently.

Wisdom and knowledge sometimes have little relationship to truth or to right and wrong. They are the result of a series of logical steps that move from observations to conclusions, or, in some cases, they can merely be proclaimed. I have encountered supposedly brilliant individuals who expound wisdom from a single observation point and altogether reject scientifically deduced knowledge when it differs from their opinion.

The growth of information provides future managers and executives with an exponentially greater amount of knowledge and wisdom than their predecessors. The challenge is how to manage this resource in a manner that provides optimum performance to their organization.

The Industrial Age was (and still is) driven by capital, labor, and non-labor resources. These are all finite and a unit cannot be used by two or more forces simultaneously. The power source of the Information Age is knowledge. Capital, labor, and resources are still part of the Information Age, but they tend to have less relative importance as knowledge allows them to be more efficiently used.

A increasingly high percentage of the U.S. population works in jobs where the chief product is information.[9] Since information, unlike capital investment, can experience almost instant exponential growth or loss in value, it is critical to continuously manage and protect knowledge. Information is not only the chief means of assessing value, it is a primary source of value itself.

VALUE—THE KEY METRIC

WHY VALUE?

Value is the primary buying decision factor. It is often made without enough knowledge, and frequently utilizes a disproportionate amount of subjectivity and emotion, but it is always the most fundamental basis of decision making. It weighs risk against reward and cost against benefit. For example, decisions on an idea, a marriage proposal, a flirtatious smile, and a political contest are all based on the perception of value.

Simply stated, *value is the worth, or equivalent, of a product, object, service, activity, idea, or a combination in its current or anticipated state.* The operative term is *state*, because value can be continuously added to or decreased from any of these things.

The world of business, commerce, and trade encompasses a continuous series of value-added activities, sometimes followed by a recycling that starts another round of value-added activities. In the linear world of the Industrial Age, these steps were more easily observed and measured. Today, value is often viewed as a *package* that blends intangibles, information, ideas, and concepts, along with products and services ranging from intellectual property to raw commodities.

Toffler, in *Powershift*, points out the type of players (including customers) now involved in adding value.

In the new economy the receptionist and the investment banker who assembles the capital, the keypunch operator and the salesperson, as well as the systems designer and telecommunications specialist, all add value. Even more significantly, so does the customer. Value results from a total effort, rather than from one isolated step in the process.[10]

At any point in the process, the net value of the transaction (or series of transactions) can be established by comparing the value of what one receives against what was paid for its acquisition or creation. This formula defines the value of the transaction to the purchaser or recipient.

$$\text{Value} = \frac{\text{What is received}}{\text{What is paid}}$$

One of the greatest challenges for every organization and most individuals is the continuous decision process on how to best utilize their resources in exchange for solutions to meet their needs. The value formula provides a foundation and the basic methodology necessary to develop the metrics.

The diagram in Figure 1.4 provides an expansion of the value formula.

Anyone who has purchased a product or service at a high price with some inconvenience and later discovered that it could have been purchased at a considerably lower price with less hassle, feels let down. One's feelings about the transaction and everything associated with it determine the assessment of value. If the customer feels great, the relative size of the

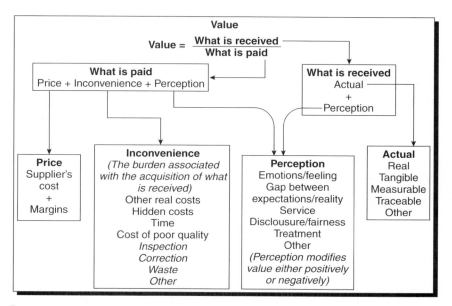

Figure 1.4   Value has many dimensions and elements.

numerator (compared with the denominator) has been increased. On the other hand, if one feels cheated or let down, the relative size of the denominator (compared with the numerator) has been increased, lessening the overall value of the product or service.

Both sides of the value formula have a perception element and a reality element. Unlike the legal profession, which uses a "reasonable person" criterion to determine fault or liability, value does not always have a reasonableness about it. It is more analogous to the "beauty is in the eye of the beholder" theory.

Price is only one factor of value. As value is continuously engineered to higher and higher plains, the value of the total package is much more important than the product or service price. W. Edwards Deming quoted Walter Shewhart for years, saying, "Price has no meaning without a measure of the quality being purchased."[11] The reason price is a poor measure of value is because it ignores not only the quality of the product or service, but the perceptions of the customer and the burden that must be endured.

When products are fabricated in an industrial process, value is created in a linear preplanned fashion. Mass industrial production requires heavy capital investment in both infrastructure and operation. In knowledge-based markets, value may be added or reduced quickly by any number of sources, including the customer or a third-party user. In an increasingly large number of cases, there is little relationship between investment size and the ultimate value added. This phenomenon is driving the reemergence of the entrepreneur as a powerful competitive force in the global economy.

As entrepreneurs' creative and innovative spirits connect more information with value and they realize their survival depends on strategic partnering with each other, they will be an increasing threat to the big organizations and institutions of the Industrial Age. Value and information are inherently linked in the Information Age as they encroach on the capital and finances of the Industrial Age. However, just as the Industrial Age required scientific management to propel it forward, the Information Age needs a *new approach to leadership.*

WEALTH CREATION AND ADDED VALUE

History provides countless examples in which someone, a team, a tribe, or a nation, transformed a prior condition into something that made everything easier or better for the human species and occasionally for the planet as a whole. There are also countless examples of transformations that resulted in loss from which the human species and the planet suffered.

Wealth creators have achieved powerful gains, such as the harnessing of fire; the discovery or invention of the printed page, language, the wheel, mathematics and navigation; and the creation of art, government, law, and music. Humankind has created wealth with transportation systems, education systems, and systems of commerce. However, none of these came without a price. Sometimes the costs exceed the gains, or a few prosper at the expense of the many. Such catastrophes are wealth destroyers—for example, most wars, crimes, disasters, and waste.

Also, on a micro level, wealth is created and destroyed. Businesses create jobs and offer products and services that benefit customers, shareholders, suppliers, employees, and society. Organizations provide joy, entertainment, security, social opportunities, and education. The medical profession saves lives and assists in healing injuries. Individuals provide high value added to themselves and others. Organizations and people destroy value also.

When a high percentage of global wealth was based on agriculture, value was primarily determined by what the land could produce. Many of the costs were human sweat and toil that accumulated from generation to generation. Lead times and cycle times were long and often unpredictable. During the Industrial Revolution, much wealth was created globally through the production of physical products. These products and the plants and machines that produced them required considerable capital investment and time. It was very expensive to retool a factory to produce a different version or a new model.

In the high-tech knowledge revolution today, value is frequently defined by speed, cycle time, and usually by acceleration, or the rate of increasing speed. The speed of change and expectations of customers are rapidly building on the wisdom of the past to essentially redefine value in ways previously unimagined. The ability of organizations to offer ample increasing value to remain competitive in the future depends on the design and implementation of integrated and disciplined systems and methods to achieve targeted outcomes. The future belongs to those organizations who are dedicated to adding real value and wealth to their stakeholders and society.

A MONUMENTAL TRANSITION

The transformation to the Information Age is still in its infancy, but penetrating changes were observed in the less-than-two-decade period between the Vietnam and the Persian Gulf Wars.

Memories of war can be very emotional. The reason for using war as an analogy is not to make a political statement or to link it with a moral lesson, but to use it to help describe the fundamental change that will eventually impact every human. The military is one of the most established forms of human organization.

The mission in Vietnam was vague; it included diverse political and military elements. It had no definite time frame. The metrics were inappropriate. The values and consciousness of the country conflicted with those of its leaders. Americans became fed up with losing their youth to a cause they did not endorse. The political agenda, with all its tampering, did not permit a military solution. The military was not a tight cohesive team. The missions and directives of its various branches did not fit together. At the lower levels, many units were confused and a low level of trust existed throughout the ranks.

The major metrics used to report the progress of the war were ineffective and eventually created their own backlash. The reported figures showing the number of bombs dropped and both the enemy and friendly "body count"[12] did not provide any indication of how the war was going.

The United States lost the Vietnam War because the basic foundation for victory was not in place. The mission was not clear, and it changed as the political climate changed. The military fought the war with restrictions that prevented them from carrying out the necessary strategy to be successful.

Much of the early strategy was based on the belief that the Vietnamese would give up once they recognized the United States was serious about the war. The American leadership believed that when the enemy realized America's overwhelming technical superiority, they would have no other choice.[13] The U.S. strategy was to continuously increase the bombing and break the will to fight. This hypothesis proved to be invalid.

Instead, the United States adopted a policy of gradualism which went against the grain of proven military strategy. This was further violated by having high-level civilians in Washington select strategic bombing targets over the wishes and desires of military strategists in the field.[14]

The Persian Gulf War was different. Not only did the war clearly show the transition toward the Information Age, but it is an excellent study of lessons learned and the evolution of improvement from Vietnam. The political and military agendas were aligned. There clearly was a military solution to the combined agenda. The military was allowed to plan and wage the war as required to achieve their mission. The politicians paralleled the military effort by gaining necessary internal and global support for the military solution.

There was one mission: to reoccupy Kuwait and seize control from the Iraqi forces.[15] The clarity of the mission permitted both the military and the politicians to perform their roles. Plans, parameters, goals, and objectives were drafted. These included understanding the mood of the American voters, the strengths and weaknesses of the Iraqi military, and the extremely complex diplomacy (and funding) that would be required on a global basis. This integration of information and knowledge was a significant difference from Vietnam.

The alignment necessary for victory in an information war includes not only political and military strength but also attention to social, economic, technological, and ethical values of many diverse groups. Once information dominance over the enemy is successful, more traditional battlefield strategies and tactics can be effectively utilized. In the Persian Gulf War, the ground battle was fought in less than one hundred hours using deception to execute a flanking maneuver.

The metrics were different. The number of bombs dropped was replaced with the number of sorties flown, hit ratios, and the number of targets destroyed. There was a continuous tally of key weapon, strength such as the number of tanks, missiles, aircraft, and infantry units. Geographical positioning and dominance, always a vital metric of any war, were continuously monitored.

So successful was information dominance, that even prior to the beginning of the ground battle, the Iraqis had lost the ability to track their own field troops.[16] With no air force and no ability to track either their own troops or the enemy, the Iraqis were quickly defeated.

The United States and the coalition forces won the Persian Gulf War with many of the advantages they lacked during Vietnam. In the Persian Gulf, leadership was committed to gathering and integrating all the necessary resources required to fulfill the mission.

Integrated leadership couples leading indicators with lagging indicators and uses information to effect goals or desired results. The more skilled and competent leaders become in integrating successful action with intended results, the more likely it is that those chartered results will be achieved. In the Information Age the linking of entire organizations with their environment to achieve defined visions is not only possible, it is essential.

SUPPORTING CONCEPTS OF INTEGRATED LEADERSHIP

SUCCESS

What is success? Success is whatever one defines it to be. A simple definition of success is the setting and achievement of a valued intention (or goal, or several goals).

To some, success maybe a world-renowned symphony concert. To others it may be a local grade-school recital. After all, music is music. A professional concert performance and a local group of musicians both use similar ingredients. Each uses the same score, since the music was created and documented by Mozart, Bach, or some other composer. They have similar instruments that are probably built to high specifications and well-tested and broken in. But the output, or results, are different.

Anyone who experiences the two will agree that the music does not sound the same. Since one is superior in almost every technical aspect, is it a success while the other fails? The answer depends on how success is defined. If the purpose of a local concert is to identify talent for a regional concert, there is a high likelihood that the local concert will be a success. On the other hand, if the success of the finest orchestra anywhere is measured by its ability to completely sell out a concert hall on a particular night, it may not always be deemed successful.

Using these criteria for success, both orchestras can fail or succeed independent of each other. It is only if the two are competing directly with each other, using the same criteria, that one must succeed and the other fail. In reality, these two will complement each other while existing in a win–win relationship. The professionals will continually motivate and help those of the amateur ranks, and the amateurs will continually produce new professionals.

Success from the standpoint of the London Symphony Orchestra may be to produce the finest music in the world, however it is measured. It may be to play to packed concert halls, or attract the finest musicians in the world, or to show a sizable profit, or any combination of measures. Success for the local school orchestra may be to produce three concerts in a season, or gain recognition as one of the finest musical developmental institutions in a four-county area, or meet the satisfaction of the local parent–teacher organization.

In a simple sense, success is measured as the output of a process that meets or exceeds the goal. A process is a series of inputs that are combined with activities, tasks and action steps that come together to produce an output. The goal may place restrictions or conditions (either implied or expressed) on the process itself, so the process must reach a certain level of efficiency in order to reach the goal.

For example, a shoe company that has a goal to gain and sustain the global market leadership position in athletic shoes has built in an efficiency requirement for itself. Theoretically, it may be able to achieve a global market leadership position by pricing below cost or through heavy advertising or by acquiring competitors. However, these strategies may be short-term or result in bankruptcy or severe downsizing. These options may not meet the sustainability goal. The sustainability portion forces or limits the options to those that are profitable or efficient.

Since leadership both sets the goals and develops and implements the methodology for their achievement, success or failure is ultimately their responsibility. Although success can never be guaranteed, there are certain principles and codes that, when followed, will provide the highest chance of success.

EVOLUTION—ACCUMULATION OF KNOWLEDGE

There probably are very few, if any, things invented or discovered today that are not dependent on earlier inventions or discoveries. Human progress is built on the continual advancement of knowledge through innovative application that builds on earlier research and invention.

Evolution is built on the notion of cause and effect. The state of anything is an effect. An effect is the result of a series of causes that were earlier effects of other causes. Every object, every achievement, every organization, and every situation are the result of a complex series of causes. The value that customers receive from an organization is the output, or *effect* of a number of processes (or causes). In order to achieve a different *effect*, or an improved result, the causes must be changed.

Not all causes are equal. Some contribute very heavily to a result, and others may have almost insignificant influence. Over time, with enough observations or enough research, causes can be measured and compared mathematically. High value improvement comes through deliberate and targeted cause modification with extensive knowledge and leading metrics of the system that produces the result.

COMPETITION

Most living things on earth are competitive by nature. Individuals in a democratic or communist environment, those employed by a regulated utility, a nonprofit organization, or owners of a neighborhood convenience store; all compete. Some may have tougher competitors than others and some may have more favorable rules or more power to support their goals, but they all compete.

The human being is designed for competition; we evolved as a species because of competition. The good news about competition is that it continually pushes the human species to new frontiers. The downside is that not everyone plays by the same rules, life is not always fair, and things can get ugly.

Individuals can elevate themselves and their organizations to a state where most efforts are directed at wealth creation, adding value and win–win relations in a defined niche where "beating" competition is not the only measure of success. This is a level where wealth creation becomes maximized.

IMPROVEMENT RATE—A KEY METRIC

The Japanese clearly won the improvement rate battle from the early 1950s through the 1980s in many areas of manufacturing. The early "baby boomers"[17] growing up in the 1950s played with toys that were stamped on the bottom: "Made in Japan." They quickly learned not to become emotionally attached to Japanese toys, because they usually failed after a few uses. The Mean Time to Failure (MTF) of the mostly bamboo and tin toys was usually a few minutes of normal use.

By the time the early baby boomers were finishing high school in the mid-1960s, they were beginning to use more and more Japanese products, ranging from electronics to motorcycles. These products were popular because they were durable and less expensive than similar products produced either domestically or abroad. In the 1970s, the Japanese had moved steadily into the production of automobiles, cameras, tools, tires, small kitchen appliances, and color television sets. The Japanese had come a long way in two decades.

In certain markets, Japanese suppliers applied integrated leadership principles better than their American counterparts during these decades.

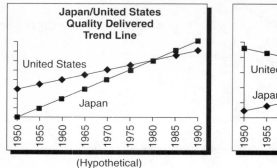
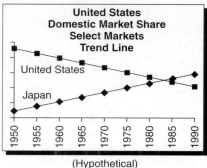

(Hypothetical)   (Hypothetical)

Figure 1.5   The enhanced quality of Japanese products in select U.S. markets helped improve their market share.

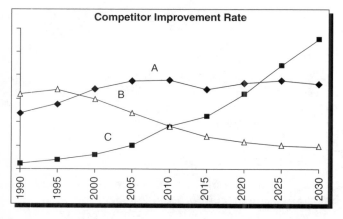

Figure 1.6   Over time an organization's performance depends on its rate of improvement against its competitors' rates of improvement.

The Japanese first noticed the increasing American demand for quality and they set their goals to meet these demands. They effectively integrated market information with the strategic positioning of delivery, which caught not only the consumer but competitors by surprise. The result was high market share gain. The graphs in Figure 1.5 show the impact that delivered quality had on market share over several decades in some U.S. markets.

Over time, market share not only depends on the absolute quality advantage, but also on the rate of improvement. The acceleration rate in comparison with other competitors determines the future of all players. The chart in Figure 1.6 is an essential control panel indicator for organizations that plan to retain or gain market leadership positions.

In the Information Age, market winners are those who use information to gain the knowledge and wisdom to improve at a rate that exceeds other market forces.

LINKING ACTIVITY WITH GOALS AND RESULTS

A few years ago, I was working with a global financial services organization where the president "negotiated" annual objectives with the executives. Each member of the senior staff were responsible for meeting five goals during the year. Each executive's performance was measured against these objectives to determine continuing employment, salary increases, bonuses, and other perks. Unfortunately, less than 10 percent of the objectives were quantified and less than 5 percent focused on results.

One goal, in particular, raised my curiosity. The top operations officer had a goal to visit 30 branch offices during the course of the year. This represented 20 percent of her objectives for the year.

The rationale for the 30 visits was based on the belief that the executive did not visit the field enough, and forcing her to go out more may somehow result in a better performance. The executive attended a conference in a metropolitan area in early March and was able to extend the trip and visit eighteen branches in one day. Similar arrangements were made on two other occasions, and by the end of May, the executive had visited more than 50 branches in only three days' effort.

She had exceeded her annual goal by 60 percent before the year was half completed. The average time spent in each branch was less than ten minutes. Her performances in her other four objectives were equal to her branch visit goals. Using the company's "state of the art" executive performance assessment criteria, she was at the top in the final rankings. She was a marvelous success, while her operational results remained flat.

Similar logic is repeated around the globe. People have goals to attend training, go to conferences, provide better efforts, work on being nicer, be a better team member, work harder or smarter, and millions of other activities that should lead to better results. This approach may help the evaluator maintain control over the assessment, since performance is not linked with results, but it does not help provide clarity to the person being evaluated. Even more tragic is that this approach breaks the causal chain that is necessary to harmonize metrics.

A goal without a plan or the means of achievement is a fantasy. Action plans without a target or a desired destination may head anywhere. To assure that goals are fulfilled there has to be action taken along a track that will lead to the desired result. This track is an action plan that is designed and implemented to cause the attainment of the goal.

For metrics to be integrated and meaningful, there must be some consistency at their origins or lower levels. This requires quantification and the ability to study cause and effect by linking action with results. In the

Information Age the integration of metrics throughout the system is essential to meet the value requirements of the market.

CREATING A NEW VISION

Chapter 10 offers some insights and predictions on how the concepts presented in the previous nine chapters will continue to evolve and how they might also be used in applications outside commerce and industry. These applications include government, medicine, science, politics, sociology, education, law, the stock market, and international relations.

The chapter provides valuable opportunities for organizations to jump ahead of competition. It presents scenarios of a world where value added and wealth creation extend into education, politics, government, social welfare, the stock market, law, art, technology, and health.

KEY POINTS   INTEGRATED LEADERSHIP

- Value is the primary metric of the Information Age.
- Information derives through understanding from observation and data and becomes the base for knowledge and wisdom. This cycle is repeated again and again to gain enlightenment.
- Value is always a key criteria in decision making.
- Value is expressed by the formula (What is received ÷ What is paid). The numerator and denominator contain both perception and reality.
- In the emerging Information Age, value does not always depend on capital investment; the potential for wealth creation is essentially limitless.
- Leadership is taking the responsibility for and performing or guiding the action necessary to plan for and achieve desired results.
- A primary role of a leader is to bring purpose, clarity, and direction to an organization.
- Success is the setting of and achievement of a valued intent (or goal).
- Integrated leadership is required to add value and create wealth in the Information Age.
- Improvement is another term for evolution. The rate of improvement is a key determinant of long-term success of an organization.
- Every living thing, by nature, is competitive.

- Any goal or result is the effect of a series of causes. Improvement is gained only by modification of the causes.
- Metrics are critical to success. The more complex the goal is or the larger the gap between where an organization is now and where it is going, the more critical metrics become.
- A control panel, or system of information integration, is necessary to understand and lead in the Information Age.
- The availability of data and the speed that data is converted to wisdom is the key to success in the Information Age.
- A control panel integrates critical metrics of an organization and assists in system balance and harmony.
- *Following are the basic principles of Integrated Leadership.*

PRINCIPLES OF INTEGRATED LEADERSHIP

- A solid organizational foundation must be carefully planned, its major elements integrated and means of implementation developed. (*foundation planning*)
- The organization must understand and be aligned with the vision, mission and plans. (*vertical alignment*)
- Customer needs and requirements and the performance of competitors in targeted and potential markets must be thoroughly understood. (*customer/market driven*)
- The organization must maximize value throughout the customer chain. (*horizontal alignment*)
- There must be a high level of understanding and application of process management tools and continuous improvement methods. (*basic value management*)
- There must be effective leadership basics that assure competency, teamwork, and communication throughout the organization. (*basic leadership*)
- There must be appropriate and consistent metrics that encompass the above principles along with their integration into a cohesive system that all can use to do their job. (*control panel*)

NOTES

1. W. Stanley Jevons, *Investigations in Currency and Finance,* Pt. 2, Cp. 4 (1884) quoted from *The Columbia Dictionary of Quotations* is licensed from Columbia University Press. Copyright © 1993 by Columbia University Press.

2. Bruce Horovitz, "Value-Minded Consumers Call the Shots," *USA Today,* 10 September, 1996, Money section, quote form Joe Wilke, executive vice president of The Bases Group, a marketing consultant.

3. The MBNQA is an annual award to recognize U.S. organizations for competitiveness and performance excellence as granted under Public Law 100–107. It is managed by the National Institute of Standards and Technology in Gaithersburg, Maryland and administered by the American Society for Quality in Milwaukee, Wisconsin.

4. Stephen R. Covey, *The Seven Habits of Highly Effective People* (New York: Simon & Schuster, 1986).

5. Alvin Toffler, *Powershift: Knowledge, Wealth, and Violence At The Edge Of The 21st Century* (New York: Bantam Books, 1990), p. 18.

6. David S. Alberts and Richard E. Haynes. "The Realm of Information Dominance: Beyond Information War." First International Symposium on Command and Control Research and Technology (June 1995).

7. James P. Womack, Daniel T. Jones, and Daniel Roos, *The Machine That Changed The World* (New York: Rawson Associates, Macmillan Publishing Company, 1990). This is an excellent text on the transformation of the auto industry to lean production.

8. See note 5, pp. 19–21.

9. Robert W. Lucky, *Silicon Dreams: Information, Man and Machine* (New York: St. Martin's Press, 1989) p. 2. In the late 1980s the estimate was two-thirds of the population. The percentage has increased since that time. It is difficult to imagine many jobs in the future where information is not the essential product.

10. See note 5, p. 83.

11. W. Edwards Deming, *Out of the Crisis* (Cambridge: Massachusetts Institute of Technology, Center for Advanced Engineering Study, 1989), p. 32, quoting Walter A. Shewhart, *Economic Control of Quality of Manufactured Product* (Van Nostrand, 1931: repr. ed., American Society for Quality Control, 1980; reprinted by Ceepress, The George Washington University, 1986).

12. James William Gibson, *The Perfect War: Technowar In Vietnam* (Boston: The Atlantic Monthly Press, 1986), pp. 125–28. This is a revealing report of the gross over-reporting of body counts driven by "production quotas" and the rewards for overcounting.

13. Gibson, *The Perfect War*, pp. 97–98.

14. See note 13, p. 268.

15. Although there may be disagreement on whether the mission was appropriate or best for the coalition forces, it was clear, concise and doable.

16. Edward Mann, "Desert War: The First Information War?" *Airpower Journal* (Winter 1994): 4–14.

17. Those born at the end of World War II, from 1946 through 1964.

Chapter 2

FOUNDATION PLANNING AND ORGANIZATIONAL ALIGNMENT

> *What is a visionary company? Visionary companies are premier institutions—the crown jewels—in their industries, widely admired by their peers and having a long track record of making a significant impact on the world around them. The key point is that a visionary company is an organization—an institution. All individual leaders, no matter how charismatic or visionary, eventually die; and all visionary products and services—all "great ideas"— eventually become obsolete. Indeed, entire markets can become obsolete and disappear. Yet visionary companies prosper over long periods of time, through multiple product life cycles and multiple generations of active leaders.*
>
> —BUILT TO LAST[1]

Long-term success is built on the right foundation. The foundation and its subsequent structure depend largely on its purpose. The same is true for organizations. Therefore, the foundation of an organization can be defined as the basis for which it stands. Once the foundation is created, the structure and the necessary integrated systems to achieve the purpose can be designed and built.

An organization is much more complex than a physical structure. In additional to internal matters, an organization, particularly one offering a vast array of products and services, exists and is driven by countless external influences as complicated as politics, human nature and diversity, regulation, competition, economics, technology, and ethics. These factors and many more all impact the structure.

THE CASE FOR FOUNDATION PLANNING

Almost every organization claims to have a long-term plan. It is an excellent starting point in the value journey, and the place to begin with any organization that wants to improve performance. However, most executives eventually admit that their current plans leave much room for improvement.

Some organizations have great plans; they have spent the proper time, resources and energy to develop, implement and adjust their planning processes. Most have not. The great organizations build and maintain a solid foundation for their organization through their approach to planning. The organizations that fail, struggle, or achieve mediocre or random success do not dedicate the required resources to planning.

In the West, we like to take a checklist or "bullet point" approach to business. If the checklist for success says we need a strategic plan, we order one up. The fact that we have one should be enough. Nothing could be further from reality. What is needed is a *winning* plan. The correlation coefficient between planning success and organizational success must be very close to 1.0.

This chapter is critical for two reasons:

1. Most organizations continually do a relatively poor job of planning.
2. The control panel required for the Information Age is largely dependent on a proper foundation.

It is based on proven models of planning that are just as sound in the Information Age as they are in the Industrial Age. However, the application of the models are significantly different in the two ages.

THE FOUNDATION AND THE VISION

The integration that a high performance organization in the Information Age requires must be built into the foundation and basic core of the organization. This step is critical for subsequent organizational alignment.

The purpose, or mission, comes first and defines where the organization fits into the larger design of a universe. Its values, or what it stands for, are the second element of the foundation. What the organization will accomplish at a future point is its vision. The vision is the aiming point that springs from the foundation. Figure 2.1 shows the vision being created from its foundation.

In many cases, both the mission and values of an organization were established when the organization was founded, and they change very little, if at all, throughout its history. In other cases, external factors or the shortsightedness of the founders may cause needed modifications. Periodically, a

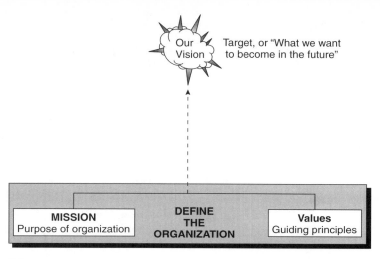

Figure 2.1   The organization is defined by its mission and values; what it will accomplished is stated by its vision.

mission and its values should be reviewed for appropriateness and continued commitment.

The establishment or modification of an organization's mission, core values, and vision must be driven by the highest level of the organization. Any number of people or levels of the organization can be involved with input, recommendations, or information gathering, but the final decision must be made or endorsed at the highest level, which represents the interests of *all* stakeholders.

Although a clear mission, values, and vision have always been important and valuable, they are becoming essential. In the Industrial Age, the only people who absolutely needed a big-picture, long-term perspective of the organization were a few executives at the top. Everyone else had a very narrow scope and basically followed orders.

In the Information Age, two dynamics exist that require more fundamental high-level knowledge of the purpose, values, and vision of an organization. The first is that substantially more information is required to conduct the affairs of an organization; therefore, the total information needed cannot be synthesized down to a few orders that can be issued to the work force. The second reflects that today's work force needs knowledge of a larger perspective in order to do their jobs. Competency is no longer determined by the ability to master a few motor skills and follow directions. Competency is driven by understanding a big picture and using creativity and the application of diverse and flexible skills to achieve targeted results.

Cross-functional teamwork is essential for a work force to compete effectively in the Information Age. It goes well beyond work teams; it requires coordination with many dissimilar and often very specialized functions. Without higher purposes, goals and values, individuals or small units cannot work efficiently together.

MISSION

The mission of an organization is its primary purpose or reason for being; it is why the organization exists. A local social club may exist to bring together people with a common hobby to share their interests and experiences with that particular hobby. The United Nations was chartered in 1945 to "maintain international peace and security and to achieve cooperation in solving international economic, social, cultural, and humanitarian problems."[2]

Every organization is unique, and every mission should be unique. It is a statement created by the organization to let stakeholders[3] and frequently the public-at-large know why it exists. It can be a simple statement such as the Newport News Shipyard:

We shall build great ships.
At a profit if we can
At a loss if we must
But we will build great ships.[4]

Or, a mission statement can describe the quality of products and services, its own values on doing business, or any personalized touch it will provide. For example:

Solectron's mission is to provide worldwide responsiveness to our customers by offering the highest quality, lowest total cost, customized integrated manufacturing services through long-term partnerships based on integrity and ethical business practices.[5]

Our mission is to grow as a global enterprise focused on developing best values through innovation, partnerships and continuous improvement in everything we do.[6] (Rubbermaid)

A mission does not have to be labeled as a mission to be one. It may be a statement of fact that an organization makes about what it does. An example is:

Federal Express Corporation offers a wide range of express services for the time-definite transportation of documents, packages and freight throughout the world, using an extensive fleet of aircraft and vehicles and leading-edge information technologies.[7]

Hewlett-Packard states a brief corporate profile to describe elements of its business.

Hewlett-Packard Company designs, manufactures and services products and systems for measurement, computation and communications. Our basic business is to create information products that accelerate the advancement of knowledge and improve the effectiveness of people and organizations.[8]

The importance of the mission is to provide focus. It is a statement for the world to see. It allows all stakeholders and potential stakeholders to see the broad parameters that define the organization. When things become fuzzy or tempting, it offers a homing beacon to help employees, whether permanent, temporary, contracted or telecommuters, steer decisions and choices. It is a critical element of long-term strategy; it provides the widest foundation for marketing.

The mission should be general in nature and extremely *long-term* or permanent. When the mission is developed several tests should be conducted. It must be *accurate;* it must be *encompassing;* it must be *enduring;* it must have *substance;* and, it must be *supported* by all major stakeholders. If these guides are not satisfied, work must continue until they are.

A mission can be as simple as a slogan; for example:

We make things that make communication work.[9] (Lucent Technologies)

Our mission is to provide simpler ways to do good work.[10] (Xerox)

Every organization should have a description of its major purpose, whether it is called a mission or purpose or some other term.

VALUES

A second element of the organizational foundation is values. These are the principles upon which the organization is based. They derive from and must be compatible with the mission. They add clarity and further define the mission.

Examples of values are: "We provide outstanding customer service," "The customer is always right," or, "We treat our employees with dignity and respect." Organizational values are not intentions or wishes; they are accurate statements that define what is important to an organization and they become the basis for policy and behavior.

Organizations have both written and unwritten values; sometimes they are confusing and occasionally they conflict. Since values are always critical, they require careful attention and deliberate clarity for common understanding. Values are at a higher level than policies or rules. They are the *basis* for decision making, not the rule itself. They are broad and designed to provide guidance.

A few examples of strong values that are openly stated by organizations are:

Innovation, creativity, risk-taking, idea sharing, entrepreneurial spirit.[11] (3M)

Simply put: Listen to the customer. Provide them with what they want. Appreciate the fact they came to your store, and do everything within your power to ensure that they're satisfied when they leave.[12] (Nordstrom)

Our management philosophy begins with two key beliefs—respect for the dignity of the individual and uncompromising integrity in everything we do.

This helps to create an environment of empowerment for all in a culture of participation.[13] (Motorola)

At Motorola, we enable . . . consumers to stay in touch, customers to delight their customers, and industries to be conceived and developed. In short, Motorola enables people to do what they want to do.[14]

The culture of our business is to understand that of others.[15] (Rubbermaid)

Not just in the United States, but from London to Vienna to Tokyo, and from Prague to Moscow to Beijing to New Delhi to Buenos Aires, no one understands or cares more than we do about our customers' requirements for document processing services.[16] (Xerox)

We're creating an environment that encourages shared knowledge and continual learning, fueled by involved employees. We've removed layers of management, widened spans of control, and given our people more responsibility and accountability.[17] (Ford)

We see competitors in our rear view mirrors.[18] (Harley-Davidson)

To respect the dignity and inherent rights of the individual human being in all dealings with people.[19] (Armstrong)

These examples use profound words, terms, and statements. They offer guidance and definition. Often they are inspirational. They attract employees who share the same beliefs; they attract investors who are searching for organizations with certain basic principles, and they attract customers who prefer doing business with organizations with certain characteristics.

Organizational policies (directives, procedures, guidelines, rules) are a more specific and directive version of values. Usually, the most important are communicated to the work force through employee handbooks, to suppliers through supplier guidelines, and to customers through product or service guides and warranty and disclosure information. The trend of value-focused organizations is toward simplicity in the communication of values and policies.

VISION

The vision is born from its mission and values. It is the cornerstone of vertical (organizational) alignment. Vision has been defined and explained a number of ways. A broad definition is provided by Warren Bennis and Michael Mische:

A vision is the articulation of the image, values, direction, and goals that will guide the future of the organization.[20]

Joseph Juran states:

Some companies have adopted the word "vision" as an expression of what they would like to accomplish, or where they would like to be, sometime in the future.[21]

Gerhard Plenert adds more definition and tends to incorporate the mission and vision into a single thought:

The vision consists of one or two sentences stating where the enterprise is going. It is an enterprise's sense of purpose, its reason for being, its guiding philosophy. A vision builds unity throughout the organization. It doesn't have to be lengthy, but it does have to give the organization purpose. The vision should provide employees with a clear image with which they can identify.[22]

Every organization approaches their vision differently. Some organizations take the Bennis/Mische approach and tend to combine it with Plenert's definition. In other words they endeavor to reduce all their images, values, directions, and goals into one or two sentences. This becomes an exercise in creative wordsmithing. Other organizations want to keep their vision so simple, powerful, and dynamic that it becomes a general statement of future intent. These organizations generally use supporting means to add the necessary definitions and messages they wish to convey.

A vision is usually relevant for a shorter duration than the mission and may be modified every three to five years, or when the current one is reached, or it has been determined that either it is no longer sufficient or that it is unreasonable to achieve.

A vision should evoke *emotion*, or, at least, be a *call for fulfillment*. It should be *compelling*, it should be *simply stated* and easily *understood*, and it should be *achievable*. It should be a *stretch*. It must *tie in with the mission*, but add a dimension of *measurability*. By definition, it is the chief, *number-one goal* of the organization. In many cases, it will be a relative measure that depends on outside forces for the goal. To be meaningful, it should ultimately *add value to society* and be *shared* among all those who contribute to its attainment.

For example, a world-class runner may have a vision of winning the 100-meter dash in the Sydney Olympics in the year 2000. The ultimate determinant of whether she fulfills her vision or not depends on her time relative to the time of the other finalists. If her vision is to run 100 meters in 10.45 seconds during the next five years, she could conceivably achieve her vision without winning the gold, or even running a competitive race. Running 100 meters in 10.45 seconds can be independent of other competitors' performance; if she runs the 100 meters in 10.45 seconds in the finals of the Sydney Olympics, she may or may not collect a gold medal.

A vision should be *measurable*; whether in absolute or relative terms. The vision should be *appropriate* for the organization. Some organizations are pioneers and have values that are longer term for the betterment of the human race; others are ruthlessly competitive and their highest values are winning the race for market share. The vision must *reflect the organization's highest values.* Some examples of vision statements[23] are:

Rubbermaid's vision is to delight customers and consumers around the world with branded products which are responsive to their trends, offer superior solutions for them, and thereby improve their living standards, as well as make their lives more enjoyable and productive.[24]

To be the world's preferred chemical company.[25] (Eastman Chemical)

Ford's vision is to be the leading automotive company in the world.[26]

We are dedicated to being the world's best at bringing people together—giving them easy access to each other and to the information and services they want and need—anytime, anywhere.[27] (AT&T)

. . . remain the unrivaled leader in the fast-growing global express distribution industry, serving more customers, in more places, more quickly, reliably and cost-effectively.[28] (Federal Express)

. . . become the world's most respected service brand.[29] (American Express)

Some organizations combine their mission and vision into one statement and may title it as either one or the other. Some enterprises use other labels, such as purpose, intent, direction, credo, aim, or meaning. Others use no term at all for their vision or mission. Setting a vision requires a different focus than the mission and values. It requires perception, innovation, and insight into a specific perspective of the future. It centers on the future and is not concerned with how anything is accomplished. It is a creative process, and therefore should have no limitations in its initial concept.

Setting a vision requires using data, information, conjecture, and speculation to create a picture of the universe in which the organization will fulfill its mission in the future. This picture includes the movement over time of technology, competition, customers' changing needs, and other external factors.

An excellent vision requires careful and deliberate planning. It should supercharge the organization. It should be the reason people work for the organization, invest in it, and select it as a provider. The achievement of the vision should contribute highly to the fulfillment of the mission.

The initial vision concept should be strongly endorsed by key organizational management and be reviewed by representation of the employee force, key customers, and shareholders. Any strong opposition should be listened to and either incorporated into the final version or explained why it will not be incorporated. By the time the final version is prepared, the organization should be anticipating it with endorsement and excitement.

The format, length, and time frame for the vision depends on the requirements and tastes of the organization. However, brevity and simplicity help understanding and communication. If the time frame goes beyond five years, key milestone targets should be communicated along with the vision. If the vision is less than three years, a longer-term perspective should be communicated. An example may be, "When we accomplish this vision in two years, we will be well positioned to. . . ."

A vision is a dream or a wish unless it has an element of measurability. If an organization proclaims it will be a "world-class" provider of widgets in four years, the proclamation has little meaning until a criteria is established to quantify what the term *world class* means in the context of the vision. It may be the market leader as measured by market share or growth, the attainment of the Malcolm Baldrige National Quality Award, or a combination of measures. The members of the organization, who will be working hard to achieve the vision, must know precisely what has to be achieved.

HARLEY-DAVIDSON—AN INTEGRATED FOUNDATION

Other than identifying the company and the report title, only 10 words fill the entire cover of the 1996 Annual Report of Harley-Davidson.[30] These are: *Heritage, Quality, Passion, Look, Sound, Feel, Relationships, Freedom, Individuality,* and *Lifestyle.* These words probably say more about Harley-Davidson than most annual reports reveal about their organization in 40 pages of glossy photos and text.

The first statement on the inside front cover outlines their *vision,* which encompasses their mission, their direction, and some strong values.

> *Harley-Davidson, Inc. is an action-oriented, international company—a leader in its commitment to continuously improve the quality of mutually beneficial relationship with stakeholders (customers, dealers, employees, suppliers, investors, governments and society). Harley-Davidson believes the key to success is to balance stakeholders' interests through the empowerment of all employees to focus on value-added activities.*

Page one consists of the following statement, overlaying a photo of one of their products.

Intangible Assets

> *At Harley-Davidson, we don't measure success with charts and tables. Financial data can't begin to describe what drives our business and builds our brand. Our balance sheet doesn't include line items for freedom, individuality and heritage, even though they're among the cornerstones of our foundation. Nor does it place a dollar value on lifelong customer relationships— those immeasurable assets that are forged with a simple handshake and strengthened by our careful nurturing of the passion that unites our worldwide family. But it is just such intangibles that define Harley-Davidson and create value for our stakeholders. This report is a review of those intangibles.*

Later in the report, they reveal their objectives for Plan 2003,[31] which outlines a strong measurable vision for their hundredth anniversary year. Like many other areas, Harley-Davidson may be unconventional in their approach, but they communicate in a crystal-clear manner their mission, values, and vision.

THE PLANNING PROCESS

The vision is the planned future state of the organization. If your vision is 5, 10, or 50 years down the road, it requires a plan. The more knowledge and information you have and the shorter time frame, the more precisely

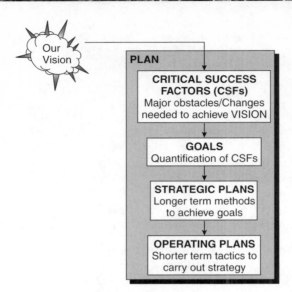

Figure 2.2 Long-term planning consists of understanding the critical success factors of attaining the vision, setting goals, and developing strategy and tactics.

you can plan. If the plan is a relatively short time frame or extremely long, the principles are the same. Figure 2.2 provides a simplistic model of a planning process to achieve the vision.

CRITICAL SUCCESS FACTORS (CSFs)

Since the vision was created within the parameters granted by the mission and values and its accomplishment will further the fulfillment of the mission, it becomes the primary focus. The path from where the organization currently is to where it desires to be must be planned, designed, and built. It is essential that the highest-level leadership in the organization participate fully in the initial high-level design phase. They may delegate data gathering and the accumulation of information, knowledge, and wisdom to others, but senior management must drive the strategic planning function.

This design phase is a very creative process. The vision is expanded by imagining what the organization will be like when the vision is reached. The key elements should be described and captured in written form. The clearer the image of the future, the more likely it will be realized.

This conceptual exercise should include defining the technology, employee competencies, leadership skills, sales, distribution, support, competitors, techniques, methodologies, systems, and resources that will exist at the time the vision is met. This may be approached using different or contingent scenarios or by carefully expanding the obvious and most likely future representation.

With an expanded view of the future organization and external factors, along with a clear understanding of the organization's current circumstances, the differences can be identified. The executive team begins answering the question, "What factors or conditions must change for us to move from our current performance levels to those outlined in our vision?"

The process should move from an extensive brainstorming exercise to a crisp Pareto[32] list of the top five to seven items, ranked in order of criticality to the attainment of the vision. This is tough to do in many cases, but it will pay dividends by establishing priorities when others are involved in the more detailed planning phase.

Critical success factors frequently fall under several broad categories:

1. *Organization-specific core competencies*—the organization sees a need to improve core competencies, develop new ones, or seize a new opportunity to capitalize on existing ones.
2. *Increasing value*—since value is the top competitive factor, improvement of value is almost always a CSF. This includes both sides of the value formula, as well as productivity, quality, efficiency, and effectiveness.
3. *Technology*—this applies to both the core products and services provided by the organization, as well as the value added and support processes that produce them.
4. *People development*—in addition to those associated with organization competencies and technology, many organizations see a need to improve leadership, team building, innovation, customer service, and general skills for individuals.
5. *Customer focus*—this includes all parts and aspects of the organization.
6. *Strategic partnering*—organizations are realizing more than ever their own limitations that can be supplemented with partners and the benefits that exist in partnership arrangements.
7. *Information management*—this ties into technology, but the massive amounts of information available and needed are increasing at explosive rates, along with processing power.
8. *Cycle time reduction*—related to value. In the arena of time-based competition, mass customization, and real time information access, speed is an increasing factor. The most focused area is usually in product or service design and delivery.

It is extremely important to achieve a high degree of consensus among the top team in its agreement that the critical success factors (CSFs) are correct and in the proper order. If there is any doubt, the issues should be worked through and resolved. On a rare occasion, the vision may need adjusting after new information or logic emerges from this process. It is also extremely important to capture the essence of why each CSF was selected and provide a short operating definition of each one.

When the senior team spends high energy in identifying and prioritizing CSFs, they begin to see the linkages among them. They are not separate issues that can be handled one by one. Each is vitally linked to the others, and the successful attainment of one usually depends on the progress of the others.

The dynamics of the senior team working through this process will become obvious. Even though there is still much work to do, they have established the proper foundation. Each member better understands the big picture and will give a much higher endorsement and support to the plans that will achieve the vision through the management of the critical success factors. Another vital step is also taking place; *the organization is building the base for its control panel.*

GOALS

High-level organizational goals are primarily the quantified expression of a successful attainment of CSFs. The key to the description of any goal is the *measured result* that is desired. In the Industrial Age, the preponderance of goals are expressed in activities; such as implement a new system, complete a project, attend a class, open a factory.

In the Information Age, goals focus on results, not activity or the completion of an event. Goals need to answer the question, "What do we want the activity or event to achieve?"

A goal should contain the following elements:

1. *What*—short description of the result, or what should be achieved
2. *How much*—where possible, an absolute or relative number; when this is not possible, a description that leaves no doubt that the goal has or has not been reached
3. *When*—an exact date or deadline that the result will be achieved
4. *Who*—the person responsible for the goal

Since many CSFs involve complex or large solutions, the goals generally are broken down into milestones. Some of the earlier milestones may be activities, or implementation steps, and the actual results may follow after a longer time frame.

Goals should tie in with value-added results. Financial performance and its measures are always appropriate goals, as long as they are not at the expense of other value indicators. In other words, a goal of a large increase in number of products shipped appears to be an appropriate subject for a goal. However, if it does not have balancing goals such as the maintenance of margins, expenses, or quality, the gains might be less than offsetting losses.

Innovation, new product development cycle time reduction, improved information systems, people development, and a decreased supplier base are all appropriate goals. However, the achievement of these goals should produce higher value products and services to customers. An appropriate control panel will measure the correlation among various factors.

STRATEGIC AND OPERATING PLANS

Strategic plans are the methods, systems, activities, and solutions that will fulfill the goals. Strategy for the most urgent goal should be developed, followed by the next most urgent, down to the least urgent. This approach allows integration of goals, so the implementation of one does not adversely impact another. Integration must take place both at high-level strategy and lower-level tactics.

Plans must also be developed to align with the organization. Strategy is generally planned and implemented at the higher levels of the organization and deployed into tactics and activities at the lower levels.

Strategy is driven by a set of subgoals that support the organizational goals. These are, in turn, supported by tactical objectives. All subgoals and objectives should contain the same four elements as goals.

DEPLOYMENT

Deployment or execution puts plans into use or action; it is the manifestation of plans. In reality, it is action, not plans, that achieve goals. But, on the other hand, action without adequate planning is frequently destined to fail. However, we know that in the real world, things continually change. Therefore, plans need constant monitoring and adjustment; exactly what a control panel does best.

Special operations may be used to help implement plans (particularly those areas that are cross-functional), explore new opportunities, act as a skunk works for nontraditional requirements, or any special area requiring attention. Any goal or objective that is measured by successful implementation instead of the result it produces should be considered a project. Projects teams are generally launched by the executive team as needs become recognized, new opportunities are identified, or plans are not being achieved. Progress of major project teams are usually reported in the control panel.

PLANNING/DEPLOYMENT MODEL

The mission, values, vision, and CSFs provide the starting point for an organization to reach an ultimate destiny of high wealth creation. The model outlined in Figure 2.3 shows the elements needed to assure that planning is completed and implemented, the results reviewed, and adjustments made so that the organization achieves its vision.

Model for Leadership Planning/Deployment

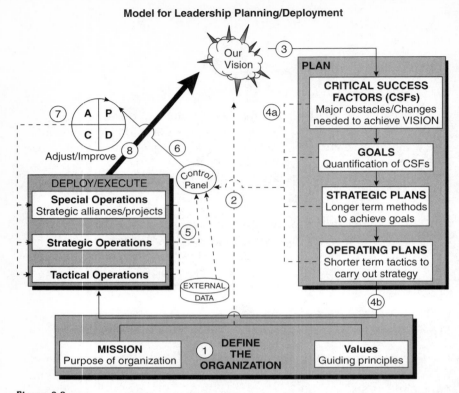

Figure 2.3 The Model for Leadership Planning/Deployment is a closed loop that allows for continual adjustment to meet plans in a changing world.

The following elements are outlined in the Model for Leadership Planning in Figure 2.3:

1. The organization is defined by its mission and values.
2. A vision is created that provides the organization with an aiming point for the future.
3. Plans are drafted that will attain the vision in a specified time frame.
4. (a) Metrics that are defined in the planning process become baseline data in the organization's control panel. (b) Plans are deployed by the operational functions of the organization.
5. Information from deployment is continuously monitored with the help of the control panel.
6. Results are continuously checked against new information from both external and internal sources and are adjusted with improvements
7. Adjustments are implemented.
8. The organization successfully moves toward its vision.

Since this model and similar versions are widely used, details of planning and deployment are not highlighted. Instead, the focuses should be on the continual monitoring of deployment against plans and the ongoing adjustment process as new information emerges.

VERTICAL ALIGNMENT

Vertical alignment assures that the organization is congruently linked with its vision through an appropriate plan. This includes a check on the soundness of the plan, along with the proper structure and communication to assure it is carried out and achieves the desired results.

Vertical alignment, is closely akin to horizontal alignment which is covered in chapter 4. The major target of vertical alignment is the vision; the primary target of horizontal alignment is the customer. Vertical alignment focuses on the organizational structure necessary to meet the long-term and short-term goals and objectives of the organization. Horizontal alignment focuses on maximizing value to the customer, while moving toward the vision. Although the two must be designed harmoniously, they continually require fine-tuning to assure optimal performance. This is accomplished with the assistance of the control panel.

Vertical Alignment is primarily assured in three main stages:

1. *Plan Deployment*—plans the deployment of the plan from the most senior level through the production level
2. *Communication*—clearly communicates the plan throughout the organization and assigns responsibility for its achievement at all levels
3. *Review*—provides ongoing feedback of plan implementation and results to allow for adjustments as necessary

Plan Deployment

The primary means of deploying plans throughout the organization is the *catchball*, or the *objective/means* method. The goals derived from the critical success factors are broken down into the various means of achieving the goal. For example, an organization may have a vision of being the market leader, and one of the CSFs to achieve the vision is strong customer focus.

A number of organizational goals may be developed under the customer-focused CSF. Some examples are:

1. Improve customer loyalty to a level that exceeds 85 percent within three years.
2. Reduce the time of new product design to less than 6 months within 3 years and to less than 3 months in 5 years while achieving a 5 percent average per-year reduction in resources dedicated to product design.

3. Improve average installation time to less than 20 days within 3 years and to less than 8 days within 5 years, while achieving an average of 7 percent average reduction per year in front-line resources used per installation.

Figure 2.4 uses a customer loyalty goal and deploys it down through the organization to the unit and individual levels. Of course, several departments, a number of units, and a significant number of individuals may eventually inherit objectives that collectively "roll up" to achieve a measured improvement in customer loyalty.

Under this system higher levels develop a means of achieving each goal/objective and pass the means down the organization, where it becomes an objective for the immediate lower level. The slang expression, *catch-ball*, to label this methodology is based on "catching the ball" thrown down the organization. The application of the system must be bidirectional, where the lower levels validate or modify the means and must either accept or help adjust the objectives to attainable levels.

This system helps assure the achievement of goals, readily identifies needed adjustments, is the base for key control panel sensors, and provides a high degree of metrics that can be used in team and individual goal setting, training, assessments, rewards and recognition, and personal development.

There must be direct linkages from the vision down to individual employee's objectives. Some training is required at each layer of the organization: first to illustrate the path and then to instruct the team leader or manager to communicate and link each performance metric. This illustration and linkage to the vision is critical *where the work is done!* If the message does not reach the individual, then the organization will not efficiently reach the stated vision.

COMMUNICATION

Communicating is an ongoing job of organizational leaders. Nowhere is it more important than the mission, values, vision, goals and plans. Communication is more than placing some words in a newsletter and providing every stakeholder with a copy. By definition, these items are the priorities of the organization. If they are not, senior management did not do its job in establishing the foundation.

The proper vertical alignment of the organization ensures that every individual, every function, every team, and every unit knows their role by preparing their own missions[33] to align with the larger organization. Alignment and shared purposes become part of ongoing communications, training, and new employee indoctrination.

A monumental problem in many organizations is the proliferation of conflicting objectives at the lower levels. When a unit creates its objectives without shared linkages, it may increase its performance at the detriment of other units. When this becomes the practice, the optimization of units drives the suboptimization of the organization. The time to avoid many of

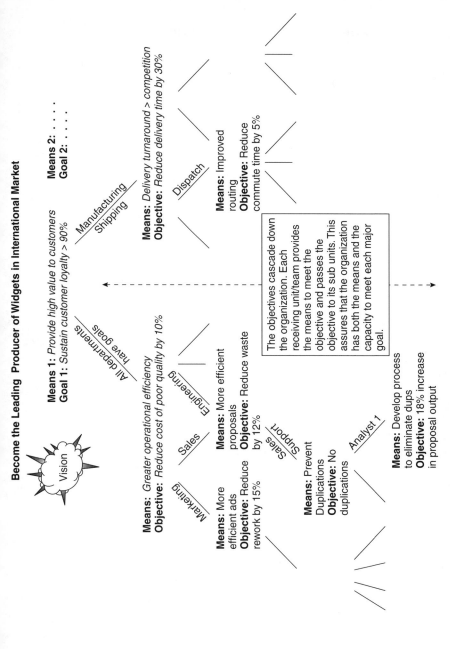

Become the Leading Producer of Widgets in International Market

Vision

Means 1: *Provide high value to customers*
Goal 1: *Sustain customer loyalty > 90%*

Means 2: · · · ·
Goal 2: · · · ·

Means: *Greater operational efficiency*
Objective: *Reduce cost of poor quality by 10%*

All departments have goals

Manufacturing
Shipping

Means: *Delivery turnaround > competition*
Objective: *Reduce delivery time by 30%*

Dispatch

Means: Improved routing
Objective: Reduce commute time by 5%

Marketing

Means: More efficient ads
Objective: Reduce rework by 15%

Sales
Engineering

Means: More efficient proposals
Objective: Reduce waste by 12%

Sales Support

Means: Prevent Duplications
Objective: No duplications

Analyst 1

Means: Develop process to eliminate dups
Objective: 18% increase in proposal output

The objectives cascade down the organization. Each receiving unit/team provides the means to meet the objective and passes the objective to its sub units. This assures that the organization has both the means and the capacity to meet each major goal.

Figure 2.4 The Objective/Means Deployment is a useful tool to deploy goals through the organization by assuring that both the means and capacity exist.

43

these mistakes is still in the planning and early deployment phases. The cost of correction is very high later.

Initially, as cross-functional units share and coordinate purposes, much confusion and animosity is reduced. This results in higher productivity and improved commitment.

REVIEW

Since the top priority of every organization is the successful transition toward its vision and the achievement of its top goals, it is critical to continually monitor the movement and the trends. Control panels should be designed and built to capture and process leading and real-time data in a manner such that progress can be both reported and predicted on a continuous basis.

Systems that are capable of capturing and processing data from the transactional and task levels can easily convert to information that correlates with goals, objectives and unlimited amounts of other factors. The understanding and knowledge gained through observation and analysis should be communicated back to the organization for input and feedback. This leads to greater knowledge. This type of cybernetic system becomes a major tool of the learning organization.

The senior management team should meet at fairly frequent intervals with the primary purpose of reviewing progress toward major objectives, goals, and the vision. During this time, updated trends in the voice of the customer (see chapter 3), head-to-head competitive drifts, and other key metrics should be reviewed and discussed for tactical adjustments and possible strategic implications.

In addition to providing sound leadership to the organization, these sessions reinforce the importance of the foundation plans and senior management's commitment to results and clearer understanding of the underlying drivers of success.

CONTROL PANEL

The top goal of an organization is its vision, and the pathway to the vision is the successful attainment of the CSFs, which are measured by supporting goals. These are always priority items on a control panel.

There are an unlimited number of ways to format information via communication displays, and each organization should tailor its communication to meet its culture and preferences. There should be a sense of priority and linkages in a control panel. In other words, those indicators that are highest in importance should be displayed as being more prominent. The indicators that drive or correlate most directly with these high indicators should be in the close vicinity of the higher indicator or somehow reflect the connection.

Most executives are familiar with and work well with charts and graphs. Learning organizations and those that are progressing ahead into

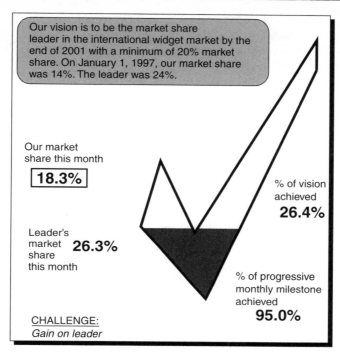

Figure 2.5 The Quality Check Company uses its logo to display progress toward its vision.

the Information Age use creative types of displays for their employees and other stakeholders. Some use cleverly designed and colorful representations to be more pleasing and appealing. Some organizations publish a periodic notebook on progress, others are formatted to be displayed on computer screens, and others continue to be a stack of charts and graphs.

Since the vision is the most serious focus of the organization, it should be continuously displayed for all those who work to fulfill it. In central work areas it can be displayed on walls, bulletin boards, in lunch and break rooms, or any common area. Since a vision is measured and has a definite target date, everyone should know the continuous progression toward the goal. Figure 2.5 shows an example of how the vision and progressive updates can be configured on a story board or display screen.

The example in Figure 2.5 only shows progress at a particular point in time. It is also important to show a historical perspective, along with some relevant information. The graph in Figure 2.6 shows the relative market share progress of the organization and the market leader over the 22 months since the vision was announced. Although the trend is favorable, the market leader has also gained market share at a level higher than the organization anticipated.

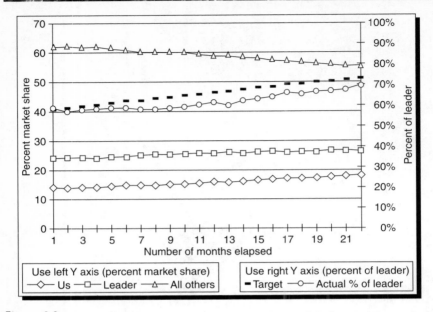

Figure 2.6 A graph will add dimension and trend information to help employees better understand the dynamics associated with movement toward the vision.

The right axis tracks the movement of the organization expressed as a percentage of the leader against a target. During the first year of vision, the market leader moved ahead of the organization's plan to close the gap in market share. However, during the past nine months the closure has improved. If this trend continues, the organization will be back on its plan within two to three months.

The control panel or scorecard concept is extremely flexible and uses a "drill down" or "roll up" approach to view the components or drivers of each indicator. For example, at a level below the vision are the critical success factors that have one or more goals associated with each one. Below the goal levels are strategies and objectives that are used to achieve and measure progress toward the goals and objectives. At any level, the capacity to drill down to lower levels or roll up the components of that level to higher levels should exist.

Along with current information on progression toward the vision, the major goals of the organization and current progress on them should be available to everyone who has responsibility for contributing to them. This should be everyone in the organization. Figure 2.7 shows an example of a format that can be used for a display board, war room, or computer display.

Other chapters offer additional examples of displaying critical indicators and visual ideas on control panels and display boards.

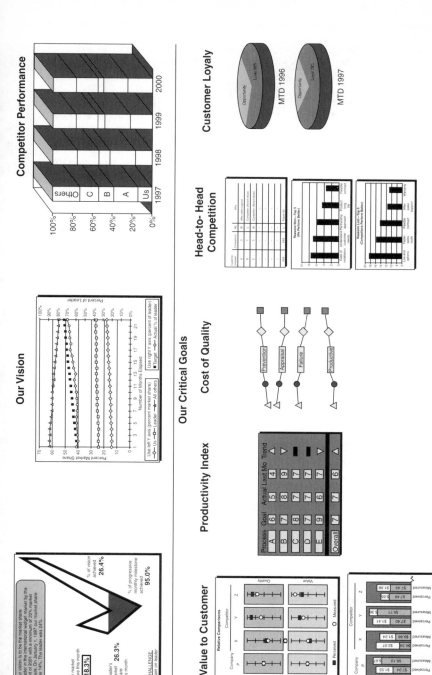

Figure 2.7 Story boards showing the organization's vision and key goals, along with linkages and results, is an effective communication tool.

THE CHALLENGES OF THE LEADER

Although there is an increased abundance of data, information, and knowledge available to today's leader, it does not necessarily make the job easier. Although these resources would provide huge advantages in the market only a few years ago, competitors are pursuing similar objectives and goals with comparable resources.

Simultaneously, customers and potential customers are experiencing new levels of products and services in identical, similar, and radically different markets. This disguises the true competitors and often masks competitive factors. For example, most product and service providers, whether public, private, profit or nonprofit, have telephone customer service operations. Many users of these operations observe a number of different providers in a variety of different circumstances over various periods of time. They form opinions based on these experiences, which lead to expectations.

If a provider only looks at its direct competitors for comparing their customer service operations, it may fall well short of understanding its customers' requirements. A survey showing it is in a top percentile of delivering service in its market may be extremely misleading and could result in disaster if an astute competitor focuses on the changing voice of the customer.

Data, information, understanding, and even wisdom can be extremely misleading and dangerous if the big picture and the changing customer are not always in the formula. Only by continually understanding the changing mind of the customer will the provider know what is driving competitive forces and be able to proactively make the right adjustments.

An organization that has established a control panel that includes its vision, and the chief drivers of success and value in its market, and has aligned its organization with that knowledge, will be well grounded and can focus on leading the operation that will create the value. Otherwise, they are always in a crisis mode and will not be efficient enough to survive when the fury of the Information Age overwhelms them.

Strong foundation planning and a well-designed control panel provides a stable internal environment while permitting a strong focus on constantly changing external factors. This permits a smooth transition to adjust the internal to external changes. This approach allows leaders to positively modify organizations and improve morale through the continual formation and reformation of an integrated team climate.

KEY POINTS   FOUNDATION PLANNING AND ORGANIZATIONAL ALIGNMENT

- Ultimate success of any organization depends on a proper foundation.
- Building the foundation is all encompassing—it must be the highest priority of the organization.
- The mission of an organization is its primary purpose; it states *why* the organization exists.
- The values are the principles upon which the organization is based; they are compatible with and support the mission.
- The vision is the chief goal of the organization over a mid range (usually 3–5 year) period.
- A vision should be realistic and a great challenge.
- A vision should be measurable, appropriate, emotional, and support the mission; it should have a definite time frame and be the rallying cry of the organization.
- The vision is the focal point of the organization, upon which its plans and strategies are based and built.
- Critical Success Factors (CSF) are the top few conditions that *must* exist for the organization to achieve its vision.
- A goal is a measurable indicator that expresses the successful attainment of a CSF.
- Strategic plans are derived from or are integrated with CSFs.
- Operating plans or tactics are derived from strategic plans.
- A project should be used as an addendum to plans or may be used to adjust to changes that emerge.
- The organization should be aligned with its vision; in other words, it should be organized to achieve the vision and everyone should know their role in fulfilling the vision. This is called vertical alignment.
- Plans are deployed throughout the organization using a *catchball* approach, where the higher level establishes an objective and a means to achieve the objective and the immediate lower level receives the means as one of its major objectives. This process cascades down the organization.
- The planning role includes a process of reviewing plan implementation and results. This ensures attainment of goals and improvement of the foundation process.
- The vision and organizational goals are critical control panel items. These should be continually monitored and communicated throughout the organization.

NOTES

1. James C. Collins and Jerry I. Porras, *Built to Last* (New York: Harper Business, 1994).

2. *The Concise Columbia Encyclopedia* is licensed from Columbia University Press. Copyright © 1995 by Columbia University Press.

3. For our purposes a stakeholder is anyone who is connected to the organization by having an interest in it. The primary stakeholders are members, employees, owners, customers, board members, and suppliers. Other important stakeholders may be the public, government agencies, and other contributors to or recipients of the organization.

4. Myron Tribus, *Quality First: Selected Papers on Quality and Productivity Improvement*, 4th ed. (Washington DC, National Institute for Engineering Management & Systems, 1992), p. 63.

5. Solectron Corporation, *1995 Annual Report*, Inside Front Cover.

6. Rubbermaid Incorporated, *1995 Annual Report*, Inside Front Cover.

7. Federal Express Corporation, *1995 Annual Report*, Inside Front Cover.

8. Hewlett-Packard Company and Subsidiaries, *1995 Annual Report*, Inside Front Cover.

9. Lucent Technologies, *First Annual Report*, 1996.

10. Xerox Corporation, *1995 Annual Report*, p. 6.

11. 3M, *Annual Report*, 1995.

12. Nordstrom, Inc. and Subsidiaries, *1995 Annual Report*, Facing p. 4.

13. Motorola, Inc., *1995 Summary Annual Report*, p. 10.

14. Motorola, Inc., *1996 Summary Annual Report*, Inside Front Cover.

15. Rubbermaid Incorporated, *1995 Annual Report*, p. 6.

16. Xerox Corporation, *1995 Annual Report*, p. 24.

17. Ford Motor Company, *1995 Annual Report*, p. 17.

18. Harley-Davidson, Inc., *1995 Annual Report*, p. 10.

19. Armstrong World Industries, Inc., *Shaking the Armstrong Tree: Reshaping for Growth; Annual Report*, 1995, Inside Back Cover.

20. Warren Bennis and Michael Mishe, *The 21st Century Organization: Reinventing Through Reengineering* (San Diego, Pfeiffer & Company, 1995), p. 47.

21. Joseph M. Juran, *Juran on Quality by Design: The New Steps for Planning Quality into Goods and Services* (New York, The Free Press, 1992), p. 31.

22. Gerhard Plenert, *World Class Manager: Olympic Quality Performance in the New Global Economy* (Rocklin, Calif.: Prima Publishing Company, 1995), p. 47.

23. Some of these are labeled as a vision by the organization and others meet the definition of a vision statement.

24. Rubbermaid Incorporated, *1995 Annual Report*, p. 1.

25. Eastman Chemical Company, *1995 Annual Report*, Facing p. 1.

26. Ford Motor Company, *1995 Annual Report*, p. 9.

27. AT&T, *1994 Annual Report*, p. 2.

28. Federal Express Corporation, *1995 Annual Report,* p. 3.

29. American Express Company, *1995 Annual Report,* p. 4.

30. Harley-Davidson, Inc., *1996 Annual Report.*

31. See note 30, p. 14.

32. A Pareto analysis is a priority ranking from the most important to the least important factor. Basically, the Pareto principle states that every effect, although it may be the result of high numbers of causes, has only a relatively few that account for or drive most of the effect. It is frequently displayed in a descending bar graph. Modern variations of the Pareto Principle are "The Concept of the Vital Few and the Trival Many" and "The 80-20 Rule." There is an excellent article on Pareto, authored by Dr. Juran, who is the first to use the term in cause-and-effect analysis. It can be found in *Quality Progress,* May 1975, pp. 8–9, and is reprinted as a chapter appendix in J. M. Juran, *Juran On Quality By Design* (New York: The Free Press, 1992), p. 68.

33. Frequently, the department and unit levels prepare their own missions and use two-way dialogue up and down the organization for input and endorsement. Teams often use the term *charter* to label their mission and individuals use the term *purpose* as part of their job description or position profile.

Chapter 3

UNDERSTANDING CUSTOMERS

> *. . . no two people see the external world in exactly*
> *the same way. To every separate person a*
> *thing is what he thinks it is—in other words,*
> *not a thing, but a think.*
> —PENELOPE FITZGERALD[1]

Chapter 3 introduces the voice of the customer (VOC) and some methods to quantify both the perceived and actual value delivered by an organization in comparison with competitors. These metrics can be further enhanced by breaking them down into price and inconvenience measures. This type of knowledge provides *real time actionable competitive advantage on a continuous basis*. These VOC metrics can be easily and immediately converted to control panel indicators that provide an ongoing visual representation of how your organization compares with competitors in the delivery and perception of value, quality, price, and inconvenience and what specific areas need adjustment.

CREATING CUSTOMER DELIGHT

Organizations with a long-term vision and mission based on creating wealth for shareholders must begin by taking care of their customers. Their target is always delighted customers. For many organizations, the target is long-term (or lifetime) delighted customers; or, more accurately, a perpetually growing base of delighted *loyal* lifetime customers.

The PIMS[2] study demonstrated that competitive success is driven by customer behavior which is, in turn, driven by perceived relative value.[3]

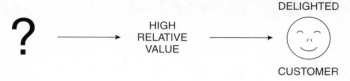

Figure 3.1   Delighted customers are the result of high value: What causes high value?

Customer delight is created from a positive perception of value that customers receive from a provider relative to what they believe they will receive elsewhere.

Only two elements are needed to provide a competitive advantage. The first is the creation of actual value and the second is the perception that the provider offers the best value. If a provider is actually capable of delivering the highest value, all the better. In the long run, perception will catch up with reality.

If the target being sought is delighted customers and high relative value is its driver, or chief cause, the search becomes, "What drives (causes) value?" This unknown is represented by the question mark in Figure 3.1.

The ultimate desired outcome of seeking value-added causal relationships is to identify and understand the dynamics among the variables that drive value in such a way that a market advantage is achieved.

CUSTOMERS AS PARTNERS

People do not buy products or services: they buy an image of themselves, enhanced with the use of the product or service.

As the Information Age accelerates, intellectual property is quickly becoming a strong competitive factor, extending to products as well as services. Physical computers, with their limitless variations of components and software, have created a vast industry, offering value-added knowledge well beyond the original creator's and vendor's intention.

Any popular software (or updated version) released today is outdated before it reaches the first paying customer. It is outdated not only because it contains bugs (flaws) that need to be corrected,[4] but also because it overlooked new opportunities and improvements that customers see at once. Thus, customers begin demanding improvements and new features immediately.

Those organizations that open real-time communications with customers and work in partnership with them in improvements and added value opportunities are pioneering a new relationship between customer and provider. They are opening channels that, in turn, provide high value-added intelligence to vendors. The sharpest ones even use this feedback to gain knowledge of their competitors and the future lifestyles and demographic trends of their customers.

The Industrial Age was built on the common law legal principle of *caveat emptor*, "Let the buyer beware." During this period, organizations based their decisions on costs and set their prices to reflect desired profit levels. The individual consumer basically accepted what the market provided and was ineffective in influencing rapid change. In most cases, business success was not driven by the needs of the customer, but by what the manufacturer or service provider decided to produce.

Today, the customer is emerging with the real power to determine market success. Consequently, successful companies are shifting from "Let the buyer beware" to "Help the buyer know."

Another emerging trend is the large growth in direct on-line computer linkage between providers and customers. Providers who are linked on-line with customers have an advantage in speed, as well as the utility of the data received being in a high-value format. These are potentially tremendous benefits if the provider has developed methods for gathering the right information in the right form and has the capability to use it to a market advantage. The challenge is to continually gather the right information from customers in a usable format.

THE LITTLE THINGS ADD UP

Wealth creation is not so much determined today by the big things, but by the little things. The big things include the basic product or service, and the little things generally make the product or service or its features more productive or convenient. Sometimes the little things are invisible, are transparent, or do not even appear as part of the product or service.

A big thing is an automobile; a little thing is the dealer taking the time and having the knowledge and ability to explain unfamiliar items and features on a new auto to customers. A big thing is a checking account; a little thing is providing customers with telephone numbers to reach their choice of either an automated telephone system or a person who can help.

The big things must be designed, built, and delivered with high quality. Without a high-quality basic product and service, a provider will certainly not survive. Ultimately, the customer is the judge of quality. All other factors being equal, quality can be measured by the value it adds to the customer. When several competitors offer quality basic products and services, the competitive difference lies in the *little* things. The *little* things become highly valued and are the new base for buying decisions.

A big thing is a round of golf; a little thing is the pencil that is used to mark the scorecard. Art Peterson, president of PSG Consulting Services of Greenwood Village, Colorado, uses an example of a clever little plastic pencil that is given to golfers in Japan along with a scorecard. Figure 3.2 illustrates the pencil; it is flat on the bottom and has a little clip to fasten to the

Figure 3.2   High value-adding pencil from Japan.

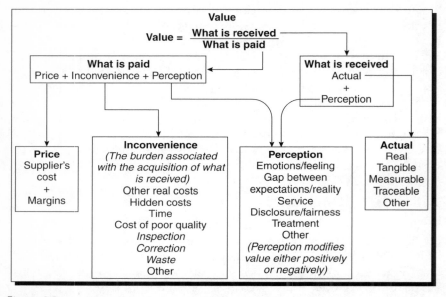

Figure 3.3   Value depends on the mathematical combination of a number of cause-and-effect relationships.

card. Unlike the round or hexagon pencil used by golfers around the world, this pencil is always conveniently located and will not easily roll away. Additionally, its lead is sufficiently hard and its point is rounded to allow clear writing on damp scorecards or the plastic type used in Japan. These characteristics contribute to a relatively long-lasting device that can be used numerous times. Overall, it provides high relative value by reducing the annoyance of searching for a pencil while engaged in a sometimes frustrating sport.

Chapter 1 presented the formula shown in Figure 3.3 that outlines mathematically how value is added and perceived. The formula is also used to establish the net value of a transaction (or series of transactions) by comparing the value of what now exists against what was paid for its acquisition or creation. This defines the value of the transaction to the purchaser or recipient.

WORKING WITH THE VALUE FORMULA

The value formula partially derives from and ties into the pursuit of *best value* by Mark Crumly of GTE. In the early 1980s, Crumly established a system of objectively evaluating vendors based on their ability to meet or exceed company quality standards in both the quality of the product and in their ability to deliver. The value that a vendor provided was adjusted by the cost of poor quality (covered in chapter 5), which was usually measured by returns, warranty work, repairs, and scrap. Additionally, it was adjusted by delivery availability, measured by the difference between the time needed and actual delivery. Both of these criteria generally uncovered high inconvenience costs. GTE quickly discovered that the bid price was a poor indicator of value, so it adjusted each vendor by its vendor index to arrive at the *best value* that an individual vendor offered. This generally resulted in business being contracted with someone other than the lowest-price bidder.[5]

The value ratio assists in measuring change and in comparing alternate choices. It is used to help increase value by increasing the relative size of the numerator (what is received) in relation to the denominator (what is paid).

The formula provides an easy and intuitive format to assess the net value of any type of transaction, product, or service. It is an evolving concept and should be tailored to the reader's situation, then built on and refined. Although the formula is a mathematical representation, it should be viewed as a template for building the cause-and-effect relationship between the dependent variable (value) and the numerous independent variables that impact it. It is a tool designed more for identifying opportunity and measuring change than for calculating precise value.

What Is Received (Actual)

Whenever anyone purchases or contracts for a product or service, there is an expectation of the output of the transaction. It may be a single product, such as a laser printer. It may be a one-time or an ongoing service, such as an insurance policy. Or, it may be a combination, such as a piece of equipment with a service contract. Expectations are set by past experiences, recommendations, requirements, or by deliberate marketing tactics such as advertising (see Figure 3.4).

```
Actual
Real
Tangible
Measurable
Traceable
Other
```

Figure 3.4   The pursuit of actual value seeks facts that are real, tangible, measurable and traceable.

Value changes over time, sometimes quickly and profoundly, and other times slowly and predictably. The formula is applied to ongoing or current products and services as well as recently completed transactions.[6] In longer term situations, it may be desirable to look at the cumulative value and wealth creation.

In many definitions of quality, *What Is Received* is equal to quality; in other definitions, quality is equal to the *actual* portion of the equation. A few quality practitioners define quality as encompassing value and use the term *total quality management* (TQM) to label their beliefs.[7] Whenever the term *quality* is used in this book it is in a context that quality most closely relates to *actual* in terms of the value formula.

Factual data should always be pursued under the *actual* portion of the subequation. Where facts are not adequately available, apply as high a level of factual observation, scientific logic, and assumptions as possible. Logic and assumptions are always subject to scrutiny and argument, but at least decisions can be made that produce a better chance of success than random guessing. The target of pursuing value is paramount *to identify and understand the dynamics among the variables that drive value in such a way that a market advantage is achieved.*

There are two commonly used methods of arriving at a close approximation of actual value. The simplest and generally the most appropriate method is to use the market price of identical or similar products or services in the market or market segment chosen. Next, adjust this price based on how much the particular product or service adds or detracts from the approximated amount. The second method is used for more unique products and services, and involves calculating the actual value based on what the customer gains from the product or service and then adjusting for the amount a buyer is willing and able to pay.

In open and competitive markets where products and services are readily available, a basic market price usually exists. This price is a good approximation and starting point to determine value. No matter what type of service or product one delivers, data or market price information exist on similar or identical services or products. Products or services may have to be broken into basic or unpackaged components to approximate their price.

The key to value differentiation is to produce high value add-ons, features, or services that augment the basic product or service by being different and new. Tremendous market opportunities exist for those who are first to market a new product or a high value-added modification. Since there is no comparison for market price or value, customers are more likely to pay actual value added, plus or minus their perception of its value.

In many commercial situations, value is estimated by its return on investment (ROI), its impact on profit and loss (P & L), its contribution to efficiency and effectiveness, or the cost impact on what it replaces. Again, these may be adjusted up or down as market value adjusts to performance.

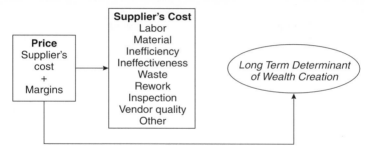

Figure 3.5 The supplier's cost plus margins determines the price the customer pays.

PRICE

From the customer's view, price is what they pay the provider in exchange for products and/or services. The price may include the product or service, its delivery, ongoing support, and warranted performance. The price is generally paid in currency, or its equivalent, or exchanged for other products or services. Price usually is simple to calculate and quantify.

From the provider's view, price is composed of costs plus margins. In the past, the customer was not involved in the costs and margins of its suppliers. Today, there is a movement toward more active participation between the provider and customer because the price of products and services by the provider becomes a significant element of cost to the customer. If a customer can assist in reducing the provider's costs, the potential for price reduction is created. Therefore, there is an emerging interest by customers in the efficiency of their suppliers (see Figure 3.5).

Strategic partnering, the emergence of preferred suppliers, and the insistence of high-quality products and services are becoming highly utilized by major corporations today. Customers know that partnering arrangements to assist suppliers with reduction of waste, rework, and reliance on inspection improves value. This practice has led to phenomenal growth in widely accepted standards and methodologies for high performance, such as the ISO 9000 series, QS9000, and numerous company-specific assessment and certification programs.

A margin, simply defined, is the difference between price and cost. It is the difference between revenue and expenses, or what is left over at a point in time to either reinvest or return to investors. From an accounting standpoint, it is profit. When this amount is adjusted for what an organization's equity could have returned in a safe investment, the amount left over is the economic value added (EVA) of the organization.

This amount becomes the foundation of determining the longer-term value or wealth the organization adds to society by surviving and growing.

```
┌─────────────────────────────────┐
│          Inconvenience          │
│   (The burden associated with the│
│   acquisition of what is received)│
│         Other real costs        │
│          Hidden costs           │
│              Time               │
│       Cost of poor quality      │
│            Inspection           │
│            Correction           │
│              Waste              │
│              Other              │
└─────────────────────────────────┘
```

Figure 3.6   The cost of inconvenience can be extremely high.

However, in reality most organizations add considerably more wealth than is shown by EVA.

The price an organization pays for products and services, including inventory, provides jobs and many other wealth-creation occasions. Of course, not all of these opportunities result in wealth creation; some result in waste, unneeded consumption, and destruction by greed. Nevertheless, a base for wealth creation and the potential for major quality-of-life improvement is established.

INCONVENIENCE

Inconvenience is the additional burden the customer endures in the acquisition of a product or service. It may be as simple as unpacking a box or may be an extremely complicated and tedious installation of a mechanical system. It may be negligible in comparison with the price, or it may be hundreds of times the price. The price of inconvenience increases by high factors when poor quality is involved. This involves such burdens as inspection, corrective activity, and waste (see Figure 3.6).

Inconvenience falls into two general categories: one ties into price and is a necessary component of a transaction (although like price it can be improved and become more effective and efficient); the other is negative value added, or value reduction. An example of inconvenience is apparent in a simple example of the purchase of a loaf of bread and a gallon of milk.

The common price of milk at the supermarket is X and the price of the bread is Y. Table 3.1 shows some examples of the final cost when inconvenience is added.

The highest price of inconvenience in the example in Table 3.1 occurs when the buyer stops to complain about the freshness of the milk. The lowest inconvenience cost is when the milk and bread purchases are combined with other shopping, spreading the cost over many items. If there is a neighborhood convenience store nearby that sells the items at a 20 percent premium over the supermarket, the buyer would pay a lower total price for the items at the convenience store in all but the two lowest-total-cost scenarios.

Table 3.1	Added cost of inconvenience scenarios.		
Scenario	**Inconvenience Cost**	**Total Cost**
Drive auto three miles to market and return	2(X+Y)	3(X+Y)
Walk to market and return (only purpose of trip)	5(X+Y)	6(X+Y)
Walk to market and return (during morning exercise)	.2(X+Y)	1.2(X+Y)
Drive to market to buy weekly groceries	.05(X+Y)	1.05(X+Y)
Market out of milk; must drive additional 2 miles	4(X+Y)	5(X+Y)
Stop to complain about lack of freshness of milk	7(X+Y)	8(X+Y)

This example assumes a smooth transaction, other than the one complaint and the time the market ran out of milk. However, things frequently do not go as planned. For example, if a mistake was made, such as the wrong calculation of the two items, or the items were placed in a defective container that leaked or split open, or if a trainee was working the checkout and required constant inspection by a trainer, the costs would increase.

There are other inconveniences that often add to the price of products and services. These include such common occurrences as tardiness of the service provider, packing/unpacking, assembly, understanding how to use product or service, miscommunications, returns, complaints, wait time, an unprepared provider (or customer), and accidents. Time almost always increases the cost of inconvenience.

PERCEPTION

Perception both adds to and detracts from value. When it increases value, it is added to the numerator; when it detracts from value it is added to the denominator (see Figure 3.7).

Unless a customer takes the effort to objectively assess value, perception is usually the strongest assessment of value. Many transactions are small and insignificant, and no one uses much time or energy to evaluate them unless something abnormal is associated with the transaction. This may happen when one feels cheated or taken, a personality clash occurs, or an enormous lesson is learned.

However, as a producer of value-added products and services, it is always critical to keep in mind that perception of value is frequently more important that reality. Often, value is very personal. One of the highest value-added services that can be provided from one human to another is a sincere expression of caring. This may manifest from the product or service itself, or from a *caring* individual.

When individuals feel positive regarding their treatment, they may use the following words or terms to describe the transaction:

```
┌─────────────────────────────────┐
│          Perception             │
│        Emotions/Feeling         │
│          Gap between            │
│      Expectations/Reality       │
│            Service              │
│       Disclosure/Fairness       │
│           Treatment             │
│             Other               │
│  (Perception modifies value either │
│       positively or negatively)  │
└─────────────────────────────────┘
```

Figure 3.7 When a perception adds value, it increases *What Is Received;* when it negates value, it increases *What is Paid.*

Good deal	*High trust*	*Bargain*
A buy	*Fair*	*Felt good*
Honest deal	*Low price*	*Highly recommend*

Personal feelings and emotions are always high determiners of perceived value. Often they may appear illogical. Frequently, they are short-term or situation-driven. They may be strongly influenced by rumor, untrue information, or selfishness. On the other hand, they may be the manifestation of a sound long-term strategy that the provider combines with the right sense of timing.

The perception of value can be linked to Maslow's hierarchy of needs,[8] in which higher needs are expressed only after lower needs are fulfilled. In other words, the needs that motivate a person at any point in time greatly influence his/her perception of value. For example, a person who is highly motivated by appearance and social interaction would probably see little value in an extra serving of high-fat food. A person who is hungry or undernourished may perceive a much higher value. Under different circumstances, perception of value may be significantly different.

Needs, motivation, situation, and personal goals and lifestyles are all notable factors that influence and drive perceived value. Social acceptance, acknowledgment, and basic courtesies are other powerful value-added traits. The bedside manners of a physician, the friendliness of a hair stylist, and the greeting by a bank teller are high value-added features for most people.

Years ago, I was involved in primary research pursuing why long-term customers of finance companies continued to do business with a finance company when they either did not need to borrow money or they could qualify for considerably lower loan rates with other financial institutions. This particular study was conducted in the United Kingdom, but was later found to be a significant factor in both Australia and the United States.

Most of the customers surveyed were given credit by the finance company at a time when they had a financial need and believed they had no other option. The decision by the finance company, in and of itself, had high value to the person, because the perceived benefit was much higher than the rates charged. In addition to granting credit, the finance company treated the person with courtesy, understood the customer's problems and was able to encourage more or larger loans.

Even if the person was unable to make a monthly payment, they were treated with respect, and the finance company worked with the customer until payments became current. As these customers became more financially secure, they continued to do business with the finance company because of the way they were treated (or the perceived value of that treatment).

Perception can be heavily influenced by information (accurate or inaccurate) such as ads, third-party testimonies, personal observation, or research. Generally, providers of products and services want buyers to have a favorable perception; buyers want to believe they received a good bargain; and competitors would like to show that their value is higher than that of others. The buyers want the big picture, and most providers emphasize only the favorable aspects they believe will make a sale or solve a problem.

A favorable perception based on value-added treatment is one of the largest drivers of customer loyalty.[9] When a high level of loyalty exists, the customer sees the connection as an informal partnership, based on win–win principles, where all parties receive a good feeling about the relationship and sense an appreciation in return.

This type of behavior is the rationale behind preferred customer programs such as frequent user programs. Usually, these programs are high value added for the customer and beneficial for the provider. This is especially true when discounts are offered for frequent use and the true benefits are available to all and disclosed.

However, frequent-use programs may eventually have a negative impact for the provider who gives obvious special treatment to one class of customers at the detriment of others. An example of this is the airline who gives preferred seating and early boarding privileges to its frequent users. This favorable treatment may add high value to those few, while taking value away from others. This type of treatment has resulted in a certain segment of the market seeking "no frills" airlines.

When customers think they will always be treated fairly and receive value, their loyalty to the provider increases. The bottom-line impact of having loyal customers is significant. However, because reality eventually catches up with perception, value must actually exist or either party may feel betrayed. When betrayal is felt, loyalty will disappear, along with the customer.

Another form of high value added is disclosure or caution that a provider imparts along with the product or service. If this is offered up front, it has an even higher value because the buyer may avoid wasting time in a decision process. To maximize the value added through disclosure, a provider must truly understand the decision process buyers go through, as well as their underlying or basic needs.

Software producers frequently face a dilemma when new software is released for sale. There is constant pressure between speed to market and the stability and workability of the product, which is further heightened when a product or service is announced before it is ready for market.

In the market, customers have different requirements; some are pioneers and are willing to work with a less stable product and assist in its evolution while others only want the product or service when it meets all of their requirements. The provider who discloses actual product or service performance and sets the proper expectation with the market adds high value and permits proper choices. The provider who is only eager to gain a time-based advantage will pay a much higher price later.

Perception's darker side reduces value. Since value, ultimately, is the result of assessment by a person, it is always subject to the parts of the psyche that influence or drive feelings and emotions. A physical object may be objectively appraised for its value; however, the acquisition, loan, or rental of the object requires a transaction (or series of transactions), the performance of which is a service. The value of a service is always subject to judgment.

A negative perception is part of the cost side of the formula. It is viewed as an increase in cost, or a *perceived* inconvenience. The degree to which negative perception reduces value ranges from a negligible nuisance to a *deal stopper*, to permanent damages that are resolved only through lawsuits or corporate feuds. Most value-reducing perceptions, like value-adding perceptions, come from feelings and emotions. When such perceptions are negative, they are frequently described as follows:

Taken	*Cheated*	*Fleeced*
Shady deal	*Burned*	*Deceived*
Hoodwinked	*Swindled*	*Gypped*

EXPECTATION AND PERFORMANCE

One of the most important criteria in the assessment of perceived value is the performance of service against *expectations.*[10] A person can perceive positive value added when dealing with a known crook if the expectation is high cost and aggravation, and the actual performance is smooth and businesslike. On the other hand, when purchasing from a retail establishment with a flawless reputation for fairness and service, one can feel let down if the store personnel do not meet expectations of friendliness or knowledge.

GAUGING PERFORMANCE AGAINST EXPECTATIONS

Figure 3.8 offers a gage for the degree of satisfaction/dissatisfaction based on whether the experience exceeded, met or fell short of expectations.

Human beings have an expectation of every transaction, or *moment of truth.*[11] The vast majority of transactions are somewhat trivial and little

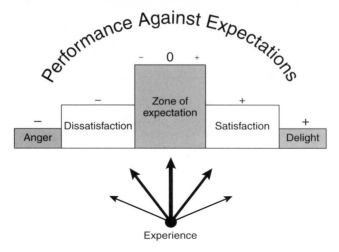

Figure 3.8   The satisfaction or dissatisfaction of an experience depends on the perception of the degree that performance exceeded, met or fell short of expectation.

thought is given to them unless reality is considerably out of proportion with expectation. Most people expect a regional bank office to be clean and tidy; a sign advertising a product to have all words spelled correctly; and, a crowded queue if one waits to mail taxes at the last minute. Little conscious attention is given to evaluating these items unless they fall outside an acceptable zone of expectation.

Performance below this zone of expectation results in dissatisfaction, and most entries into the zone of *dissatisfaction* tend to leave lasting impressions. This does not necessarily imply that all is lost, the response to dissatisfaction has an expectation that can be exceeded, or can again fall short. Each time the customer is disappointed, the recovery is tougher.

The zone of dissatisfaction is usually perceived to be the result of a mistake, misinformation, incompetence, or carelessness. Once it reaches wanton disregard, a total lack of caring, intention, or a higher level of emotion takes over, it enters the zone of *anger*. Here, even though the perception or expectation may later prove to be false, the memory remains and colors future perception. On the other hand, if performance is beyond the zone of expectation in a positive sense, perception enters a zone of *satisfaction*. In this zone, something triggers a reaction in the customer who says, "I like this," and makes a mental note of the feeling. It does not have the permanency of an experience of dissatisfaction, but it does register on a mental scorecard.

An even more positive reaction beyond satisfaction is *delight* which usually results in an exclamation, "Wow, this is great." Usually, this occurs when a need is met that the customer did not realize they had or did not believe the provider could meet. Fairly recent examples of delight are a loan that can be approved in minutes and beepers that are handed out at a restaurant to notify patrons when a table becomes available (this may be little or no help, depending on how long the wait against expectation). An experience with delight is usually associated with a perception that the provider was motivated to develop or introduce the delightful product or service out of a sense of concern for customers. Consequently, delight provides extreme high value and is a loyalty building experience.

The apex of delight is excitement. Excitement is new territory, and customers feel they are on the leading edge of a breakthrough product, feature, or service. They feel appreciative of the experience and want to tell others. Examples are a new innovative ride at an amusement park, the acceleration and low-cost operation of an electric car, or the initial experience of a surround sound movie theater.

However, providers should be cautious of overselling expectations on breakthrough products and services. The key to high satisfaction and delight is an element of surprise. Wherever possible, set expectations high and be sure they can be exceeded.

SHIFTING EXPECTATIONS

Over time, as performance exceeds expectations, the new level of performance becomes the expected level and is less satisfying than it was previously. The same effect results when competition consistently delivers higher levels, or if the customer receives higher performance from a similar service, even if it is a noncompetitive source. Performance that used to be delight becomes a source of dissatisfaction if it does not meet the new expectation.

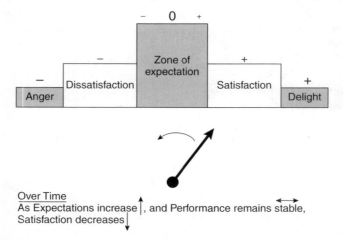

Figure 3.9 As higher and higher levels of performance are delivered they become the new expectation and the previous lower levels are less satisfying.

LOYALTY

Repeat business, long-term relationships, and loyalty are desired by most providers of products and services. These characteristics are cost-effective and usually profitable. The longer the term and the more transactions and moments of truth that occur with a provider, the more pluses and minuses a customer has recorded on the scorecard. Customers do not like to change providers. For the most part, they prefer to find one they are happy with and remain faithful to that provider.

An element that always seems to be a major factor in the decision to stay or leave a provider is the perception of how one is treated. One recent study found that a high degree of loyalty existed in the banking industry, in spite of negative experiences with products and services. The loyalty was attributed to former positive human interactions experienced at the bank.[12]

Loyalty is a function of overall high satisfaction and cannot adequately be measured with traditional satisfaction surveys. However, anything lower than a very high overall satisfaction level should be a concern for providers. Loyalty is more a feeling of a beneficial partnership than satisfaction with a transaction or series of transactions. Loyalty measurements require an understanding of loyalty drivers in different niches and must be observed from an integrated standpoint.

REFERENT POWER OF SATISFACTION[13]

Dr. Gary McCain, professor of Marketing at Boise State University, added a competitive dimension to the degree of satisfaction diagram by viewing the movement from low satisfaction to higher satisfaction as increasing the competitive advantage. His contribution is shown in Figure 3.10.

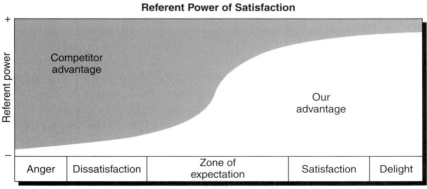

Figure 3.10 The Referent Power of Satisfaction shows how competitive advantage is lost or gained by movement along the satisfaction scale.

Referent power is defined as our ownership, control, or strength of loyalty, subject to our influence, to withstand competitive strategy and tactics. It is, to a large degree, ours to keep or lose by our delivery of value. As performance against expectation increases, satisfaction increases, and our power to withstand competitive factors is strengthened. This power is "referred" from our performance to competitive advantage or disadvantage. Using observation and information from the strategic VOC (covered later), an organization can empirically identify both dimensions with metrics and adjust tactics and strategy to gain advantage or minimize competitors' advantages.

VOICE OF THE CUSTOMER/QUALITY FUNCTION DEPLOYMENT

The voice of the customer (VOC) is a methodology that provides valuable customer and market information to organizations in an actionable form. VOC looks at the market from its basic need level. It deploys this knowledge throughout the organization from the initiation of product/service planning to the end of its life cycle.

The application of using VOC to design, build, and support the processes that create world class products and services is called quality function deployment, or QFD. Initially, VOC was the foundation for QFD and was considered inseparable. Today, VOC is frequently used outside its connection with QFD in such applications as customer surveys, executive control panels, and organizational performance evaluation.

Our use of the voice of the customer is an expansion of its original application with QFD. The greatest difference is its longer-term focus. VOC, in a QFD project, is a one-time snapshot of customer priorities and requirements, along with an assessment of how well each is met by the organization and its major competitors. The strategic use of the VOC looks at the changing priorities and requirements of customers at the detail level on a dynamic basis. This view provides extremely valuable strategic information and offers tremendous advantages over competitors who do not pursue a similar approach. The movement aspect of the VOC provides both acceleration and change of velocity indicators of all major competitors at the value attribute level. Over time, this clearly indicates each competitor's market strategy (or lack of strategy).

The use of QFD is rapidly growing around the globe. Because of this expansion, many improvements and variations have emerged since its conceptual introduction by Yoji Akao in the mid-1960s and its first practical use at the Kobe shipyards in 1972. QFD reached the United States in the mid-1980s with the introduction of the concept at Ford Motor Company. Two training organizations, the American Supplier Institute and Goal/QPC, began offering courses in QFD in 1986.[14]

The voice of the customer is one of the most robust tools devised to understand the essence of value. VOC is a planning technique that helps establish the target points for horizontal alignment of the organization. Its underlying purpose *is to understand the basic needs of customers and the capabilities of competitors (or competitive forces) in such a quantifiable and actionable manner to design, build, or modify products and services that offer higher value than the others in the market.* It is specifically designed to provide a competitive advantage.

In a sense, VOC uses fundamental market research and many traditional marketing models and techniques; however, its focus is different. Traditionally, the aim of marketing research is to provide information to management on market opportunities, marketing effectiveness, and marketing problems.[15] The challenge of management is to sort through too much information in some areas and not enough in others in order to make marketing decisions.

VOC is much more specific and direct. It begins with a market or market segment and searches for the drivers of value in the minds of the customers in that market. Once drivers are established and prioritized, current performances of competitive forces in the market are assessed and competitive opportunities are identified. VOC does not take the place of basic market research, but it does provide much needed direction, efficiency, and effectiveness. The primary tool of VOC is a complex matrix called the house of quality, which correlates needs with solutions and assesses current performance and desired performance in certain areas.

In its elementary stages, VOC uses surveys, focus groups, and customer interviews for data gathering. As it progresses, it captures customer behavior and motivation during moments of truth and dissects them for expanded knowledge. The aim of a mature VOC process is to understand the needs and motivation of customers in their use and potential use of products and services.

One innovative method of capturing this data is the hands on, eyeball to eyeball, observation of customers using products and services and their reasons for and reaction to key attributes that are inherent in or displayed by the products and services. As organizations become better aligned horizontally, every employee becomes the eyes and ears of the organization in collecting and reporting customer observation.[16]

Customer service encounters, both centralized and in the field, offer great potential for continually understanding customers. Of course, the more realistically customers are grouped in segments and profiled, the better the organization can serve their changing needs and expectations.

FOUR POWERFUL CUSTOMER/COMPETITIVE METRICS

In the long run, loyalty is a function of continuous satisfaction and satisfaction is a function of value. Although value may be based on both perception and reality, the provider who is capable of delivering value has the advantage of one who focuses on primarily managing the perception of value. The one who does both is unbeatable.

In the Information Age, every organization will need to know where it is in both the delivery and perception of value. They also need to know what must be done to improve both and they need to know where their competitors stand in relation to all other competitors. These are extremely tough metrics to gather. They can only be gained through VOC observations and methodologies at the attribute level of purchase and use points. They cannot be gathered through surveys, or existing internal or external data sources alone.

The following four indicators are powerful, competitive tools that provide high strategic value as well as tactical information. They should be key instruments on the organization's control panel alongside the vision and top goals.

(The detailed methodology involved in assembling the data and information that rolls up to these four indicators is beyond the scope of this book. However, Appendix A provides a high-level overview of the process that goes from the house of quality to the indicators. Readers with a basic knowledge of QFD should find it easy to follow.)

VALUE AND QUALITY DELIVERED—ACTUAL AND PERCEIVED

Probably the most insightful indicator on an organization's control panel is the current competitive level of relative value and quality from both a perceived and actual standpoint. Figure 3.11 is an indicator on Company P's control panel that shows how well they measure against their three major competitors in the overall delivery and perception (stated) of value in their consolidated markets and product lines.[17] Of course, this information is available by segment, territory, and product lines as one "drills down" into specific information. Most real opportunities are found at the detail level, although each ascending level leads the route to larger opportunities.

This indicator clearly states that market improvement is essential for Company P. Although the organization's stated quality and value lag at a dangerous distance behind Competitors Y and Z, its measured quality and value are closer. A detailed analysis closer to the source matrices at the VOC level will provide areas that require immediate attention and will also show both strategic and tactical advantages, as well as the most severe causes for concern. It also will identify efforts that may best be abandoned where resources can be redeployed to gain other advantages.

Since value is a function of quality, price, inconvenience, and perception, Company P must select the right blend to achieve maximum gain. Additionally, there appear to be some perception opportunities that might improve short-term performance through marketing and sales emphasis, while the company continues to work on the quality and price gaps.

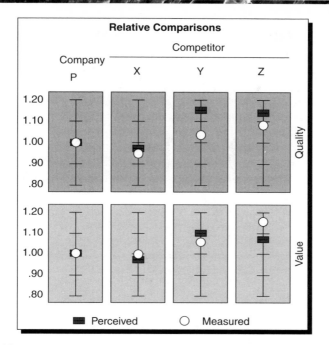

Figure 3.11   A control panel indicator showing comparative quality offers insight into improving value.

PRICE/INCONVENIENCE SPLIT

Value is based on the total package of products and services that customers receive. In the Industrial Age how they are bundled, or unbundled, is a marketing decision. In the Information Age, customers will assess value in a manner that renders deceptive bundling ineffective. In the past, providers may have been able to pass costs or their own performance limitations to customers as an inconvenience cost. As customers gain superior information, they will not be fooled by marketing disguises and will seek knowledge of their actual costs, including inconvenience. Providers must keep up with the true and perceived prices and inconvenience costs in order to gain advantage.

Figure 3.12 clearly shows the cost of a similar bundled product or service, along with the breakout between price and inconvenience (both measured and perceived) among each of the four companies.[18] The value of the comparisons must be understood for the price/inconvenience split to be meaningful.

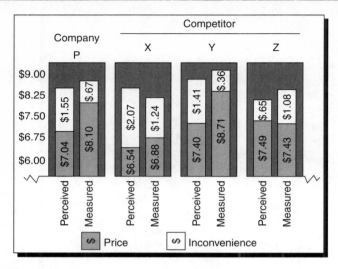

Figure 3.12 Understanding the elements of price and inconvenience offers value improvement opportunities.

Company P's marketing and sales functions may be able to reduce its high inconvenience perception while it improves the other value drivers. It may select Competitor X and Z's products or services to help demonstrate its superiority on inconvenience factors, while it studies Competitor Y for knowledge on how to improve its own performance. In the longer term, it must reduce both the perception and reality of cost in relation to competitors.

MOST IMPORTANT ATTRIBUTES TO CUSTOMERS AND HOW THEY PERCEIVED THEIR DELIVERY

Since the perception of value is ultimately driven by needs, those looking at the big picture of the market must continually be aware of changing needs. This is becoming more important in the Information Age because of the accelerated momentum of change.

Executives who do not keep pace with change quickly find themselves trapped in an ancient paradigm. This is extremely dangerous when intuition based on the past conflicts with the rapid enhancement of value and its drivers. Therefore, solutions that allow executives to monitor customer behavior are among the few essential indicators on control panels.

The graph in Figure 3.13 is used by a restaurant called Us to compare customers' perception of competitors' performance (including Us) in ten need categories. The graph uses a Pareto approach to rank the needs based on the demand weight taken from VOC metrics.[19]

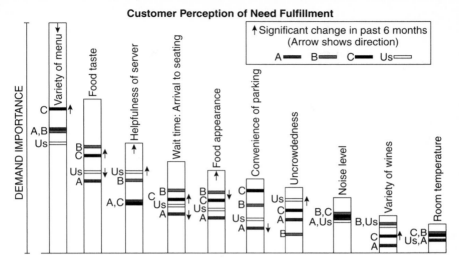

Figure 3.13   This graph shows restaurant customers' perception of how well four competitors perform on each of ten identified needs for a particular geographical segment.

The demand weight offers a priority of attention Us should give each customer need based on the importance of the need to customers, the improvement needed by Us, and the sales point of the need. In this particular example—although its importance is falling—menu variety is still the highest priority, and Competitor C is pulling farther ahead of the pack.

Senior management of Us should be very concerned about customers' perception of both the menu variety and food taste, and should deploy resources to close the gap and gain an edge. These concerns cannot be the sole responsibility of the chef or the food director; they must be concerns of senior management, because these are the areas that will ultimately influence the market.

If senior management's largest consideration is the next quarter's revenues, and it fails to look at what is driving those revenues, US will eventually lose to the competitor who understands value and the production of value.

There are unlimited ways to display this information on a control panel. Each organization needs to design its own methods and elevate critical information so that leaders will understand and be able to act on it. Without a consistent and reliable methodology, information will selectively move to the top and poor decisions will be made.

The solutions to customers' needs come from products and services or various features of products and services. Key solutions, as identified in VOC analyses, should be *quantified* in terms of the needs they address. After objective assessments, competitors can be compared based on measurements of their actual delivery.

DRIVERS OF VALUE AND HOW WELL
EACH IS DELIVERED BY COMPETITOR

The house of quality correlates each priority need against each major solution (feature, product, or attribute). Any one solution may address several needs. For example, a certain engine for an automobile may meet the need for acceleration, quietness and maintenance. The more needs a solution meets, the greater it meets each need and the more critical the needs are, the more important the factor is in driving value.

The graph in Figure 3.14 uses a Pareto approach to rank the solutions based on how highly each correlates with value as defined in a local restaurant market.[20]

The information in Figure 3.14 tracks with most of the perceptions in Figure 3.13. However, it appears that Us has made gains over the past six months in the appropriateness of food and variety of menu. It may be time to help perception catch up with reality through the use of clever advertising or positioning. Or it may be strategically better to wait until the gap has narrowed more or Us has moved ahead of the competition and taken them by surprise. Options derived from knowledge are always superior to those resulting from conjecture.

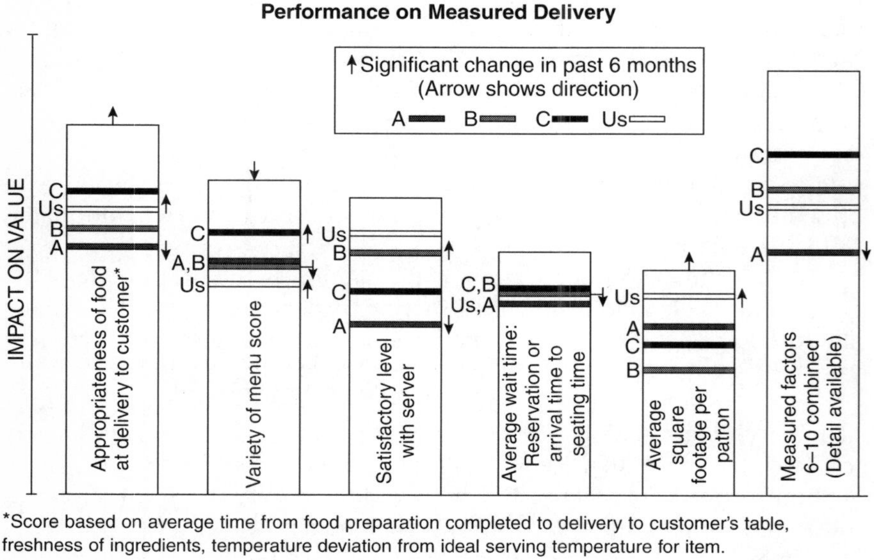

*Score based on average time from food preparation completed to delivery to customer's table, freshness of ingredients, temperature deviation from ideal serving temperature for item.

Figure 3.14   This graph shows the actual measured performance of four competitive restaurants in their delivery of different buying attributes offered in a particular geographical segment.

THE CHALLENGE

There are countless innovative and creative ways to gather data, analyze, and understand the changing needs and expectations of customers. The Information Age has elevated the importance of using an integrated systems approach to the challenge. Today, consumers are bombarded with so much information that they cannot absorb all of it. Many are rebelling by insisting on having unlisted telephone numbers and addresses, filing privacy lawsuits, and not responding to the endless barrage of requests to supply information and opinions.

The corporate customer, on the other hand, continues to insist on higher and higher value from producers and service providers. They continually demand higher quality and higher convenience while squeezing prices. The answer to these challenges is to work with customers as partners while continually improving the management of value.

As value management evolves globally, along with the elements of quality, efficiency, and effectiveness improvements, the challenge to compete will become tougher. As organizations continue to move toward strategic partnerships and work together in the management of value, those who ignore this revolution will survive only in local specialized niches, and only until a better organization comes along.

The way for producers and service providers to prosper in the Information Age is to continuously study changing customers and markets and devise methods to communicate the findings throughout their organization. The best technique yet created for synthesizing and elevating information to the decision level is the control panel. An organization without a VOC indicator on its control panel is like an airplane without a direction indicator.

KEY POINTS UNDERSTANDING CUSTOMERS

- Competitive advantage depends on both actual value and the perception of value.
- In the Information Age, *caveat emptor*, or "Let the buyer beware," is being replaced with "Help (add value to) the buyer by disclosing actual quality."
- The key to adding value is by understanding the causal relationship among the variables that drive value.
- Feeling positive about a purchase is value adding; feeling negative reduces value.
- Total payment for any product or service always includes the price, plus all inconveniences experienced by the purchaser in connection with the product or service.

- Satisfaction or dissatisfaction with an exchange of value depends on the degree that actual performance meets, exceeds or falls short of the expected performance.
- As customers experience higher levels of performance of products and services, their future expectations become higher.
- The purpose of the voice of the customer (VOC) is to understand the basic needs of customers and the capabilities of competitors in such a quantifiable and actionable manner to design, build, or modify products and services that offer higher value than others in the market.
- VOC is high value-added knowledge; therefore, it must be continuously gathered and analyzed in a timely manner at a rate that exceeds other market competitors.
- The control panel should always have indicators showing the actual and perceived value and quality provided by the organization relative to major competitors.
- The organization should always know the true cost of its products and services to the customer by understanding both the price and inconvenience costs. This information should be available on major competitors.
- The most important buying attributes to customers and competitive performance on each one should be a major control panel indicator.

NOTES

1. Penelope Fitzgerald, "Shippey," *The Gate of Angels,* chapter 6 (1990). The Columbia Dictionary of Quotations is licensed from Columbia University Press. Copyright © 1993 by Columbia University Press. All rights reserved.
2. Profit Impact of Market Strategy, see note 4.
3. Robert D. Buzzell and Bradley T. Gale, *The PIMS Principles* (New York: The Free Press, 1987), p. 111.
4. Stephen Manes, "Software Today: It's All Beta," *PC World,* October 1996, p. 346.
5. This information came from personal discussions with Mark Crumly of GTE Telephone Operations in Ontario, California during the Spring, 1996.
6. In this case the formula should read "What Has Been Gained/What Has Been Paid."
7. The pure definition of TQM (Total Quality Management) implies that quality is totally managed. I attended a presentation by Dr. W. Edwards Deming on July 31, 1989, in Costa Mesa, California, when a gentleman

asked Dr. Deming to provide his definition of TQM. Dr. Deming initially gave the appearance that he did not understand the question. After the gentleman insisted on a response, Dr. Deming replied, "Hogwash, there's no such thing." I agree with Dr. Deming.

8. Abraham H. Maslow, "The Theory of Human Motivation," *Psychological Review*, vol. 50 (1943), pp. 370–396.

9. Customer loyalty goes beyond customer retention. It is defined not only by continually doing business with a provider, but by relying solely on that provider for all products and services one needs that can be furnished by that provider.

10. Much of the material in this section was derived from the Kano Model of Quality with the original reference: Seraku Kano and Tsuji Takahashi, "Attractive Quality and Must-Be Quality," 1984. Presented at Nippon QC Gakka: Twelfth Annual Meeting. A very well-presented western source for the Kano Model is Kurt Hofmeister of the Total Quality Group, 13061 Glenview Road, Plymouth, MI 48170, USA. Mr. Hofmeister presented the model at the Second and Fifth Annual Service Quality Conferences for the Service Industries Division for the American Society for Quality Control.

11. Originally coined by Jan Carlzon, it describes any encounter between a provider and customer where the customer has an opportunity to form an opinion about the services or products of the provider. Jan Carlzon, *Moments of Truth* (Cambridge, Mass.: Ballinger Publishing Company, 1987).

12. Carol A. Reeves, David A. Bednar, and R. Cayce Lawrence, "Back To The Beginning: What Do Customers Care About In Service Firms," Quality Management Journal vol. 3, Issue 1 (1996), pp. 56–72.

13. My thanks to Dr. Gary McCain, marketing professor at Boise State University, for this concept. Dr. McCain attended a presentation I made to the Las Vegas Section of ASQC in September 1996 and drew out the diagram in this section as an extension to Figure 3.8. It helped explain the potential degree of impact each zone offers as an advantage or disadvantage and lays the foundation for some interesting metrics.

14. Stan Marsh, John W. Morgan, Satoshi Nakui and Glen D. Hoffherr, *Facilitating and Training in Quality Function Deployment* (Methuen, Mass.: Goal/QPC, 1991), p. 18. Two organizations that I have associated with who are among the current leaders in QFD in the United States are the American Supplier Institute of Allen Park, Michigan, and The QFD Institute of Ann Arbor, Michigan.

15. Philip Kotler, *Marketing Management: Analysis, Planning and Control* (Englewood Cliffs, N.J.: Prentice-Hall, 1980), p. 627.

16. On a management study tour to Japan in Spring 1986, I toured the Kawasaki motorcycle assembly plant. During the time spent on the assembly line, I discovered that a large percentage of the workers spoke English. The workers were interested in learning more about the needs and preferences of Southern California bike users. Since I had no experience as a user,

I felt I had little to offer. However, the questions continued as the workers asked about hobbies, color preferences, and lifestyles of Americans and Southern Californians. I wondered who was studying whom.

17. Refer to Appendix A, Table A-2, to see how these measures are obtained.

18. Refer to Appendix A, Table A-1, to see how these figures are obtained.

19. See Figure A-1, in Appendix A; demand weight is the far right column.

20. The attributes from Figure 3-14 are prioritized in the house of quality. This is shown in Appendix A, Figure A-2 and is labeled *Importance of each Solution in Improving/Meeting Customers' Basic Needs.*

Chapter 4

VALUE-ADDED PROCESS ALIGNMENT

> *You want to see an example of a perfect process. You already have a perfect process. Every process you have is perfect. They are perfect for the results you are getting.*
>
> —W. Edwards Deming[1]

Once the organization is aligned with its vision, goals, and plans and has a credible voice of the customer, the next step is to ensure the organization produces maximum value for its customers and is building the methodology of continually improving value. This adjustment process is called *horizontal alignment*. Chapter 4 focuses on the numerator of the value formula by aligning with the voice of the customer and providing high value products and services that meet their needs. Chapter 5 will work on the denominator.

HORIZONTAL ALIGNMENT

Vertical alignment ensures that directions and plans are developed and communicated. Horizontal alignment ensures systems are designed, implemented, and refined to carry out the plans. The vision and major organizational goals are the focus of vertical alignment, whereas delivering value to customers is the focal point of horizontal alignment (see Figure 4.1).

Horizontal alignment assures the organization is properly positioned with external elements to optimize the creation of value. The two major classes of external forces are suppliers (which provide input) and customers (which receive value). This concept is shown in Figure 4.2.

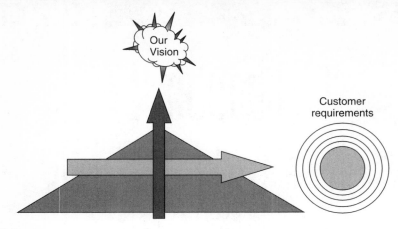

Figure 4.1 Vertical alignment focuses on the vision and its supporting plans; horizontal alignment targets meeting or exceeding the requirements of customers.

VALUE-ADDED PROCESS—THE MEANS OF ALIGNMENT

A process is a series of steps or actions that produce an output that is different from its inputs. A value-added process produces an output that is more desirable than its inputs. Examples abound: An assembly process yields a product that is more valuable than its unassembled components. Scattered data that have been grouped through a statistical analysis become more valuable as they transition to information. A hot meal, properly prepared and served, is more valuable than its uncooked ingredients.

Each product and service that is offered, available, or delivered is the result, or output, of a process. The term *process* can be applied to a small series of steps or can be used to describe a number of parallel operations that produce a complex output. The term is used to describe production or servicing from answering a telephone to manufacturing an oceanliner.

Processes consume our lives. Life itself is a process, or the result of a large number of processes. The transition from waking up to going to work is a process. Thinking is a process. Shopping is a process. Driving an automobile is a process. So is studying, courting, breathing, sleeping, working, relaxing, and everything else we do during our lives.

I lived and worked in England in 1987. My first trip to the grocery store was an experience in adjusting to a different process than I had been used to. I easily found a shopping cart and the food items I needed and headed to the checkout clerk. As he tallied the items and moved them to the end of the counter, everything sat there.

Something was missing in the process. My lifetime experiences with grocery shopping conditioned me to present the items to the cashier, pay the total, and pick up the items in bags at the end of the counter. The items were not in bags and there were no bags or containers readily available. The

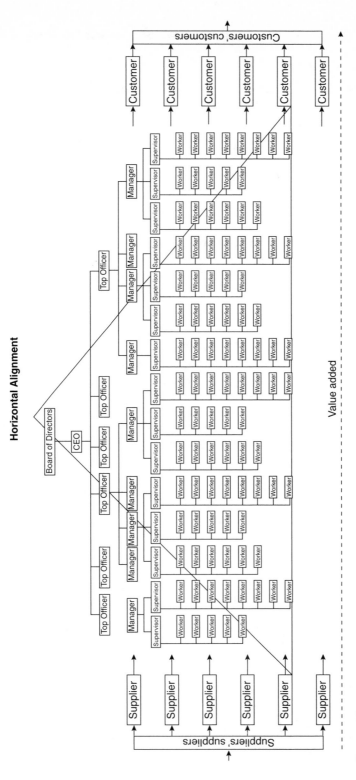

Figure 4.2 Horizontal alignment assures the organization is most efficiently and effectively arranged to deliver value to customers.

81

groceries sat at the end of the counter, and the clerk was helping the next customer.

It took a relatively short time for me to realize the store's process usually ended a step or two earlier than the process ends in the United States. After purchasing a few bags from the clerk, I completed the shopping process and was able to carry my purchase home.

I had a similar experience the first time I bought a small electrical appliance. When I went to use it, I discovered it had no plug at the end of the electric cord. Once again, I completed the process (after a few additional purchases, some inconvenience, and a little training).

I had some fun with the local Marks & Spencer in Reading during the next 11½ months with some customer feedback opportunities, and slowly they began to offer a little higher value service at the checkout counter (to the delight of a few customers).

Value-added propensities and value-added opportunities generally last long after the sale. If these are understood, they can be targeted and built into the process.

CUSTOMERS—THE TARGET OF ALIGNMENT

Any organization that views the customer exclusively or even primarily as the person or entity who pays for the product or service may find itself in trouble. Those organizations that look at every person who remotely or directly comes in contact with the organization as a customer, will have an advantage. A tight definition of a customer is the person who pays; a broad definition includes those who may benefit, endure an inconvenience or loss, or even form an opinion of the organization.

The broad definition includes suppliers, the general public, employees, and anyone subjected to information about the organization including advertisements, news, investment opportunities or research data. We saw in chapter 3 that customers are not all equal, but their requirements and ultimate influence should be well understood.

For example, under normal operating conditions, the primary customers of an airline may be paying passengers. However, many of these passengers have relatives, friends, or business associates who have close interests in the timely and safe arrival of the passenger. They may contact the airline for information regarding the flight status; they may have scheduled a business meeting that coincides with passengers' arrival times; or, they may be driving around the terminal waiting for the passenger.

When an airline incident or accident occurs, the immediate family and government regulators become high priority customers. They both have a critical need for data and information. Relatives and friends may have an additional need for understanding or comfort. For long-term success, organizations must design processes that consider the dimensions of the situation, as well as time, priority and meeting normal operational needs.

A few years ago, a persistent and apparently competent salesperson spent months selling a personal computer system to a friend who had recently started a home-based mail-order business. My friend finally ordered the $12,000 system and requested that it be delivered via overnight express at an additional cost of $140, since she would be traveling for the following few days. She was on the telephone the next day when the door-bell rang, but quickly ran downstairs to open the door. As soon as she did, she saw the delivery van drive away, with her computer.

She called the delivery company to make arrangements to have the computer redelivered and was told that the earliest they would try again would be the same time the next day. She explained what had happened and the short time she was given to answer the door. The delivery company rep said since she lived in a residential neighborhood, delivery personnel were instructed not to wait since most people were not home during the day anyway. When she complained, she was told that she was not the customer and the delivery company had no responsibility to her, and if she did not agree she could take it up with the sender.

She ignored all future attempts to receive the packages and they were returned to the manufacturer. When the salesperson called again to help with the problem, he was told, "Obviously neither you nor your delivery company know or care who the real customer is." She did not make the same mistake with her company. When she opened several warehouses and expanded inter-nationally, she did not conduct business with the shipping company who refused to acknowledge her as a customer. Neither the delivery company nor the computer supplier did all of the work necessary on the VOC.

THE CUSTOMER CHAIN—THE LINKAGE

The internal/external customer chain is widely understood and used. How-ever, it is rarely used effectively to integrate processes through the use of the metrics required to master control panel thinking. This chapter will intro-duce some techniques for high value application of the chain.

All organizations have primary customers. A primary customer is one who is the immediate recipient, beneficiary, or user of the organization's value-added processes. Frequently, it is the paying customer, but this is not always the case.

The primary customer for most retail trade is the person who orders, purchases and receives goods and services. When these are different people or functions there may be more than one primary customer with different needs. The primary customer for a learning institution is the student. Another person or organization may pay for the education and will be a customer, but generally not the primary customer. All customers are impor-tant, but are not necessarily equal in importance. The key to satisfying all of them without any distinction in class is by understanding and managing the customer chain.

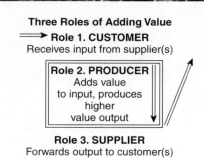

Figure 4.3 Each link of a customer chain has three roles: customer, producer, and supplier.

The customer chain, or value-added chain, is often very long and very complex. However, any single organization will primarily be concerned with a relatively small number of segments. The customer chain is composed of links, which, in turn, are comprised of smaller links. These links are processes, subprocesses, microprocesses, and so on. Each link depends on the links that precede it and each creates a situation where subsequent links depend on it. The customer chain is a causal series of dependencies.

A link on a chain can be an organization (any size), a division, unit, individual, activity, transaction, or even a step or procedure. Each link plays three distinct roles: supplier, producer, and customer. A link's primary role is producer, where it adds, or produces, value. This is the purpose or mission of each link. However, in order to produce value it requires some form of input or assistance. These are furnished by suppliers. Once its role as producer is completed, it hands off its output to a customer. As it hands off this output, the link functions as a "supplier" to its customer(s) (see Figure 4.3).

The customer chain is the result of linking several producers through the process of receiving input from suppliers, adding value, and handing off output to a customer. The chain is illustrated in Figure 4.4.

A simple example of a high-level chain is shown in the illustration in Figure 4.5. The targeted customer is a traveler who is in town for a few days staying at a local hotel. One of the needs of the traveler is hot meals with fresh vegetables. The supplier of a meal is the hotel restaurant. One of the suppliers of the ingredients of the meals may be a local transport company that delivers fresh vegetables it purchases from local farmers (or a farmers market).

The actual high level chain is more complex because there are a number of suppliers, in addition to the transport company, who directly furnish goods and services that are required in the value the traveler receives. Also, there are a number of customers, in addition to the traveler, who will receive value from the hotel restaurant over a period of time. Figure 4.6 shows an expanded list of customers and suppliers.

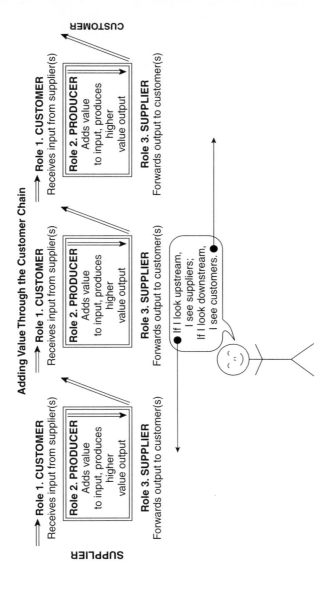

Figure 4.4 The customer chain, or value-added chain, is a long series of handoffs from suppliers to producers to customers.

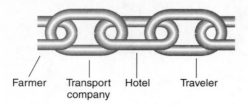

Figure 4.5   A high-level customer chain from the farmer to the hotel restaurant serves a traveler.

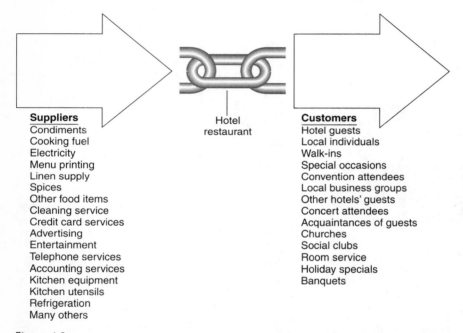

Figure 4.6   A restaurant has a large number and different types of both suppliers and customers.

The customer chain is a high-level process that increases value. Each link in the chain contains a series of processes, each of which is a value-adding step to the ultimate value added by the chain. For example, the critical steps needed to serve a hot meal to a restaurant customer may consist of the steps shown in Figure 4.7.

Each step has a series of activities that must be completed in order to complete the step. For example, the preparation of food may include the activities shown in Figure 4.8.

Each activity can be broken into a few tasks. Each task can be given a measured goal or standard and its completion can be documented, studied,

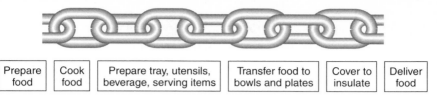

| Prepare food | Cook food | Prepare tray, utensils, beverage, serving items | Transfer food to bowls and plates | Cover to insulate | Deliver food |

Figure 4.7 These are major steps the restaurant completes from the time food is prepared until the customer is served.

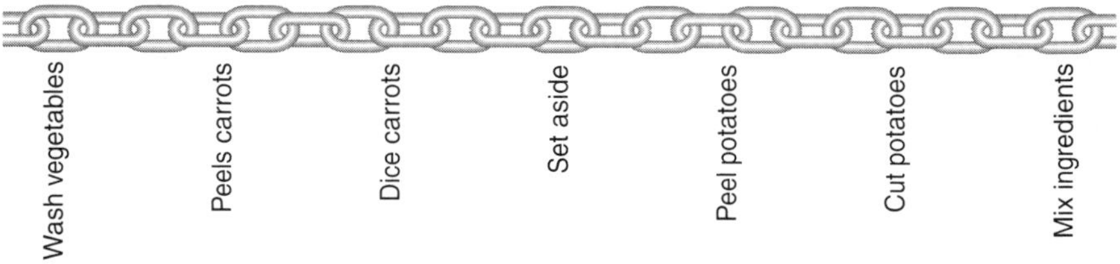

Wash vegetables | Peels carrots | Dice carrots | Set aside | Peel potatoes | Cut potatoes | Mix ingredients

Figure 4.8 Preparing the food requires a number of activities.

and improved to a degree where it is acceptable or meets the standard. Employees can be trained to follow the procedures and meet the standard. Although every task does not require a measured goal, each is capable of being quantified into goals.

In a complicated organization, processes become very complex. They are not a simple linear flow. They consist of parallel processes that come together at an assembly or merging point. These are prevalent in manufacturing organizations, but exist in almost every organization. An example of a typical organization's process flow is shown in Figure 4.9.

There are numerous loops where a producer is both a customer and a supplier to another producer. The customer service role is a prime example. It receives training and knowledge from many parts of the organization and sends back information as customers provide feedback. Any time one process hands off an output, information, or a resource to another and sees it again, it is part of a closed loop.

An accounting service (or department) receives data and information from an entity. It may perform calculations and reformatting of the data into a prepared report and return it to the entity. The accounting role is both a customer of and a supplier to the entity.

Other large process roles in organizations are fulfilled by support roles. They may not be considered as part of the major critical process[2] of the organization, but they may contribute to the overall value added by the organization. Examples are a personnel department that provides generic training and assistance in filling open job positions or a legal department that drafts the language of a contract or reviews warranty information.

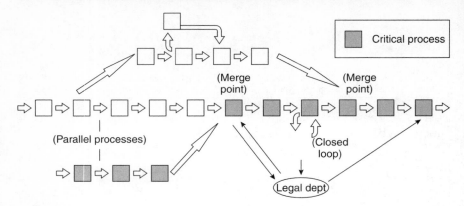

Figure 4.9 The critical process of most organizations is not a simple linear flow, but a combination and consolidation of a number of support and parallel processes.

CUSTOMER REQUIREMENTS—THE METRICS

Understanding the proportions of customer requirements is a neverending quest. As soon as an organization has some comfort in its understanding of customer needs, customers begin to change. However, a solid base of understanding allows observation of trends. An organization that has well-positioned listening posts, as well as continuous analysis of data and information, has tremendous advantages over those who do not.

To be meaningful, requirements must be translated into some form of a measurable goal. With an objective in mind, a route can be established and a stable and repeatable process can be designed. Customer requirements are discovered through a VOC process. In the final analysis they must be the voice of the customer, whether stated, implied, or created for the customer.

PRIORITIZE

The first step is to prioritize the segments themselves. This step is used when segments share resources such as sales and support operations. It is not necessary if each segment is unique and separate. The criteria for importance should be decided by the organization based on its longer-term strategies and goals. A very good method of prioritizing that is used frequently in Pareto analysis is to force the field to 100 points, or percent. This provides a quantified *relative* priority among the various choices.

Each segment should then be viewed separately and the top five to ten requirements identified and prioritized using the Pareto approach. Once this is completed for all segments, similar requirements can be combined among the various segments, and a weighted priority can be calculated for combined segments.

| **Table 4.1** | The left table outlines the priority of segments, as well as the priority of requirements within each segment; the right table consolidates percentage totals from all segments. |

Importance Ranking of Top Requirements

Customer segment	Importance of segment	Requirement	Importance within segment	Overall importance	Percent of total
A	15	Requirement 1	12	180	1.8%
		Requirement 2	25	375	3.8%
		Requirement 3	4	60	0.6%
		Requirement 4	35	525	5.3%
		Requirement 5	24	360	3.6%
B	8	Requirement 1	9	72	0.7%
		Requirement 2	31	248	2.5%
		Requirement 4	38	304	3.0%
		Requirement 5	16	128	1.3%
		Requirement 6	6	48	0.5%
C	30	Requirement 1	7	210	2.1%
		Requirement 2	18	540	5.4%
		Requirement 3	10	300	3.0%
		Requirement 4	35	1050	10.5%
		Requirement 7	30	900	9.0%
D	22	Requirement 2	12	264	2.6%
		Requirement 4	17	374	3.7%
		Requirement 6	11	242	2.4%
		Requirement 7	28	616	6.2%
		Requirement 8	32	704	7.0%
E	25	Requirement 2	14	350	3.5%
		Requirement 4	12	300	3.0%
		Requirement 6	14	350	3.5%
		Requirement 7	21	525	5.3%
		Requirement 8	39	975	9.8%
Total	100			500	100%

Requirement	Combined total	Rank
Requirement 1	4.6%	7
Requirement 2	17.8%	3
Requirement 3	3.6%	8
Requirement 4	25.5%	1
Requirement 5	4.9%	6
Requirement 6	6.4%	5
Requirement 7	20.4%	2
Requirement 8	16.8%	4
	100.0%	

Table 4.1 provides a sample format using five segments, with five requirements per segment.

The information in the righthand matrix from Table 4.1 is viewed in a Pareto format shown in Figure 4.10.

The major objective of relentless prioritizing is to provide a sequence to follow in assuring that customer requirements are met. The cumulative line in the Pareto chart in Figure 4.10 shows that more than 80 percent of the

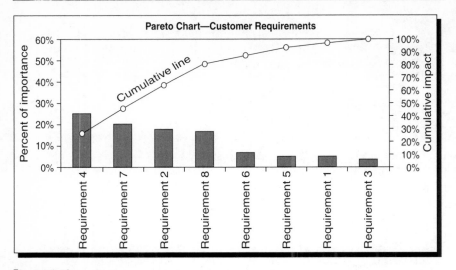

Figure 4.10   Pareto chart showing priority of customer requirements from information in Table 4.1. (The generally accepted format for a Pareto chart displays connected bars; these are separated for greater clarity.)

total importance of the top eight customer requirements are found in the top four requirements. *These must be met.*

QUANTIFY

To be meaningful and actionable, requirements must be stated in a measurable form. Many requirements can be easily measured; some are difficult, but none are impossible. There are only a few metrics that are commonly used to measure requirements. They are all based on time and physical properties. They are frequently stated in relative terms such as accuracy, productivity, and position.

Time is generally stated in terms of cycle time, which is the measure of elapsed time from the start of a defined cycle to its completion. Physical properties include the measure of material, matter, energy, and space and the various ways they are used, either separately or together. In service examples, cycle time is usually stated as *response time,* which is the time measured from the communicating of a service request to its acknowledgment, provisioning, or completion. *For many services response time is the key metric.*

After requirements are quantified, the organization makes decisions on their desired performance levels, or targets. These targets are based on customer priority and current performance levels against both actual and perceived performance levels of competitors from the VOC. Generally, these targets are expressed in the language of the customer.

TRANSLATE

However, customer requirements from the VOC must be translated into the language of the organization. Initially, this is the step in the quality function deployment process that follows the VOC. If QFD is not used, this step must still be completed or reviewed.

Requirements should be measured from two separate viewpoints; first, from the customer's; then, from the organization's. Although the two measures can be the same, they also can be very different.

For example, a person calling a customer service facility may have a requirement for the telephone to be answered "quickly" by a customer service representative. However, the term *"quickly"* to a customer placed on hold may be remarkably dissimilar to that of an overworked and undertrained customer service representative.

Several elements drive requirements. A major one is the desire of the customer. Others include the perceived expectations of the customer, the disclosure and anticipation set by the provider, and the levels that are provided by competitors.

Standards are applied differently than goals. There are several types of standards and none, some, or all may be used to support a goal. The most commonly used standard is the work or production standard, which is used internally by the organization. This is the targeted lowest acceptable output level of a process or individual job. An increasingly used standard is the service or warranty standard. This is either a promise or a guarantee by the provider to the customer to deliver the goods or service to a certain level. These range from an advertised promise to a contracted specification.

Although the organization should understand the voice of the customer with accuracy and empathy, it should use its own language and methodology in assuring that its processes deliver the desired output. In this example of the customer service facility, the customer is not the least concerned with all the challenges that the organization endures to answer telephones quickly. However, the organization must be very concerned.

Those working in customer service know that the speed of answering telephones quickly and accurately is a function of a number of variables. They may measure and control some variables; others are either not measured, are immeasurable, or remain in some other mysterious domain of the organization.

Customer support functions measure and report talk time, resolution time, rate of call abandonment, calls per incident, speed of answer, and hold time. These are a few of the day-to-day measures that directly impact how long it takes for a customer to speak with a representative of the organization.

Other internal measures also impact the cycle time of answering telephones. These include staffing levels, nonproductive time, training time, meeting time, absentee rate, tardiness, overtime, morale, tenure, lighting and noise levels, comfort, technology and availability of information.[3]

However, by far, the most important elements of customer support are not these measures but what is driving the causes for the call in the first place. Customer support is a major customer of most of the other functions of the organization. Every design flaw, every manufacturing or service error, every deficiency in support or instructional material, every element overlooked in training, and every perception of lack of caring or attention by anyone in the organization can create a call to customer service.

The major element on a customer support function's control panel is an ongoing Pareto analysis of the root reasons for the call in the first place. Although these are in the language of the organization, they ultimately translate into the language of the customer.

LINK

The highest requirement of airline passengers is that their airplane lands safely at its destination. This requirement is usually followed in importance by an on-time arrival and the satisfactory delivery of checked baggage. As long as the higher requirement is met, or the customer perceives it is being met, it is not a strong motivating factor. Requirements, as in Maslow's hierarchy of needs, are driven by those that are unmet.

In an emergency, or perceived emergency, checked baggage and time of arrival become insignificant. Other needs become dominant. Depending on the emergency, customers need information, instructions, assurance, and leadership. If a plane is late, customers' requirements change. They need information, understanding, perhaps a telephone, and some direction. The duration of the delay triggers and influences other sets of needs. A person whose baggage did not arrive has different requirements than the person whose luggage is safe and sound at the pickup area.

The situation almost always drives requirements. When things go wrong, or do not work as promised, the customer needs solutions and may need an apology or some sort of acknowledgment from the provider. Unmet or unfulfilled requirements always create other requirements. However, these situations can be studied, needs can be understood, and the necessary processes developed to meet the new requirements that changing situations demand.

There are two separate phases for mistake correction. The first is a form of triage, or service recovery. It is important to deal with serious errors based on likely damage to customers and make corrections or amends as soon as possible. The longer-term solution is to fix or improve the process that created the error so it is not repeated. The organization that understands the multifaceted requirements of customers and knows how to meet them will win in the long run over those who do not.

CRITICAL PROCESS SPECIFICATIONS

The major process that delivers value to the customer is the critical process of the organization. That does not diminish the importance of the other processes, but it does establish focus and priority.

Every organization has a different critical process chain but most have common elements that vary in sequence, terminology, and application. The most common are (see Figure 4.11):

1. Strategic/tactical/customer planning and alignment
2. Product/service design
3. Marketing[4]
4. Manufacture or service production
5. Sales
6. Delivery/installation
7. Support

The ultimate desired output of the critical process is high value to customers. It is defined by products and services that meet or exceed agreed upon requirements delivered in an effective and efficient manner. These requirements are prioritized, quantified, and expressed in metrics and verbalized specifications.

Critical processes are designed and built to meet requirements and they are continually improved to deliver higher and higher value to customers. Specs are defined in the planning process and become the goal of the totality of the critical process.

A simple example is illustrated in Figure 4.12. The customer requirements for a widget are defined through a VOC analysis and then translated into company specifications.

More comprehensive specs may include several layers of customers, such as jobbers, distributors, wholesalers, retailers, freight movers, salespeople, insurance providers, and regulators. With clear and comprehensive specs, processes can be built and adjusted to ensure compliance.

With a large number of customers and diverse and sometimes conflicting requirements, it is essential that the organization take an integrated

Figure 4.11   Many organizations have these critical processes or variations of each.

Major requirements for VOC

A widget that is compact enough to fit in a hand, light enough to carry, waterproof, durable, has a long battery life. If it ever malfunctions, day or night, I need immediate assistance and/or quick replacement.
It should be delivered to me within a short time of ordering.
I should be able to install a widget quickly with a minimum of training.

High level specifications

A widget that is no larger than 3" x 4" x 2"; less than15 oz. net weight. Waterproof to a depth of 25 feet; battery life that exceeds 2 hours continuous use using 4, or less AA alkaline batteries. MTF of 10,000 hours of use. Customer support line available 24 hours/ 7 days with average resolution time of less than 5 minutes from time dialed until problem solved. Up to 100 units must be delivered within 2 days in Continental U.S.; instructions should be clear enough that average 10th grade education can install in less than 12 minutes with less than 2% error. The delivered cost per widget on the first 10,000 produced will not exceed $xx.xx.

Figure 4.12 An example of translating customer requirements into high level specs or standards for the organization.

approach to meeting specs. In many cases, quality function deployment will be used to ensure coordination, but QFD may not be practical in every case. When QFD is not practical, there has to be a methodology for spec compliance among all functions.

Each spec should have a function assigned with primary responsibility for its achievement. This may be mostly a coordination role, or it may be an implementation and delivery role. The illustration in Figure 4.13 offers an example of the coordination and integration of specs in an organization. Ultimately, all areas should share the responsibility for the achievement/ failure of meeting or exceeding specs.

TWO VIEWS OF AN ORGANIZATION

ORGANIZATION CHARTS

Many organizations use an organization chart to depict how they function. Unfortunately, most organization charts are very limited in what they communicate. They outline reporting structure and job titles, but do not show how work is performed, how value is added, or how different roles work together. Additionally, an organization chart is little use in providing meaningful metrics to a control panel. Since organization charts usually only contain employees of the organization, they exclude both external suppliers and customers.

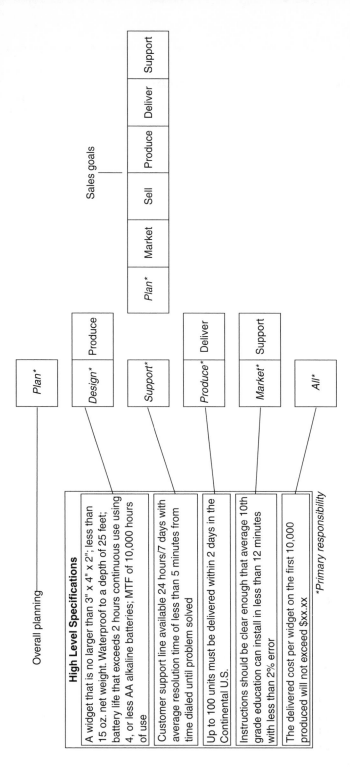

Overall planning

High Level Specifications

A widget that is no larger than 3" x 4" x 2"; less than 15 oz. net weight. Waterproof to a depth of 25 feet; battery life that exceeds 2 hours continuous use using 4, or less AA alkaline batteries; MTF of 10,000 hours of use

Customer support line available 24 hours/7 days with average resolution time of less than 5 minutes from time dialed until problem solved

Up to 100 units must be delivered within 2 days in the Continental U.S.

Instructions should be clear enough that average 10th grade education can install in less than 12 minutes with less than 2% error

The delivered cost per widget on the first 10,000 produced will not exceed $xx.xx

*Primary responsibility

Plan*

Design* Produce

Support*

Produce* Deliver

Market* Support

All*

Sales goals

| Plan* | Market | Sell | Produce | Deliver | Support |

Figure 4.13 Since specs cover a wide range of customer requirements, they should be assigned as the responsibility of major functions that can deliver or coordinate their fulfillment.

95

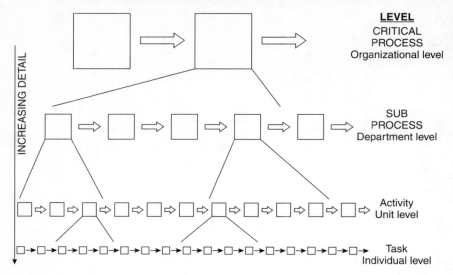

Figure 4.14 Processes can be mapped from high level with little detail to lower levels with much detail.

A typical organization structure is depicted in a pyramid structure (see Figure 4.2). It is constructed showing vertical silos that represent organizational units such as divisions, departments, and work groups. It is difficult to ascertain how work flows and which functions provide support and which produce and add value along key processes. The only common connection points tend to be at the top of the organization.

PROCESS MAPS

Other tools are required to show how work is accomplished, value is added, roles work together and meaningful metrics are provided to a control panel. The primary tool is the process flow chart or process map. Figures 4.9 and 4.11 are examples of high-level process maps. These are a visual representation of the flow and sequence that transform inputs to higher value outputs.

Process maps can be extremely detailed or they can be high level. Figure 4.14 outlines various process levels in an organization. At the highest level, they appear smooth and homogeneous. At the lower levels they can become cluttered and confusing. An analogy is traveling by plane versus travel by automobile. The view from ground level is full of detail; one can see signs and buildings and people. The view from 35,000 feet shows entire cities, mountain ranges, and huge lakes. Of course, we can use a microscope to see even more precision when needed or use telescopes to see billions of miles across space. All these views have their purposes, advantages, and disadvantages.

Process maps have numerous applications and are pivotal tools used from business process reengineering to process improvement.[5] When meaningful

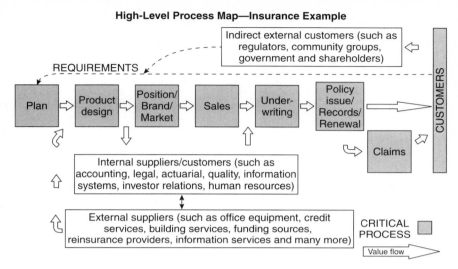

Figure 4.15   The major external suppliers of the organization and major customers of the organization, along with internal units, will become pieces of a process map.

metrics are added to key output points, they provide a multidimensional tool that becomes a critical part of an organization's control panel.

A practical method to apply this valuable tool is to begin with higher level maps at the organization level and work your way down to any level of detail necessary to improve performance. It is important to begin at the top, or highest level, as that will provide the path to lower levels. Beginning at a lower level is an exercise in futility and mostly a waste of time and energy.

The value of starting at the top is the improvement potential of critical processes. They have the largest and most far-reaching impact on customers and will, in turn, feed through subprocess and activity improvement. Careful prioritization will provide the best return for the effort.

The core of the highest level process map is the critical process. It should be drawn first, as it is the cornerstone from which the other parts come together. Once the critical process is mapped, the next step is to identify the major external suppliers and other customers of the organization. These customers may not pay the organization for the benefit they receive. They include any person, group, or other organization that benefits from the organization or is in a position to demand performance or compliance from the organization. Additionally, all internal units, functions, and individuals will eventually become part of a high-level process map.

Figure 4.15 shows an example of a critical process and the various types of customers and suppliers that comprise the value-adding processes for an insurance company. This approach is a good beginning point for a high-level process map. Once all players are identified, each can be linked to either the critical process or the role they support.

The major objective of process mapping is to view graphically how value is added throughout the organization. A sensible way to begin is by answering the question, "Who are the primary suppliers to the major steps of the critical process and what is the relative importance of each?" The best place to begin is with the VOC. Determine who or what areas deliver or are responsible for the value that the customer ultimately receives.

In the example shown in Figure 4.16, the highest values added to customers come from the production and sales areas, followed by support, design, and planning. The relative impact of each is shown by the thickness of the line; dashed lines and thinner lines are less critical than heavy solid lines.

As more suppliers are identified, additional internal units and external suppliers begin to appear on the map (Figure 4.17).

By the time the top suppliers for the beginning process steps are charted, the diagram begins to appear complex. It clearly becomes a complex system that continually adds value forward down the customer chain while building and modifying feedback systems that provide adjustment data and information. The diagram in Figure 4.18 shows a sample of a customer–supplier map, where five to six top-priority suppliers are identified and charted for the six major critical process steps between planning and the target customer.

The number of flow lines increases tremendously when the critical process steps are broken into smaller units and the customer–supplier relationships go beyond the top five to six suppliers or customers. The dynamics increase further if one attempts to record these relationships at the individual level or the transaction level.

During the value-adding process alignment phase, higher-level maps serve the purpose of identifying key relationships that should be quantified and tracked at high levels. Similar techniques can be used at all levels of the organization to assist leaders in the understanding and management of their operations.

Simple maps should be performed at every level of the organization and periodically updated as changes occur. At the lower levels, the maps are transactional and activity-flow charts. At the highest levels, they are used for proper process engineering of the organization, as well as serving as key sensors for strategic indicators on the executive control panel.

Every leader in the organization should have at least two high-level process maps (they may be combined). These consist of a map of their area of responsibility and a map above their area that contains all functions that embody either customers or suppliers. These provide a "big picture" view of their organization and shows how work is performed and value is added. This aids in communicating to each individual how their efforts link to the value chain. This information will enhance decision making and performance on a daily basis.

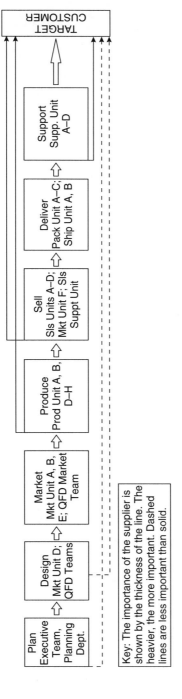

Figure 4.1b Begin developing a comprehensive view of how value is added by identifying the key suppliers to each process step, starting with the target customer and working up the process chain.

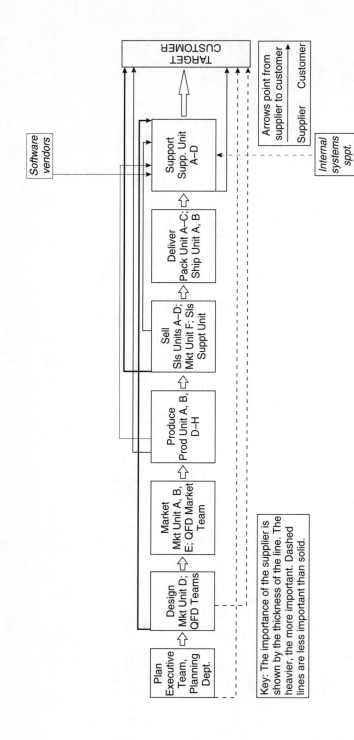

Figure 4.17 As mapping proceeds up the supplier chain, additional suppliers appear.

100

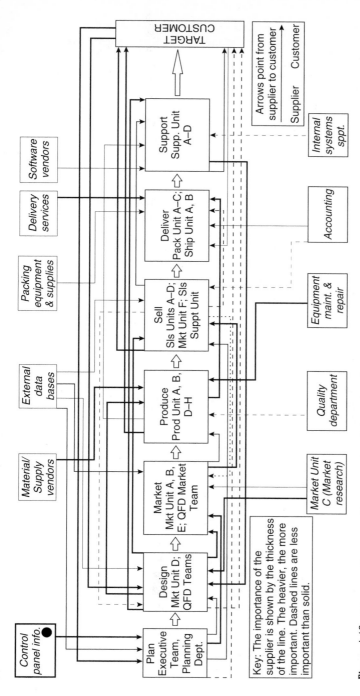

Figure 4.18 The top few suppliers to each of the critical process steps are shown, with a relative indication of each supplier's importance to each step.

Every function, whether a support or a direct step in a critical process, should appear on a customer–supplier map. This serves several purposes: it accounts for the role of everyone, it allows everyone to see how they contribute to the value-adding propensities of the organization, and it offers a basis for leadership and improvement.

ESTABLISHING AND TRACKING PERFORMANCE TO MEET CUSTOMER REQUIREMENTS

Senior management needs a system to concisely look at the high-level performance of the organization in order to spot trends and adjust as required to keep the organization on track. Every person below the highest level has the same requirement for their areas of responsibility. Those at the top of the organization must have the means to delve into the lower levels, and those at the lower levels must be able to see what they are expected to merge with in the pursuit of higher value. All should be members of a common team in pursuit of common goals.

Since value is ultimately delivered to target customers, and they make the final determination on its utility, effectiveness, and worth, they are the best place to begin performance tracking. However, as customer/supplier mapping reveals, everyone is a customer and everyone has opinions and observable metrics of what they receive from their suppliers.

If those at the early stages of the customer chain are not receiving required value, it is unlikely that those at the end will receive their required value. For this to happen, someone down the chain will be involved in rework and correction, and the system will be inefficient. Inefficient systems are not high value producers.

In order to observe the efficiency and effectiveness of a system, sensors must be placed strategically throughout the system to provide data to a central point for integration, consolidation, and collaborative assessment.

PERFORMANCE INFORMATION SENSORS

Using the Pareto principle, there is no need to have sensors everywhere. We must find the key drivers of value and monitor them. High-level customer maps offer a solution. Using the example in Figure 4.18, the diagram in Figure 4.19 adds sensors at a few strategic points. These are critical areas that have evolved through much observation and analysis that indicate key performance.

How sensors are linked with a control panel depends on the size, complexity, and type of organization and the organization's progress in the Information Age. Most organizations today have centralized processing systems, as well as localized area networks and stand-alone personal computers. Information, data, and knowledge may be processed at the control panel level or it may reach the control panel in a high level state. It may be

Key Suppliers to Critical Process Steps with Sensors at Critical Metric Points

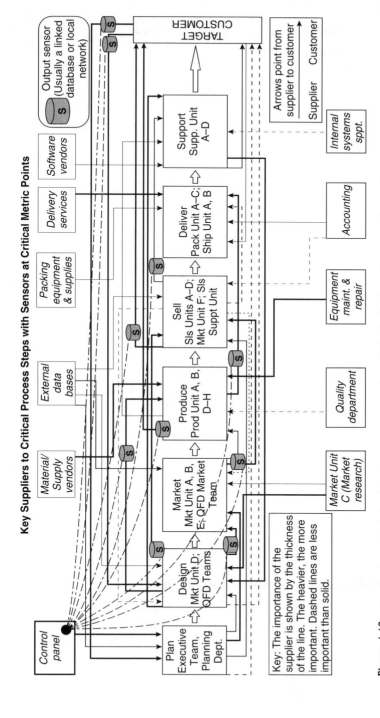

Figure 4.19 Output metrics of critical process steps should be linked to the control panel.

displayed in a fairly raw form, or it may be synthesized or consolidated into indices or a combination of both. It must be high level, manageable, meaningful to the organization and clear.

A few examples of performance sensors are:

- Call management systems—these automated systems track hundreds of data points on a customer service function, including type of call, wait time, response time, percent resolution on first call, and many others.
- Operation cycle time reports—the time that elapsed from the receipt of input until delivery to customer. This is a common sensor in production lines, batch processing. It can be used in almost every process and may be automated or manual.
- Defect rate—this may be the result of automated or manual inspection, statistical process control charts, or customer feedback.

Performance indicators exist throughout every organization at all levels. The key to assuring that every control panel has the best blend of sensors is to utilize those that will provide data and information on the priority results of the most critical processes, provide a balance among leading and lagging indicators, and ensure that the data or information collected is statistically sound and representative of the process output.

REPORTING PERFORMANCE AGAINST SERVICE STANDARDS[6]

An organization tracks and reports performance at any and all levels. Major recipients should always include downstream customers and higher levels of management who can help assist in improvement. Charts and graphs should be used in the workplace on a frequent basis. These can be continuously updated to show monthly, weekly, or even hourly or minute-by-minute results. At the lower levels more frequent reporting provides quick feedback for adjustments when needed.

There are no limits to how information can be displayed or communicated. The Japanese traditionally tended to use fishbone diagrams, matrices, and flowcharts to show several dimensions of performance. Americans have preferred result charts. However, these are changing, as both are being used more in both countries to show a greater level of cause-and-effect.

In those processes where sensors are automated and production flow is continuous, display boards can provide a constant display of performance. On processes that have longer cycle time, or rely on manual input or manual review, the results will be displayed over a longer time frame.

More organizations are beginning to publish results to a wider audience than in the past. This creates several opportunities and advantages:

- It promotes greater cooperation and a feeling of teamwork by showing how linked processes must work together in order to produce results.

- It presents a larger picture of the critical process that flow together. Individuals and small units can readily see how their contribution makes a difference.
- There is a higher spirit of openness and trust when everyone sees both the objectives and performance against either standards or objectives.
- There is little doubt to what is important to the customer and higher management.
- It promotes the building of an enlarged team as customers and other recipients of the information are encouraged to contribute ideas and suggestions to help further improve results.
- It provides a solid, measurable basis for collateral benefits such as performance assessment, training, gain sharing, process improvement, and future planning.

Of course, senior leadership must be committed to achieving overall goals. It must be consistent in its approach to openness and information sharing for high value to be added through communication of goals and results.

Figures 4.20, 4.21, and 4.22 are examples taken from an early edition of a publication on the monthly results of an organization's six critical and thirteen supporting processes at the division level of a major corporation. This publication later evolved into a newsletter-type format that featured more information on results, as well as projects being undertaken through improvement teams and personal interest stories of selected employees who worked in these processes, as well as their leaders. Periodically, the newsletter published overall process maps, as well as the mission and major longer-term goals of each unit.

The document was initially distributed internally and later sent to key customers. Ultimately, it became a marketing tool, as the organization discovered that competitors did not track or disclose the standards they would provide to customers. The fundamental philosophy of the publication was communication of results and sharing of ideas to improve results.

Each unit or process step published monthly performance on the top three to five of their critical goals. The graphs were usually bar charts showing the previous running twelve months performance as well as the standard, or goal. As performance improved above existing standards, some were raised or other goals emerged. Periodically, a historical review showing the evolution of standards and results was compiled and published. Figure 4.22 is a sample page from an early edition showing three of five goals of one unit.

CONTROL PANEL

So far, we have several major types of elements on a control panel. In chapter 2, we established a mission and values as boundaries of a control panel

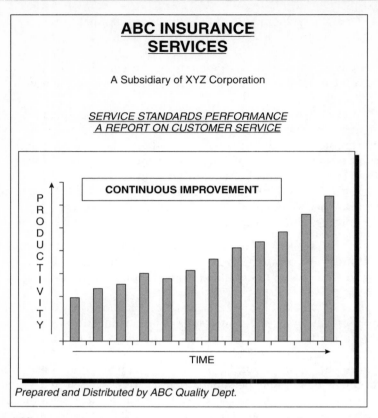

Figure 4.20   The cover of the document showing monthly results of service standards performance shows continuous improvement is the intent.

and a vision as its chief longer-term focus. The CSFs (critical success factors) were converted into top organizational goals that are tracked and continually updated.

In chapter 3, we added the VOC (voice of the customer) and established methods for observing both actual and perceived performance on the most important attributes of value delivered to customers.

Additionally, we have added the dimension of the customer–supplier chain, which connects the internal value-adding processes of the organization with external suppliers and customers. Value is added through a series of steps that link together. Each step has measurable inputs and outputs. Although the ultimate goal of these processes is to add value to customers while meeting or exceeding their requirements, we may translate their requirements into an internal organizational language that is different from

---

ABC SERVICE STANDARDS

OUR QUALITY PHILOSOPHY

Never-ending improvement of our performance on all our products and services to all customers, both internal and external. Quality at ABC Insurance Services is *defined by our customers and is always measurable.*

This publication was created by our management and employees to communicate to both our customers and ourselves how well we are performing in those areas that are important to all of us. At ABC, we believe that we must all continually improve our service and the value we deliver to customers; it is as much a part of our jobs as performing our assigned tasks. We look at the customer who is paying premiums as the ultimate judge of our performance. However, along the way, each employee is the customer of other employees and we rely on each other working together to constantly improve our process and performances to the point where we are clearly ahead of competition.

In the spirit of improvement, we encourage the reader of this publication to communicate to any individual or department, including our President on ways we can improve or on standards of measurement that are meaningful to you, as a customer. You may communicate directly or may contact our Quality Department at:

ABC Quality Dept....

Figure 4.21   The first page of the service standards publication outlines its philosophy and intent.

customers' language. This provides the ability to observe and measure performance throughout the organization.

The elements on the control panel are beginning to overlap. For example, an important attribute outlined in the VOC may also be a CSF and, in turn, may be the output of the critical process. Although this is frequently the case, there are examples where this does not exist.

One of the greatest values of a control panel is its integration power. This will become more apparent later. It is the master integrator of the organization; particularly in the Information Age. At this point, we are compiling a catalog of high potential sensors, meters, and metrics for a control panel that will provide the information and knowledge required to drive and support leadership decision to keep the organization on course to fulfill its mission. There is still much more work to do.

ABC SERVICE STANDARDS

Collateral Command System

Results–199x

THE COLLATERAL COMMAND SYS-SYSTEM (CCS) HAS BEEN OUR INSURANCE TRACKING OPERATION SINCE 1976. WE CURRENTLY PROVIDE OUR SERVICE TO 90 FINANCIAL INSTITUTIONS AND THEIR 3,200,000 AUTO, MORTGAGE AND LEASE CUSTOMERS.

OUR COLLATERAL COMMAND SYS-SYSTEM HAS BEEN MONITORING THE QUALITY AND PRODUCTIVITY OF OUR OPERATION FOR OVER FIVE YEARS. OUR PERFORMANCE HAS LEAD TO EXCEPTIONAL GROWTH DURING THIS PERIOD.

****

Service standard: Speed of telephone answer

Goal: Under 20 seconds

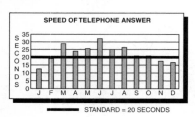

Customer service: Daily, we monitor the time between first ring and availabilty of a customer service representative. Our response rate is calculated as a monthly average.

****

Service standard: Documents processed/Hour/Person

Goal: 60 Documents/Hour/Person

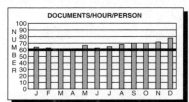

Data entry: Daily counts of each operator's work are divided by the number of task related hours worked. The measurement combined with quality achievement creates the basis for performance evaluations.

****

Service standard: Data entry accuracy
Goal: 98% accurate

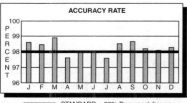

Data entry: Each week mail updates are reviewed for each operator. An error could be one or more of 17 possibilities per document. Our 98% goal means that for every 100 documents we may allow 2 errors per 1700 possibilities. (Less than .12%)

****

Figure 4.22   A sample page showing a brief introduction to the unit and monthly results of three of its five goals.

KEY POINTS   VALUE-ADDED PROCESS ALIGNMENT

- In addition to the organization being aligned to its vision, mission, and value (vertical alignment); an organization must also be aligned with its suppliers and customers (horizontal alignment).
- The focus of all alignment is value to the customer.
- Horizontal alignment is achieved along the customer–supplier value added chain. Each link in the chain is a producer who receives information, material, produces, or services from a supplier, adds value to them and sends the higher-value product or service to a customer.
- The end customer, the person or organization that receives the final product or service in the process, defines the requirements through the satisfaction of basic needs. Each producer upstream sets the requirements of its suppliers in order to add the value necessary to meet the requirements of their customers.
- Internally, customer requirements are converted to standards that the producer must meet in order to deliver acceptable products and services.
- The customer–supplier chain should be mapped to show how value is added, how much, and by whom.
- Critical process maps outline the most important process(es) of organizations, along with supporting suppliers, both internal and external to the organization.
- Information sensors should be placed at strategic locations to continually update progress against performance requirements.
- These sensors should be connected to the organization's control panel to monitor critical performance information for consolidation and analysis with other strategic information of the organization.

NOTES

1. Paraphrased from Dr. W. Edwards Deming during his four-day seminar, *Quality, Productivity and Competitive Position,* on the evening of August 1, 1989, at the Red Lion Inn, Costa Mesa, California.

2. The critical process is the process that produces and delivers the highest portion of value that is added to the customer. It is usually the core process of an organization.

3. These measures include computer response time, computer up/down time, telephone capacity, use of headsets, accuracy, and accessibility of data and clarity of display.

4. In many organizations the marketing function includes sales. Here marketing refers to the process of market research and positioning the product or service for sale, which may include such functions as sales support, advertising, pricing, and packaging.

5. This includes productivity enhancement, improved efficiency, and effectiveness and value improvement. These are covered and used throughout chapters 5 and 6.

6. Service standards may also be called performance objectives, goals, or targets.

Chapter 5

VALUE MANAGEMENT

> The new breed of managers has learned that it is possible to lower costs by increasing quality. This means that the higher-quality producer has a double advantage. The higher-quality product can command a higher price, yet because it has a lower cost to the producer, it gives the enterprise a much larger profit margin than its competitors. It can use this margin in several ways, including the option to finance growth internally as it moves into new product lines. It can also keep the competitors on the verge of bankruptcy as it slowly lowers its prices and gains market share.
>
> —DR. MYRON TRIBUS[1]

Value management is a continuous activity involving everyone in the organization. In order to optimize value, everyone must understand value and how it is added and delivered by the organization. However, the understanding of value includes the understanding of customers, as well as the understanding of the effectiveness and efficiency of the processes that deliver value. Chapter 5 primarily focuses on the denominator of the value formula.

The denominator is composed of costs to the buyer, whether associated with price, inconvenience, or perception. In the Industrial Age, price is straightforward. When producers call the shots, they determine price by calculating their costs of producing and delivering, then adding in a target profit, or margin. If their costs increase, they pass them on to customers through price adjustments. There are many creative ways to disguise price with inconvenience, so the customer remains confused and baffled.

In the Information Age, pricing will not be so simple. The customer is only interested in their total costs, including all prices and inconvenience. They will look at the total package as well as its components. As information increases and value is the determining factor, price will be based primarily on its return to the customer, not its cost to the producer. Growth, return, and wealth will go to those who are most effective and efficient, not those who can best disguise, shift, or postpone costs, or overstate benefits.

We saw in earlier chapters that many elements come together to determine value. At first glance these may appear to be primarily applied to a purchase point, where a customer receives delivery of a product or service. In reality, the components of value, including actual quality, perception, and inconvenience, apply at every critical process step, subprocess step, activity, and task. In other words, every customer in the customer chain requires maximum value.

Value management has two major focuses: the *meeting or exceeding of customers' requirements* at the *lowest total cost* possible.

TRADITIONAL APPROACHES TO COST

Every step at every level in every process has a cost associated with it. At the lower levels the cost per transaction, step, or task may be minuscule, but the costs add up. On the other hand, every process, transaction, step, and activity should add value to the overall output. Those that do not are waste, and are either not needed or require rework. Of course, rework is a process and has additional costs.

Each customer along the value-added chain inherits the cumulative costs of all the processes that have produced and delivered the goods, services, or information to the customer. The customer may or may not pay a price that reflects these costs. In the long run, if the price is less than the costs, the owners of the critical processes will either disappear or abandon them. Although there may be a number of reasons for short-term prices being lower than costs, no organization can survive if that condition continues.

Since every process step has a cost and the cost of all steps is cumulative (see Figure 5.1), each process step added will increase the overall cost of the process. On the other hand, process steps can be added or modified that change the overall process and make it more efficient, reducing *overall* costs. Of course, change itself is a process and has a cost.

Cost is one large element of price; margin (profit) is the other. Margin is always the balancing figure—it is what is either leftover from revenue after all costs have been paid or it is the shortage that must come from precious reserves or additional debt. In reality, a considerable portion of most organization's margins are costs. If they are invested back into the organization, they immediately become costs; if they are paid as dividends, they leave the organization and can be considered the cost of attracting investment or rewarding the owners. If they are retained as surplus, they become the cost of assuring a better future.

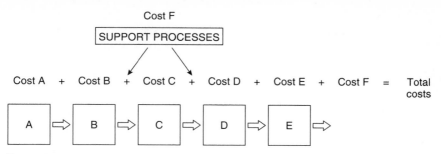

Figure 5.1 The costs of a process are the sum of all the costs of the process steps and processes that support them.

In accounting terms, costs are called *expenses*. Expenses are either recorded when they occur or they are capitalized over a period of time. Expenses are expressed as a monetary measure of assets, usually cash, that flows out of an organization. Expenses fall under categories such as rent, salaries, insurance, cost of materials, and telephone expenses. Most organizations report expense records for the various divisions, units, and subunits of their organization.

The traditional approach to expense management is the budget. The expense goal of management is generally to perform at or below their budget while meeting their other goals. Most organizations have tight controls to ensure that expenses are closely monitored and budgets are met.

The costs of all employees and managers are organizational expenses. Generally, a large number of employees are directly involved in the major production or servicing areas of an organization and another large number are involved in supporting them. Another segment of the employee and management work force is involved in revenue generation. Revenue generators are usually a portion of marketing personnel and sales personnel, and sometimes they include service personnel.

In an organization, accounting systems, like all support systems, merge with and become part of political and social systems. The pursuit and the ultimate use of accounting information is always subject to these characteristics.

Human nature tends to focus behavior toward rewards and recognition and away from punishment. When a manager or a worker competes against peers for recognition and that recognition is partially based on performance against budget, individuals will do what they can to look good. In most organizations there are many ways to pass costs on to other units with little knowledge of the consequences to the larger organization. This behavior is not considered negative; it is a byproduct of unlinked and poorly integrated systems. It is a carryover of the Industrial Age. In order to better assure higher productivity, alternative accounting methods are needed.

What is missing in traditional accounting practices? A few examples may help answer the question.

- Operation A and Operation B sell, produce and service similar services in different geographical areas. They both use a shared information system that was jointly developed three years ago. Since they are evaluated against each other, they do not readily share knowledge. Recently Operation B independently began working with a systems consulting firm to develop a new information system. It is estimated that the new system will cost more than $20 million for its first two years of operation. What does the organization gain and lose by maintaining the two independent systems?
- Employee A and B both receive pay of $11.35/hour. Both produce about 36 units per hour. Unknown to anyone, A has an error rate of .1 percent that goes undetected until customers discover them within about six months after installation. Half of discovered errors result in a call to customer support and the other half require a field visit. Employee B's error rate is less than 10 percent of Employee A's, which is about average. Are the true costs of A and B equal?
- At XYZ Company, middle managers have to battle hard for their budget every year. They know they better not exceed their budgets throughout the year but they do not want to end the year much below their budget, because it might reflect poorly on their budgeting skills and it would probably reduce their next year's budget. A high status symbol in the organization is the number of employees who work for a manager. One team discovers a more efficient method that results in eight members doing the work that required nine previously. After one employee left the organization, the manager decides to hire a secretary that will share support for both the manager and the team. Is the operation better off with the change?
- Corporation P's sales staff are compensated totally on commission based on a percentage of sales revenue. Almost every year, Sales Agent 16 produces the highest commissions. In addition to an income that is close to the president's, SA16 receives a nice incentive bonus and gets an extra two weeks' vacation to attend the all-paid corporation's first-class vacation trip. Sales Agent 21 is always in the top 20 percent of all sales agents, but never quite reaches the top. In reality, SA16's annual customer retention rate is less than 80 percent, while SA21's approaches 95 percent. Additionally, the average margin per account of SA16 is less than 11 percent, while SA21's is almost 45 percent. Over the past ten years, SA21 has contributed more than $12 million more to the bottom line than SA16.
- In the past, the training department's expenses were charged back (allocated) to the various operational departments based on their budget size. The chief financial officer decided it would be more equitable if allocated expenses were charged to departments based on attendance at training events. One of the larger departments

soon discovered it was less costly to have a few trainers attend a training session and later deliver the material to other department personnel. How did that decision affect overall costs, learning retention, and interdepartmental cooperation?

- What are the costs of employee benefit reductions, layoffs, downsizing, allocating expenses, artificially creating profit centers, departments competing for budget dollars, forced ranking of employees, and hundreds of other programs that ignore the big picture? What are the true costs of lost opportunities that every organization misses because it is chasing less valuable pursuits or not optimizing its time?

Solutions to these examples require greater knowledge of the true costs of decisions and activities. This can certainly be improved in every organization. However, it can be achieved only to a limited extent with existing (or commonly used) financial tools alone.

THE COSTS OF INEFFECTIVENESS AND INEFFICIENCY

Organizational leadership needs to know the true costs of decisions. A common management error is to deal with a number of factors at once with insufficient thought given to how each one impacts the other. In other words, an organization may correctly foresee that it can successfully implement undertaking A or B or C. Perhaps a different section of the organization is a champion of each undertaking, although the three sections are all part of the same cross-functional process. In reality, the combined demand on resources may exceed the capacity of the organization to successfully achieve all three. When such an endeavor fails, traditional Industrial Age management usually blames someone for the failure. This, combined with the suboptimal use of resources, is a high and unnecessary cost to the organization.

Generally, the highest unnecessary costs incurred in an organization are the results of failure to see big picture changes affecting the organization and its market(s). This is caused by either moving too fast, too slow, or in the wrong direction on major new initiatives. The organizational culture, combined with the velocity of market change, drive many companies to move too fast or aggressively, while other cultures procrastinate and take too long to modify the obvious. This huge burden is the *cost of ineffectiveness* and it is the *result of not doing the right things*. The second highest unnecessary cost in most organizations (sometimes the highest) is the *cost of inefficiency*. In reality, it is the cost of *not doing things right the first time*. The cost of ineffectiveness is the highest cost in any organization. However, its opposite, the rewards of seized opportunity, are the greatest potential assets of any organization.

Organizations that survive and prosper do so because they are more effective and efficient than those that do not. They make an effort to establish processes that add high value to customers and drive waste and rework out of their systems. On the other hand, organizations that focus on outcomes other than value and do not spend attention on creating and improving effectiveness and efficiency generally end up out of balance and cannot compete. Key barriers to effectiveness and efficiency include the following.

DELEGATING RESPONSIBILITY

One of the biggest failures a leader can make is to delegate the responsibility for effectiveness and efficiency to others. The leader cannot say to anyone else in the organization, "You take care of the effectiveness and efficiency of the organization, I have more important things to do." There is nothing more important than to ensure the organization does the right things right the first time.

GROUP THINK*

Group think is a term used to describe the psychology of following the leader because of the leader's position, even when other factors signal that it is not the wisest choice. One often-referred-to example, is the Bay of Pigs failure during the Kennedy administration. Even though Kennedy's closest advisors believed separately the invasion of Cuba would fail, they agreed as a team that it was the proper choice. Years later the term *group think* was coined to describe this phenomenon.

The more charismatic and respected the leader, the more likely group think will occur. This is definitely a likelihood as a leader moves from closed leadership style to a more opened or coaching role. In the Industrial Age, a leader frequently knew more about most variables facing an organization than others, or had the information available. In the Information Age, the leader needs to continually process data in order to have the necessary information and facilitate the activity that leads to the knowledge required for decision making. If group think occurs, the result will be less than optimal decisions.

DUPLICATION OF EFFORT—THE LEFT HAND NOT KNOWING WHAT THE RIGHT HAND IS DOING

Applying Industrial Age mentality, a favorite method of selecting the best person for the next promotion is to give all the candidates the same objective, or project, and let them compete for the prize. Although it may be both fun and entertaining to observe several individuals compete for achievement and then be the judge and jury of the outcome, it is not the most productive.

Many organizations carry this competitive philosophy to the unit, division, and company levels. When rewards are based on the internal criteria

*Also referred to as groupthink.

of performing higher than other units (individuals, divisions, companies) instead of cooperatively outperforming external competitors, cooperation becomes superficial and results in duplication of effort. Duplication always costs more than cooperation.

THE NEED TO BE RIGHT

We are taught from infancy what is right and what is wrong. In many cases, right and wrong are based on values that have been passed down from previous generations. In our formal education, we spend years learning facts, figures, laws, rules, theorems, logic, and conjecture. We look up to our teachers as being more knowledgeable than we are (at least in specialized areas). In turn, they judge our ability to learn through various means of assessment.

Through our early years most of us develop a psychology that accepts apparent superior knowledge as being accurate. We learn to believe there is *the* correct answer, *one best* choice, or an actual explanation for every situation. This conditioning remains with most of us throughout our lives. Even in our early organizational experiences we learn there are rules and guidelines that are expected to drive our behavior. For example, it is right to raise your hand before speaking and it is wrong to take a break at any time other than 10 o'clock.

In business, as in life, there is no *one* right or wrong way to do things. What method might be best at a point in time might result in failure at another time. Today's solutions may be inappropriate for tomorrow, and tomorrow's may be inappropriate for today. What works for one organization may fail for another.

If the goal is being right, then the goal is wrong. The goal must be a specific result that is superior to the current condition and meets the requirement of those who have the need for something different. In the case of efficiency and effectiveness, the goal should be increased efficiency and effectiveness.

MANAGING EFFECTIVENESS

Leadership is 80 percent effectiveness and 20 percent efficiency. Many managers today have these elements reversed. They believe if an organization is efficient, it will become effective. The opposite is true; being effective leads to becoming efficient. This is based on common sense. If you do the right thing, you can work on doing it right. On the other hand, if you do the wrong thing, how important is it for you to do it right? The Principles of Integrated Leadership are the road map, and their application is the way to higher effectiveness and greater efficiencies.

Senior leaders should never stray far from high-level strategy. In the Information Age, everything moves too fast. Planning is continuous. The modern organization is like an army at war; it must be led by strategic thinkers who view every dimension.

Unfortunately, in the world of competition, time is frequently a major distraction. Therefore, the decision-making process of an organization should be both *thorough* and *speedy*. Most organizations can deal effectively with real emergencies but seem to struggle or postpone decisions on routine concerns, those that are in the symptom stage, or the large opportunities of the future.

The organization must establish a process to move change through the organization quickly and efficiently. Those things that are recognized as requiring modification must be carried out upon recognition. Those things that are no longer needed or are no longer adding value should be abandoned or modified. Procrastination is extremely costly.

Strategic planning should be an ongoing process where new data, information, and knowledge continuously enters the organization and merges with the results of current strategy and tactics. However, since many organizations do not commit strongly to their strategic plans, are heavily influenced by shorter-term pressures, or believe they should be ready to pounce on every opportunity, they need a linked system to maintain focus and sort out the endless barrage of opportunities, problems, and demands coming toward them.

An element should be developed as part of the control panel to continuously prioritize and manage the progress of major projects that are proposed, approved, and implemented. This keeps senior management, and others, informed about the major undertakings that supplement or modify existing plans. In reality, every undertaking of the organization that requires or consumes a certain level of resources or impacts a certain percentage of the organization should be identified and continuously monitored for communication, coordination, and integration.

Only if each significant action, potential action, and trend is understood and managed based on its ultimate value and its integrating propensities can a high degree of effectiveness exist.

THE COST OF INEFFICIENCY—TWO SUPPLEMENTAL COSTING METHODS

Although traditional accounting systems are ideal for financial control and supporting statutory accounting principles, it is not very useful for understanding the ever-changing concept of value. Its chief limitation is caused by one of its greatest strengths, which is its demand for precision or exactness. Our current accounting systems allow Industrial Age managers to know the line-item cost of everything and the value of nothing.

On a given day, any Fortune 500 company can provide its annual sales, expenses, assets, liabilities, net worth, and any number of other financial indicators to the nearest dollar, using generally accepted accounting practices (GAAP). With a few exceptions, most could not report within the nearest $10 million their annual cost of ineffectiveness and inefficiency. Most leadership decisions are made with considerably less accuracy in their supporting information than those required by GAAP.

Two supplemental costing methods to GAAP are Activity Based Costing (ABC) and the Cost of Quality (COQ). ABC provides a system for accounting for costs by activity in addition to the traditional method of breaking costs down by line item and function. COQ seeks continual reduction in waste, rework, and the cost of their correction by moving these high costs into the lower cost of prevention or detection; this can be a valuable assist with process improvement and reengineering. Since both methods are widely used and there is much information available elsewhere, just a few points and some knowledge gained through experience will be offered on each.

ACTIVITY BASED COSTING

Activity Based Costing is an evolved tool from the past fifty plus years of cost accounting. It is a superb method for better understanding and managing costs. It focuses on pursuing the costs of *activities,* instead of the traditional approach of primarily reporting functional unit expenses. This allows a more in-depth view of factors that drive costs, as well as a superior cross-functional accounting of process costs.

It provides excellent techniques for comprehending unit costs, which leads to higher knowledge of product and service costing. This information can be used to assist the improvement of process efficiencies, as well as reducing the cycle time of new product design and implementation. Another huge advantage of understanding costs at the activity level is its benchmarking potential with the ability to compare with other similar processes and learn from best practices.

> *Activity accounting assesses a company's activities to determine if they are being performed cost effectively in comparison to alternatives both inside and outside the company. Activity accounting enhances the understanding of new process technologies. The introduction of a new technology (such as the flexible manufacturing cell or the computerized production control system) changes the factors of production or the performance of activities.*[2]

It is a superior system to traditional accounting in cost allocation because it assigns costs based on actual performed activity instead of historical cost formulas or derived algorithms that may be misunderstood, disagreed with, or manipulated. Most organizations consolidate many *overhead* costs under a category labeled General and Administrative (G&A), or a similar title. This practice tends to disguise true costs and sources of inefficiency. Additionally, ABC has a methodology to help identify value-added activity from nonvalue-added (NVA) activity.

Another large advantage of ABC is its insistence on identifying cost drivers. A cost driver is an activity that causes or strongly influences the costs of subsequent activities. This characteristic provides a linking propensity among costs that is not available through traditional methods.

For all its advantages, ABC has some drawbacks. First, and foremost, it is a secondary system. As long as GAAP and statutory accounting requirements exist, traditional accounting will be the dominant accounting system. Other limitations include the following:

- ABC is expensive to implement on a widespread or organization-wide basis. In addition to the cost of the system, it requires considerable timekeeping, manual tracking, and entry, and has its own set of procedures and controls. This should be significantly reduced in the Information Age.
- ABC requires tremendous employee support and involvement to be used effectively. Unless the values of the organization are based and practiced on a win–win philosophy for all stakeholders, with a high degree of trust, employees and many management personnel will resist and generally reduce its benefits.
- Although it has a methodology to help identify value-added activity from nonvalue-added activity, it is extremely tedious and difficult to utilize.
- Like most other accounting tools, it does not readily provide answers on how to effectively re-deploy resources that are identified as waste or nonvalue-added activity.

ABC is most effective at the process or subprocess levels. In practice, it becomes less useful to account for costs as one moves up the organization chain. One reason is because most management and executive personnel are extremely resistant to maintaining any type of timekeeping of their activity. The larger reason is the far-reaching impact of many management decisions that drive or influence costs that are essentially untraceable or require high resources to follow their impact trail. Although the discovery and analytical expenses may be rewarded on a few high-impact costs, little or no positive payback will be realized on most. In most cases, the best solution to minimize or optimize far-reaching decisions is better up-front planning.

COST OF QUALITY

The cost of quality is often called the cost of poor quality (COPQ) or the cost of nonconformance (CNC). It is defined as the *cost of doing things wrong,*[3] or *those costs that would disappear if our products and processes were perfect.*[4]

In the real world, we may not yet be ready for perfect products and processes that always do things right (their cost may be prohibitive). We may be better served by working on a system that provides us relative superiority to competitors and minimizes our risk against catastrophic loss.

COQ, or the term *cost of nonconformance,* has been used by the Japanese for some time. I attended a presentation in Tokyo in the mid-1980s using handouts dated from the early 1960s explaining these costs. Figures 5.2 and 5.3 evolved from those illustrations.

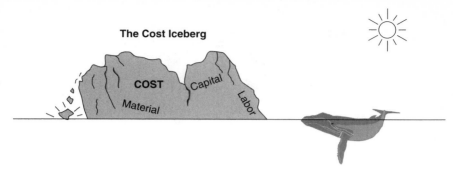

Figure 5.2   Many costs are like a huge iceberg; a majority of them cannot be easily seen.

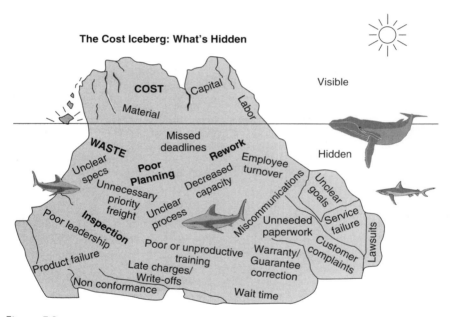

Figure 5.3   Discovering true costs and their drivers requires different tools than traditional methods provide.

Traditional accounting has a fairly standard approach to line-item expenses that place costs under certain categories, such as supplies, salaries, taxes, and many others. It makes no provision to judge the appropriateness of expenses. Since all expenses are categorized under their descriptive title, many true costs are not revealed. Additionally, many expenses are postponed, delayed, or capitalized over time to further disguise their real

Cost of Poor Quality: Money Spent at Each Stage to Prevent or Correct

| Prevention | APPRAISAL
Audit process | APPRAISAL
Inspection | INTERNAL
FAILURE | EXTERNAL
FAILURE |

Figure 5.4 Wisdom gained through cost of quality shows that the earlier in the process problems or errors are prevented or corrected, the less costly they will be.

impact. In reality, it is the invisible costs that may cause the most damage, because they cannot be readily detected using traditional methods.

Although there are many variations of COQ, most break down the costs of poor quality under the following categories (see Figure 5.4):

- Prevention costs
- Appraisal costs
- Failure costs

Generally, prevention costs are considered "good" or necessary costs under the assumption that if poor quality can be prevented, the cost will be small compared to its eventual discovery later on. This is a practical concept in theory, but its application is not that easy. However, it is doable and quite inexpensive if the process is linked to the VOC and various listening posts throughout the organization.

Like ABC, the cost of quality can be time-consuming and may sometimes be costly for organization-wide application. However, it is an invaluable tool if it is applied in areas where the cost of quality is suspected or known to be high, or to any complex process that requires a notable degree of rework or is highly frustrating to employees or customers. On the other hand, it can be used to improve the cost of any size and type of process. COQ is an important tool to supplement reengineering or process modification techniques. Additionally, it can be used to access the realized impact of the change.

The practicality of COQ, unlike traditional accounting, is that it is root-cause oriented. In other words, a cost of quality assessment or review will identify opportunity for cost reduction and, perhaps, capacity improvement. Once the causes of poor quality costs are discovered, the process is modified and the improvement results are confirmed, it usually becomes a maintenance issue until the next opportunity is pursued.

A cost of quality assessment, or even ongoing reporting of the COQ, is a fairly simple endeavor, but it requires a commitment[5] on both management and those performing work because of the data-gathering effort. The

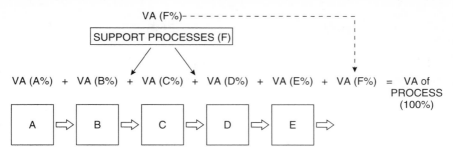

Figure 5.5 Step 1 in assessing Value to Cost ratio is to determine the relative value added by each step in relation to the total value added by the process.

objective is to determine the amount of effort the organization expends in nonproductive activity. The only way to ascertain COQ with any degree of confidence is to understand activity at the level it is performed.

IDENTIFYING HIGH COQ OPPORTUNITIES

There are several "short-cut" techniques to find likely areas in any organization where high-quality costs exist. The first two searches begin at a high level in the organization, by looking for smoke or warning signs, then exploring their source(es). The third begins at the lower levels and moves up. All begin with subjective methodologies and progress toward more objective assessment.

ASSESSING VALUE ADDED RELATIVE TO COST

This technique begins with a high level or critical process map, usually depicting five to eight process steps. The following question is asked, "What percentage of the total value added by the process is added in each step?" (see Figure 5.5). This generally requires discussion outside of the normal way of looking at the organization. Using nominal group techniques, facilitated matrix analysis, or any workable team approach, this should be answered to a fairly high degree of consensus. Of course, the more data available, the better. Usually, it is best to include end customers or downstream users of the process output in determining relative value.

A workable method for estimating value is to determine a fair market price for the product or service at the beginning of the process and again at the end. The difference is an estimate of the market value added. This should be adjusted for life cycles, competitive forces, and other factors.

Once the relative value added by the major process steps are determined, the relative costs of each process should be calculated (see Figure 5.6). Generally, a higher degree of accuracy is available on the cost side.

VA (A%) + VA (B%) + VA (C%) + VA (D%) + VA (E%) + VA (F%) = VA of
  15%   7%   40%   12%   18%   8%   PROCESS
                                                                        (100%)

Figure 5.6 The sum of the separate relative percentages for each process step should equal 100%.

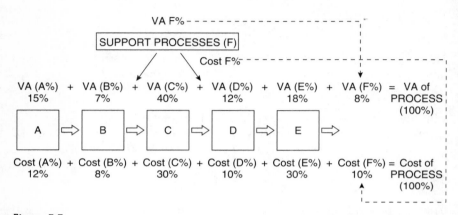

Figure 5.7 Step 2 in assessing Value to Cost ratio is to determine the relative cost incurred by each step in relation to the total cost of the process.

Once both the relative value and relative cost figures are estimated (see Figure 5.7), the ratio between each should be calculated for each process step (see Figure 5.8).

This analysis provides an excellent starting point to begin a cost-of-quality assessment. In and of itself, the analysis offers very little regarding the cost of quality and the relative value-to-cost ratio has little meaning other than identifying a point to begin more detailed exploration. In Figure 5.8, Process E appears to be extremely inefficient, whereas Processes A and C seem much more efficient. But, in reality, initial looks may be deceiving.

The major reason the initial process selected may not be the chief driver of a high COQ is that it may be the main recipient of poor quality and not its cause. However, the major receiver is a great place to begin. The greatest contribution of a COQ analysis is its far-reaching ability to locate drivers and root causes of the high cost of quality. The initial search is not to locate all of the causes of poor quality and where they exist, but to plot their trail. Assessing value added relative to cost provides a quick and productive means to find the right trail.

Depending on the size and complexity of the initially targeted process(es), the next step may be to begin a detailed COQ assessment or to break the targeted process into its major subprocesses and repeat a relative value/cost analysis for the subprocesses. If there is any doubt, it is better to

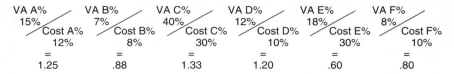

VA A%	VA B%	VA C%	VA D%	VA E%	VA F%
15%	7%	40%	12%	18%	8%
Cost A%	Cost B%	Cost C%	Cost D%	Cost E%	Cost F%
12%	8%	30%	10%	30%	10%
=	=	=	=	=	=
1.25	.88	1.33	1.20	.60	.80

Figure 5.8 Step 3 in assessing Value to Cost ratio is to divide the relative value % by the relative cost % for each process step.

conduct a relative value/cost analysis for the subprocess and find a better starting point for the detailed analysis.

REVIEWING PROCESS MAPS

Another way to locate prime areas to conduct COQ assessments is to identify likely high COQ processes through a review of process maps. This approach is generally used as organizations begin to pursue greater knowledge of process documentation and improvement.

This requires a fairly detailed review of middle-level process maps to determine bottlenecks and inefficiencies in process flow. Generally, routes that loop back, require approval or inspection, include management personnel, contain frequent decision points, or appear confusing or complex, or where the process is not well documented or is outdated, are prime suspects for a COQ assessment.

OTHER HIGH-LEVEL INDICATORS OF HIGH COQ

Other major indicators of high COQ include high employee turnover, low morale, or high absentee rate. Although these may be symptoms of other problems, they generally are seen in conjunction with high COQ. No one enjoys working in inefficient processes that add little or no value.

High customer complaint rates potentially point to areas of high COQ. These may not be obvious and the complaints may not hint at the source, but generally, most are attributed to high COQ. Areas that are supervised or managed by individuals with little background experience in the expertise they are managing or where management/supervisor tenure is short and turnover is high frequently experience high COQ. This is a caution point only, as new managers and supervisors often incorporate high value-added improvements.

Any area that requires higher manual operations than it should; any area that does not have an up-to-date operating manual, documented on-the-job-training, objective performance measures or growth goals and objectives are all prime candidates for COQ assessment.

Questionnaire—Cost of QUALITY

The Cost of Quality is the cost associated with delivering quality. It includes the cost of waste, wasted time, money and effort. It includes the cost of not doing things right the first time, the costs to find and correct them as well as productive costs.

To help determine the cost of quality in your work area, please complete the following:

WHAT PERCENTAGE OF YOUR AVERAGE WORK DAY IS SPENT ON:

1. **REWORK caused by such factors as:** Unclear scope or definition of requirements; incomplete/contradictory information; changes in data or information; complaint handling or information follow-up; correcting mistakes; or, unnecessary expediting.	%
2. **PRIORITY CHANGES caused by such factors as:** Start, stop start work load; management interference/priority changes; pressure from other groups; sudden pressing needs; confusing directions or instructions; or, interruption to your own planned agenda.	%
3. **LACK OF CLEAR PROCEDURES causing you to:** Find out what to do and how to do it; reinvent the "wheel"; get the run around feeling; be unable to locate the right person; or, need training to perform the work.	%
4. **WAITING ON OTHERS caused by:** Needing more information; playing telephone tag; awaiting a management decision; indecisiveness by others; or, interdepartmental bickering or unresponsiveness.	%
5. **UNPRODUCTIVE ACTIVITIES, MEETINGS, REPORTS, DOCUMENTATION** with no clear purpose, agenda or written outcome, unnecessary attendance/preparation required, no definite action assigned, little actually implemented, or little value-added information gained.	%
6. **PERFORMING ACTIVITIES SUCH AS:** Checking, reviewing, auditing, testing or inspecting delivered work (vendor or internal); performing unneeded steps; handling complaints, returns, late pays, lawsuits; or, working on unnecessary/unused projects/reports.	%
7. **WORK THAT ADDS VALUE TO THE ORGANIZATION'S CUSTOMERS by:** meeting the value-added needs of the customer and/or adding value to the end product or service.	%

TOTAL 100%

Figure 5.9 A simple instrument that helps pinpoint areas to begin a COQ assessment.

BOTTOM-UP TOOL

A tool that I have used for years to assist in identifying COQ opportunities is a simple inventory instrument that asks front line and production workers how they spend their time.[6] The instrument, outlined in Figure 5.9, has been used with countless individuals in the past and a solid relationship between their responses and the actual COQ in their work areas has been established. The survey is not intended to accurately measure COQ, but it provides a relative perception and a fairly accurate representation among different units in an organization.

The more participative the organization, the more the instrument represents reality. Generally, production workers in manufacturing organizations have a relatively higher overall percentage of productive work, averaging between 65 percent and 85 percent. On the other hand, those in service support areas tend to be less productive, as they are pulled in numbers of different directions and their roles are less defined and seem to change continuously. They generally range from 40 percent to 70 percent productive.

Although the instrument seems to work well with both hourly and professional employees, it is less insightful or accurate with management, unless it is accompanied with an interview to understand how and why they spend their time. Individuals who spend most of their time in rework or inspecting others' work generally have very low value-added percentages.

When using this instrument, it is recommended to interview a small sample of those completing the instrument to understand their approach to the survey. This offers insight into their feelings toward management, their jobs and what they perceived as priorities and causes of the cost of poor quality. These factors should be used to adjust their responses.

Once a credible sample has been gathered, the responses from the various sections, work units, and departments can be tabulated and compared. The insight from this analysis, along with the size and financial impact of each, can be used to determine the need for a more detailed COQ assessment.

CONFIRMING OPPORTUNITIES—A SHORT PRIMER ON ASSESSING THE COST OF QUALITY

My first experience with the cost of quality was based on Phil Crosby's *Quality is Free*.[7]

In 1984, I continuously struggled with the conversion of a primarily manufacturing concept to the financial services area. Although all the gurus acknowledged that the emerging quality movement applied to service as much as it did to manufacturing, there was little credible knowledge and few studies available on service.

The large global financial services company I worked with in 1984 spent a couple of months gathering data and estimating its cost of quality (which it labeled as the cost of nonconformance). When the estimates began exceeding $135 million and we had barely scratched the surface,[8] we figured we would be better off by beginning to correct them. We redirected the resources we had been deploying to understand them to help reduce the cost of nonconformance. Since we did not fully appreciate the Pareto principle in those days, we were not as productive as we could have been.

We later discovered some techniques through the American Society for Quality Control (ASQC) in the area of COQ in vendor relationships. Much of that work was compiled into a book titled *Principles of Quality Costs*.[9] The book is a such a wealth of information that its use throughout a cost of quality endeavor is recommended.

The first step after making the decision and gaining commitment to identify the COQ is to prepare an inventory of all activity that is performed in a process, and perhaps the customer's process(es) and supporting processes.[10] This is usually outlined as a flow chart or lower-level process map, and can be converted to a check sheet for recording data such as time spent, resources utilized, and other costs in each activity.

After the data gathering, the cost of each activity should be evaluated as either productive (value added) or falling under the heading of prevention, appraisal, internal failure, or external failure or their subcategories. Those activities that correct failure are failure costs. These may be broken into subcategories such as documentation, auditing (by type), source of failure, rework, waste, and reinspection. Although there may be provisions to split categories by activity, it is better to split the activity into categories. An example is a meeting that is held weekly for an hour. If 40 minutes is waste and 20 minutes is value added, it should be split under the activity of "weekly meeting."

In addition to the employee costs, all other costs such as material, supplies, overhead, rent, and capital investment should be gathered. Although some of these may later be subjected to the endless debates on capitalized costs and fixed versus variable expenses, they should be recorded. Analysis of these costs usually reveal the long-reaching tail of past decisions and point out the high need of integration and linkages in the organization.

The form shown in Figure 5.10, or a variation of it, can be used to track the type(s) of costs associated with each activity or process (flow chart) step. By listing all activities or flow chart steps, no costs will be overlooked and it is easier to determine the categories and subcategories that are important for your process(es). Additionally, this step tailors the form to fit the specific organization.

Once data is gathered, it can be easily rolled up into departments, units, products, or any other organizationally defined category. The COQ can be periodically updated and reported or continuously monitored until targeted goals are reached or it has been reduced to an acceptable level.

BEING THE LOW-COST PROVIDER

Being the low-cost provider is a strong desire of most organizations and many have it as a strategy with goals to achieve it. But, what is the low-cost provider, how is it attained, and how is it measured? These questions must be answered for this strategy to be effective.

The term itself is usually misused. The issue generally is not the *low-cost* provider. It is the *high-value* provider. Only if every organization delivered precisely the same level of actual and perceived quality would the term *low-cost provider* be appropriate.

One of the goals of the marketing organization of a large public utility company was to reduce their expenses in relation to similar organizations.

Process: _____

Cost of Quality—Data Gathering

Activity/Flow chart step	PREVENTION COSTS							APPRAISAL COSTS							INTERNAL FAILURE							EXTERNAL FAILURE							Value added/Productive costs	TOTAL COST OF STEP
Quality cost category	Design quality	Training & Education	Supplier qualification	Technical manuals	Other prevention costs	Other prevention costs	Other prevention costs	Inspection	Testing	Review inspection data	Safety checks	Other appraisal costs	Other appraisal costs	Other appraisal costs	Rework	Scrap	Reinspection	Abandoned programs	Other internal failure costs	Other internal failure costs	Other internal failure costs	Customer complaints	Customer service unit A&B	Returns	Client lawsuits	Other external failure costs	Other external failure costs	Other external failure costs		
Activity step 1																														
Activity step 2																														
Activity step 3																														
....																														
....																														
....																														
Activity step 25																														
Activity step 26																														
Activity step 27																														
Total subcategory																														
Total category																														

Figure 5.10 The above matrix offers a format to record the cost of quality for each activity or process step.

They commissioned a rather expensive study that compared the size of their operation (as measured in number of employees) with other utility and nonutility companies. They compared the expenses of marketing operations with such factors as revenues, total organizational expenses, energy output, mix of business, and other financial and operational indicators. Their goal from this impressive benchmarking study was to reduce their expenses relative to other indicators to fall in the top x percent of the benchmarked organizations.

As they became more knowledgeable in control panel concepts, the cost of quality, the VOC, and integrated leadership, they began to realize their benchmarking study was severely flawed. First, marketing is acquisition and growth oriented. Its costs should primarily be driven by strategy, not benchmarked data that are not linked with strategy. Second, in customer-driven organizations, marketing contains a high percentage of preventive costs (such as QFD, design quality, support characteristics, and prototype testing). Third, in many organizations, marketing costs are capitalized over long time frames, so comparisons have little meaning. Fourth, every organization has a different definition of what falls under "marketing" in an organization.

In reality, benchmarked data that is not integrated with strategy is misleading and can be extremely dangerous. On the other hand, accurately integrated benchmarked data is very expensive and difficult to obtain. Even if it is accurate, it still may have little value unless it is correlated with results. For example, the proof of investing dollars in marketing should have demonstrated payoff in greater sales and less failure costs. Additional costs incurred in product, service, and process design should have a multitude of savings in customer support and service areas.

A superior metric for being the low-cost provider is the measure and comparison of actual and perceived value covered in chapter 3.

HIGHLIGHTING COST METRICS ON THE CONTROL PANEL

Cost (expense) is the most observed and scrutinized metric in almost all organizations. In and of itself, cost is meaningless. It is only what a cost provides, produces, or offers that has meaning. In spite of this, we continue merrily along, being satisfied with reporting cost primarily against historical trends, budgets, and, in some cases, against artificial or consolidated revenue. We tend to categorize costs as fixed or variable, controlled or "outside" our control, or as planned or unplanned. We hold some people accountable for pennies and give others blank checks. We fire productive people for not being able to account for a dollar, while "carrying" others for years until they can gracefully retire with full benefits or leave the organization with years of compensation disguised as a golden parachute.

The biggest reason we do these things is because we do not generally have the means to account for the benefit derived from the cost. The aim of the control panel is to identify high opportunity areas or likely downside concerns in time to capitalize on the opportunities or to avoid or minimize the downside. Since the control panel is an evolutionary tool, the sooner the pursuit begins, the more long-term return and the quicker more meaningful metrics will be found.

Following are some control panel indicators that provide valuable insight into costs.

PROFITABILITY BY PRODUCT/SERVICE LINE

Although this is recognized as a desirable indicator by most organizations, it is almost impossible to obtain an accurate reading of profitability of product/service lines using traditional accounting methods. In order to obtain a much higher accuracy level, ABC is required.

Initially, as better accounting methods are being formulated, it is most important to gather input and a strong level of agreement and commitment from all cost centers that contribute to products and services being tracked for profitability reporting (which, in the long term, should be all).

At the control panel level an important calculation is cost per product or service (which may be stated in historical, current, and marginal terms). This allows viewing cost movement in relation to current sales velocity and acceleration, as well as current actual and perceived prices for the organization and competitors. Using VOC indicators, actual costs and margin factors can be factored into value and price analyses. This type of indicator provides great opportunities for high short-term gain.

PRODUCTIVITY

Productivity for any organization, department, unit, or individual is expressed by the formula:

$$\text{Productivity} = \frac{\text{Output}}{\text{Input}}$$

In chapter 4, we saw the importance of developing service standards that meet the requirements of customers. If every slice of the organization has key output metrics that can be measured, then a productivity measure is easily calculated by simply dividing the output by the monetary cost of the unit, or resource that produced the output. For example, if a work unit has a standard of 22 units per person per hour and its eight employees produce for a 35-hour work week at a level of 22.6 units each that meet quality standards, it produced 6,328 units for the week ($22.6 \times 35 \times 8$). If the total cost for the unit was $7,840, the productivity level was .807 units per dollar spent (6,328 units / $7,840), or a cost of $1.239 per unit.

One method of monitoring productivity on the control panel is the reporting of a few key process performance indicators, such as those outlined in chapter 4. Another method that provides a wider view of cost impact is to consolidate a larger number of indicators through a productivity index. The ongoing monitoring of a productivity index provides a big-picture panorama of organizational productivity on a frequent basis and can be zoomed down to observe any level.

The simplest and most effective index I worked with was a financial services operation in the United Kingdom in the mid-1980s. It reported data on ten different operations that were weighted against each other in importance, consolidated, and converted to a 100-point scale. Index scores were reported and managed on a monthly basis.

The index had three major categories: productivity (55%), customer satisfaction (30%), and employee satisfaction (15%). Forty percent of productivity measures were based on individual units (with various weightings) and 60 percent was based on overall performance such as delinquency rates, customer complaints, capacity, expense ratios, growth, retention, profitability, sales closing rates, and liquidations (with various weightings). This was quite forward for a service organization in the mid-1980s.

COST OF QUALITY

Organizations that pursue cost of quality, even for segments of their operation, should report progress on their control panel. This is such a powerful indicator and tool that it will easily demonstrate reduction results in a short period, as well as the vast potential for greater productivity gains. These should be shown in actual monetary terms, as well as expressed against overall expenses, sales, and historical results. Improvement in COQ should always be a morale booster for everyone it impacts.

TRADITIONAL ACCOUNTING METRICS

Key ratios and analysis of important financial indicators that include cost measures (or the results of expense control)—such as actual vs. budget, projected cash flow, balance sheet and income statement—should be included on the control panel.

Overall, the control panel should always attempt to put costs in the perspective of their value, or their ability to provide a benefit to stakeholders. Again, it is important to remember the balance needed between financial and nonfinancial measures. The key is to understand their relationships.

KEY POINTS VALUE MANAGEMENT

- Value management focuses on meeting or exceeding customers' requirements at the lowest possible cost.
- Traditional accounting methods have no methodology for reporting the appropriateness or value-added propensity associated with costs (or expenses).
- The two primary roles of senior leadership are to ensure the organization does the right things (effectiveness) right (efficiency). Their focus should be on effectiveness.
- The primary tool for minimizing the cost of ineffectiveness is integrated strategic planning; followed by a system for incorporating and managing change.
- The key causes of ineffectiveness and inefficiency include abdication of responsibility, group think, duplication of effort, and the search for the right answer.
- Two important tools for managing inefficiency are activity based costing and cost of quality.
- Activity based costing views expenses from the angle of "activities," instead of the traditional approach of line items or expense categories.
- The cost of quality provides a methodology to view unnecessary costs in producing and delivering goods and services. It focuses on the prevention or early detection and correction of errors that may later result in failure or customer dissatisfaction.
- Cost of quality should be approached using the Pareto principle; the largest opportunities should be identified and addressed first.
- Productivity, profitability by product/service line, and cost of quality are key control panel indicators.

NOTES

1. Myron Tribus, *Quality First: Selected Papers on Quality and Productivity Improvement* (Washington D.C.: National Institute for Engineering Management & Systems, 1992), p. 155.

2. James A. Brimson, *Activity Accounting: An Activity-Based Costing Approach* (New York: John Wiley & Sons, Inc., 1991), p. 70.

3. Philip B. Crosby, *Quality is Free: The Art of Making Quality Certain* (New York: Mentor, 1980), p. 15.

4. Joseph M. Juran, *Juran on Quality by Design: The New Steps for Planning Quality into Goods and Services* (New York: The Free Press, 1992), p. 119.

5. Gaining the commitment of those actually performing work may be the most difficult part of COQ. Very few individuals are willing to enthusiastically conduct extra work when they perceive one of the outcomes may be a reduction in the number of people assigned to the process. Chapter 7 explores some ways to deal with this challenge.

6. The original source of this tool is unknown, although current versions have evolved over time.

7. See note 3, p. 15.

8. The organization had recently experienced huge downsizing, the divestiture of numerous core businesses, had thwarted a hostile takeover at a huge cost, and was being threatened with the loss of its license in one foreign operation and a key state (due to questionable business practices). Although the early quality initiatives were controversial and resistive, they ultimately helped overcome these challenges.

9. ASQC Quality Costs Committee, Jack Campanella, ed., *Principles of Quality Costs*, 2nd ed. (Milwaukee: ASQC Quality Press, 1990).

10. Some organizations have a difficult time distinguishing processes from jobs. An alternative, less preferred method is to produce an inventory of all activities, or even tasks, performed by different jobs in a work area. The challenge frequently involves political sensitivities, but often there is no choice. When competitors add more value to the market, changes must be made for everyone's survival.

Chapter 6

CONTINUOUS VALUE IMPROVEMENT

> *Throughout the past, as successive stages of social evolution unfolded, man's awareness followed rather than preceded the event. Because change was slow, he could adapt unconsciously, "organically." Today unconscious adaptation is no longer adequate. Faced with the power to alter the gene, to create new species, to populate the planets or depopulate the earth, man must now assume conscious control of evolution itself. Avoiding future shock as he rides the waves of change, he must master evolution, shaping tomorrow to human need. Instead of rising in revolt against it, he must, from this historic moment on, anticipate and design the future.*
>
> —Alvin Toffler[1]

Survival has always depended on adaptation, change, and improvement. All of the important breakthroughs in history were either followed by improvement or they disappeared. How many would attempt a transoceanic flight today if the airplane had not been radically improved from its early flights? The disaster rate in commercial aviation as late as the middle of the twentieth century would be considered catastrophic if applied to the large volume flown today.

The phenomenal evolution of aviation from the Wright Brothers' initial flight at Kitty Hawk to the astronauts on the moon during a single century demonstrates the remarkable ability of the human species to successfully integrate hundreds of disciplines into a single endeavor. And that was accomplished prior to the actual advent of the Information Age.

IMPROVEMENT 101

Improvement is as natural to us as breathing, eating, and socializing. The first thing we do when something is improved is to try to improve it more. We have continuously studied and improved the methodology for improvement itself. We invented a scientific method and we have learned how to transfer knowledge, both of successes and failures, from generation to generation and around the globe. With today's communication systems and databases, it is possible for the critical mass required for change in practically any field to have the latest knowledge and wisdom on a real-time basis. This greatly increases productivity as it minimizes wasted duplication of effort.

THE STRATEGIC POWER OF IMPROVEMENT

How an organization selects the deployment of its resources to improve its value is one of its most critical strategies. The ability to improve and how this ability is used must be managed as a critical resource.

There are two important aspects of improvement to consider to effectively utilize it as a strategic asset. The first is the *ability of the organization to improve* and the second is *where to focus its application*. The first is the easier of the two and takes care of itself if the second is managed properly. It is rare, if ever, that the second evolves from the first.

Thousands of organizations have trained a large percentage of their employees on continuous improvement methods over the past ten years. They later reduced or abandoned these efforts because they did not achieve the results they expected or were promised. In almost every one of these reductions, the major cause was because *improvement was not properly positioned in the organization*. In most organizations, since no one, including senior management, knew where to strategically apply the new knowledge, it became a secondary tactical tool instead of a strategic resource. We have proven over and over again that the acquisition of improvement skills alone does not lead anywhere close to its optimum use. The maximum benefit of this knowledge can only be realized by strategically planning and executing its delivery.

LEARNING IMPROVEMENT SKILLS

The acquisition of knowledge of continuous improvement methods is readily available today through hundreds of training organizations, community colleges, textbooks, software, on-line databases, and internal training departments. The basic resources needed are trainers, the commitment of time, and availability of training facilities. Generally, improvement skills are taught with team skills, since organizational improvement depends on teamwork.

Imagine that you have never sailed before but you have a passion to be a crew member, or captain, of a large competitive racing sloop. You sign up and begin training and preparing to realize your dream. You learn the theory of sailing, all the terms, how to handle all the positions, navigation, racing techniques, and basic leadership. Every day, you and a small crew practice in no wind conditions as your boat remains docked. The sloop never leaves the dock, yet you continue to prepare and practice.

1. How long will you continue to pursue this madness before you find another boat or abandon your dream?
2. If you and your crew finally left the pier for the first time and somehow reached the beginning point of a race, what chance would you have against seasoned veterans?

Sailing, like any acquired expertise, must be mastered in a logical sequence. It is a combination of theory, demonstration, and application of the most basic techniques, which develop into more and more advanced skills. Each subsequent skill builds on the cumulative progression of those that preceded it. Teamwork and continuous improvement are similar, because both require a blending of diverse skills and knowledge focused toward a common goal.

One must learn the theory, then apply the knowledge to the "real" world; learn from experiences and mistakes and use the knowledge gained to apply to the next level, and so on. The real beauty of a team is that not everyone must be a master of every skill. The masters of one skill set can help those who are almost masters, who can help those who are at an intermediate level, who can help the beginners, and so on. This is the development process by which organizations master improvement skills.

Yet, most organizations provide large numbers of people with classroom training in many of the improvement skills and then release them back on the job with no practical experience, no model to follow, no mentor to support and encourage them, no metric system to link efforts with results, no meaningful reward system to compensate them for their headway and confusion on how improvement fits into their job. After a period of time, someone makes an observation, "That doesn't work." In some organizations, mandated training without supporting structure lingers for years; it still fails, because it was never designed for success; regardless of the intention.

The key to successful improvement training follows a few simple procedures. First, train executives, managers, supervisors and those zealots in the organization who demonstrate a penchant for quality, statistics, and customers. These individuals should be well grounded and tested in problem solving, teamwork, and facilitation skills. They should be given exposure, but not necessarily in-depth training, to all of the quality tools.

However, they should know where to go or send others to receive detailed education, as needed. As the demand for additional knowledge increases, it should be provided to everyone with the need for the knowledge, primarily using internal sources who have actually applied the skills in the work environment. Within a relatively short period of time, (if, and only if, the organization builds and implements the systems needed to utilize the knowledge on an ongoing basis) improvement will be as much a part of everyone's job as the work they perform.

From Education to Improvement

As stated earlier, knowledge of improvement tools without meaningful application offers little value to an organization and no strategic advantage. How does an organization transition from education to practical knowledge and valuable results?

The question can be partially answered by sharing some painful experiences in what does not work well. Other than some experimentation with quality control circles in the late 1970s, my first experience with large-scale training came in 1984 when I was part of a small team that launched a massive training effort to educate more than a thousand team leaders over four continents within a period of one year. Although the training was successfully conducted, the results were mixed, and the organization did not succeed in gaining strategic advantage. There were noteworthy accomplishments and the efforts certainly launched the organization on the road to a more open environment and paid for itself several times over; however, it fell well short of its potential.

There was one obvious shortcoming. There was poor integration among the team program, the formal organization structure, and corporate strategy. In most cases, management made sure they retained control over the program by treating it as something separate from real work and business issues. Consequently, most teams worked on insignificant projects. When teams did achieve brilliant successes, management generally took credit. In spite of endless challenges, the program survived intact for years and still exists in pockets in the organization.

The primary lesson learned from this and later experiences is that a team and improvement process must be completely integrated into both the formal and informal organizational structures with a defined basis for its existence and with solid plans and goals. This must happen on an organization-wide basis, beginning at the strategic planning level. On the other hand, improvement tools can be brought in at any level of the organization to greatly assist in localized gains. However, they will only approach their full potential when they are integrated cross-functionally.

Improvement in Perspective

There are several pressure points driving the need to improve. The earliest pressure comes from customers. Customers always seek greater value.

Usually the most intense pressure comes from competitors, who constantly bring higher value to the market. The third pressure comes from owners, who always want to ensure their investment and increase their returns. Other pressures come from vendors who want to help in the value formula by bringing the latest and greatest products and services to the organization. Additional pressure comes from the community, regulators, and other special interest groups.

The organization that does not improve does not prosper long. We saw earlier that the long-term performance of an organization depends on its improvement rate compared to other competitive forces. This is especially important in global competition and Information Age markets.

In the Industrial Age, management could order (or ask) people to work harder and produce more. They could also bring in specialized expertise when needed to help increase productivity. In the Information Age, working harder may not produce needed results, and specialized experts are more likely the people already performing the work or handling information.

The bottom line: Improvement is as much of a job in the Information Age as production was in the Industrial Age. Some improvement comes through individual effort, but not enough to remain competitive. The level needed must evolve from the integrated efforts of the organization led by teams and assisted by the documentation of the improvement process. With so much opportunity available and so much riding on improvement results, organizations must be learning how to greatly improve their improvement.

THE FOUNDATION OF IMPROVEMENT TOOLS

There are many tools for improvement[2] and they are extremely varied. However, their applications all link to an improvement model. All improvement models are based on cause-and-effect relationships and follow a cycle of improvement that includes planning a change, implementing the change, observing the impact of the change and either readjusting or keeping the change. These two models most commonly used are the PDCA Cycle and problem solving, which are actually variations of each other. For an example of the use of an improvement model applied to value enhancement, see Appendix C.

CAUSE-AND-EFFECT

Every condition, element, and situation that exists today was created or caused by a combination or transformation of previous conditions or activities. In turn, as new actions and activities occur, they form new permutations and conditions that are different, and frequently more complex, than the previous ones. Consequently, any condition that one targets to improve is the result of countless former conditions and actions. In most cases, planned improvement comes through the understanding and select alteration of the principal causes of the targeted condition.

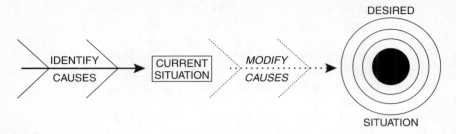

Figure 6.1 The fishbone diagram shows possible causes of the current situation and offers insight into what must change to obtain the desired situation.

Figure 6.2 The Shewhart Cycle or Deming Cycle is a logical approach to improvement.

Many possible causes are frequently brainstormed through the use of a fishbone diagram,[3] and the drivers or major causes are identified through the application of the Pareto principle. By identifying the desired effect and understanding the causal relationship between current causes and effect, the drivers (causes) can be modified for a new effect (desired result). This is illustrated in Figure 6.1.

PDCA CYCLE

The *Plan-Do-Check-Act Cycle* (or PDCA) was founded in the late 1930s by Walter A. Shewhart in the United States and introduced in Japan in 1950 by Dr. Deming (see Figure 6.2).[4] It basically explains improvement as a process of planning the improvement (*Plan*), implementing the plan (*Do*), checking the results of the implementation (*Check*), and acting on the results by making the change permanent or completing the cycle again until the targeted results are achieved (*Act*).[5] Once the improvement is made, another round of improvement begins.

1. Define what exists and what is desired

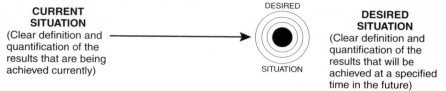

CURRENT SITUATION
(Clear definition and quantification of the results that are being achieved currently)

DESIRED

SITUATION

DESIRED SITUATION
(Clear definition and quantification of the results that will be achieved at a specified time in the future)

2. Discover the primary causes of current results, validate with data/information

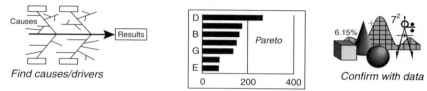

Causes

Results

Find causes/drivers

Pareto

Confirm with data

3. Modify drivers (implement solutions)

4. Assure modifications provide desired results

5. Adjust as required

6. When results achieved, change process

Figure 6.3   Most problem solving/improvement models are variations of the outlined process.

PROBLEM SOLVING

Problem solving begins not by jumping from problem to solution, but by understanding how and why the current situation exists. Most basic problem solving or improvement models follow a five- to eight-step process and the same basic logic as the PDCA Cycle. Although there are a number of distinct models, they all use the same methodology but are broken down into different titles or number of stages. The number of steps is not important, but the underlying logic is critical. The illustration in Figure 6.3 outlines a typical approach.

IMPROVEMENT—THE ADVANCED COURSE

WHAT TO IMPROVE

The secret to organizational improvement is *knowing what to improve*. With limitless improvement opportunities available and restricted resources to spend on improvement, how does an organization decide where to focus its efforts? The future of the organization depends on the answer.

The answer is becoming more complicated. In the past, the answer was basically that any place the organization improved was fine, because after the improvement, the organization was a better organization than it was before. However, if the future depends on an improvement rate that exceeds competitors, more logical effort should be expended than random selection.

Improvement should be viewed from several angles. In the absence of great opportunity or immediate or total disaster, improvement efforts should be directed at achieving or exceeding formal goals and improving the value the organization delivers to customers.

RELENTLESS PRIORITIZATION—THE KEY TO DOING THE RIGHT THINGS

The life blood of any organization in the long run is innovation and the implementation of new ideas. Some organizations are like a jet ski and can change direction in a split second. Others are like a battleship and require considerable time and distance to alter course.

Without a stable process to sort through the countless opportunities and options available to an organization there are two dangers:

1. Decisions may be made that will help part of an organization to the detriment of another. The overall impact on the organization may be negative or considerably less gain than other alternatives. If a decision is a gain for one portion of the organization at a loss to another, the overall cost must be considered. Cost always impacts value.
2. The cumulative impact of change that is not coordinated may shift or confuse the strategic direction of the organization (strategy creep). Prioritization will only be effective if its impact on other variables is considered.

These two dangers can be minimized by a frequent review of all major projects and modified activities of the organization by reaffirming or changing their priorities and reviewing their progress to see if they are on schedule and achieving their targeted results. *In an environment of rapid change, it is wise to see if past decisions are still valid.*

A few years ago I worked with a very innovative organization that always looked for opportunities and located an abundance of them. A major concern with their philosophy was the speed in which they always believed they had to make decisions. They believed the "window" of every great opportunity was closing and they had to move quickly before it was gone forever.

Their corporate offices were in the Midwest and they employed around 500 employees. One opportunity they identified was in Hawaii. They moved quickly, closed the deal, and sent resources to Hawaii. Within a few months the Hawaiian business was in trouble. The financial projections went from an astoundingly high return on investment (ROI), to a low positive ROI, to break even, and, eventually, to losses. These extremes all occurred within a few months. In the meantime, they had shifted highly productive resources to attempt to salvage the new operation to the detriment of profitable operations.

After a few more similar experiences, they were acquired at a bargain price. They failed to prioritize their opportunities and integrate new projects or undertakings with existing activities and plans. They, like many similar organizations, paid dearly for this failure.

The acquisition of or merger with another organization is an improvement opportunity and should be assessed using value criteria. It is much more than a financial exercise. The major driver of a high return acquisition, like any other opportunity, is integration.

The highest level of any organization, whether a single individual, a global corporation, or a department within an organization, should have an ongoing process for incorporating the knowledge and wisdom gained from all information sources (a control panel) with the day to day operation of the organization and the countless opportunities for innovation and creativity.

INTEGRATION

Since a major benefit of the control panel is the ability to see a wide perspective spanning current activity with future goals and results, it must be utilized to assist in prioritizing and integrating improvement opportunities. Opportunities, whether newly discovered or buried within organizational processes, compete with each other for resources. Therefore, the overall issue is, "How do we properly allocate the organization's resources?" The evolving decision must weigh new creative opportunities against current and planned projects and operations. Decisions must be made on what to *retain, reduce, abandon, and enhance.*

One reason for indecision can be explained by culture. Most growing problems and great opportunity ideas are first observed or generated in the lower echelons of an organization. Some germinate from customers, third parties or vendors, but they enter the organization through the producing parts of the organization. Because of the apparent large number of both opportunities and problems, executives tend to ignore the whimpers and suggestions until they become screams or obvious opportunities. Usually, when viewed from a high-level perspective, most have common roots and, in reality, there are a relatively small number of opportunities and problems that warrant the involvement of senior leadership.

As organizations rush into the Information Age, more leaders recognize that valuable data, information, and knowledge enter the organization from a number of sources. They are learning that innovation and creativity expand proportionately to the amount of effort with which they are pursued and the freedom that idea sources are granted. They build better systems to identify and harvest these precious resources by moving them quickly and efficiently to decision points.

Since there are millions of bits of information and hundreds of ideas for every true gem, how are the most profitable ones identified? The answer has evolved over the past 40 years, beginning with the great breakthroughs made in Japan in the 1960s and 1970s. In the 1990s, the answer may be based on the disciplines acquired by "learning organizations."[6] First and foremost, a learning organization is a "system thinking"[7] organization where individuals pursue "personal mastery"[8] while "building shared visions"[9] and "developing extraordinary capacities for coordinated action."[10] A learning organization implements worthwhile ideas at the lowest possible level; it does not need to propose or push them up the organization.

When great ideas or necessary changes are identified and they cannot be implemented locally, they are routed to the appropriate level or function. In this system very few radical concepts go to the top because they are handled at more practical levels. Those that are elevated are able to command the attention they deserve. However, even with a high level of "systems thinking" throughout the organization, some ideas must go to the top, as that is the only place in the organization that has the integrated knowledge and power to act appropriately on the idea.

THE TRANSITION FROM THE PRESENT TO THE FUTURE

The movement to the future depends to a large degree on the starting point. An obvious first step is to implement and practice the principles of integrated leadership. As this is being done and a control panel is being planned and built, a formal decision support process system can be created that will later mesh superlatively with the control panel.

Since decisions have always been made, an early step is to understand how they are made currently. In most organizations, they are formed by a variety of methods spanning from the top executive with an idea who says, "Do it," to a committee who mulls over certain topics year after year. Some decisions are well researched and documented, proceeding through a formal process based on predetermined criteria backed by ROI scenarios; others seem to come out of nowhere and, seemingly, are implemented before anyone knows they were even being considered.

Even more puzzling in many organizations is how decisions are implemented, how, and if, they are ever evaluated, and what lessons (good or bad) are learned from the experience. A few years ago, I became a member of a corporate executive committee. At the first meeting I attended, a critical issue was discussed and an important decision was made. A few months later the same issue came up again, and some of the previous discussion was repeated. Someone asked, "Haven't we already decided that?" No one had recorded the decision or implemented the change.

In the absence of a *formal decision and implementation process,* anything may happen, including lost opportunities and a high cost of ineffectiveness and inefficiency. The solution is to build and manage the process.

SOME CONTROL PANEL INDICATORS IDENTIFYING IMPROVEMENT OPPORTUNITIES

The VOC contains a prioritization matrix with improvement goals (see chapter 3). Therefore, if a VOC is in place, it has a built-in system for selecting improvements. However, an organization has other improvement needs that the VOC will not identify. Additionally, a working and meaningful VOC can be neither quickly nor easily implemented in an organization, and updates may not approach real time for years. There are some feeding, or linking, systems of a mature VOC that can be fairly easily readied in a short period of time. As the VOC evolves, these should be major information sources for improvement. These include high-priority information from sales, support, and other sources showing customer information, including surveyed information.

WON–LOST REPORTS

Every organization has sales reports outlining sales from every conceivable angle. Most are used by sales and marketing management to lead, operate, and improve sales performance. There are a few that help the entire organization improve. One, used with a sales force that primary deals one-on-one with customers, is the won–lost report. When used to its full potential, it provides some of the most valuable information available to an organization. The difference between high-value information and worthless information in a won–lost report is usually determined by investing significantly less than 1 percent of the time that is spent on a sale or prospective sale to document why the sale was made or not made and the performance of the key competitors.

The sales force must participate in the management of such information to help improve the value of the goods and services the organization delivers. It must be a positive experience for the sales rep or the data may become unreliable and worthless. Reasons should be explained to the point where they are at a root sales attribute level or are clear to anyone reading the report. After a period of time, the input form can be simplified by using reason codes, although there should always be opportunity to communicate creativity or competitive advantages.

The value of the won–lost report and the manner that it is displayed on the control panel (see Figure 6.5) is designed to maintain score with top competitors and provide an updated Pareto analysis on improvement opportunities. For example, most sales are won or lost for one of two major reasons; either a value issue or a sales issue. Either can be won or lost based

Won–Lost Report

Name of client or prospect	Primary selling factor(s): List top three in order of importance	List in order of finish; provide short explanation why winner won and others lost			Where we finished (if not in top 3)	Comments
		Winner	Second	Third		
		Competitor: Reason:	Competitor: Reason:	Competitor: Reason:		
		Competitor: Reason:	Competitor: Reason:	Competitor: Reason:		
		Competitor: Reason:	Competitor: Reason:	Competitor: Reason:		
		Competitor: Reason:	Competitor: Reason:	Competitor: Reason:		
		Competitor: Reason:	Competitor: Reason:	Competitor: Reason:		
		Competitor: Reason:	Competitor: Reason:	Competitor: Reason:		

Figure 6.4 The Won–Lost Report shows the outcome of head-to-head competition by outlining who won and why.

| Competitor Head-to-Head Standings | | | | |
Competitor	Won	Year to Date Lost	Pct.	Last Year
C	83	40	.675	.714
Us	84	51	.622	.587
A	56	48	.538	.545
D	48	54	.471	.404
B	18	31	.367	.201
E	31	96	.244	.467

Figure 6.5 This is one of countless ways won–lost information can be shown on a control panel.

on perception or reality. Additionally, there are countless subissues and combinations of factors that can be identified and prioritized in order to select high-return improvement opportunities.

If a competitor begins making market gains, it will appear quickly on the won–lost score sheet while there is time for adjustment or damage control. On the other hand, if your organization begins making gains on its competition, the sooner the gains and their reasons are discovered, the more the organization can gain larger advantages.

The Pareto charts in Figure 6.6 prioritize both current organizational strengths and opportunities for improvement. However, they require more work and study that must be gathered in the improvement process. Many questions, such as why and how much, need to be answered in the data collection effort. In Figure 6.6, *flexible contracts* appear as one of the top reasons for both wins and losses. Additional research or more detailed data gathering will resolve where contacts are an advantage and where competition has the advantage (real or perceived).

There are unlimited creative opportunities in a well-managed won–lost system that is shared with the organization and appears on the control panel. Additionally, the won–lost report is a quick feedback system to organizational changes and provides information that may help validate or challenge the ongoing work on the VOC.

SALES PROCESS STORY BOARD

Another example of value improvement that may be less global but is an excellent method of finding improvement opportunities is by studying process flow in a critical process. Three areas that are excellent for this type of analysis are sales, delivery (particularly where installation is involved), and support. A sales example is outlined as follows.

An excellent sales system is called *strategic selling,* which is described in the book by the same name.[11] The strength of such a system is its ability to

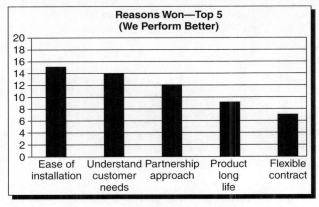

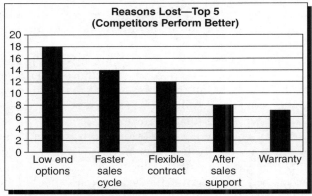

Figure 6.6 A Pareto chart outlining reasons for both winning and losing sales always offer opportunities for improvement.

tie selling skills into a process that can be observed, measured, and improved.

The sales process is one of the most linked processes in an organization. It depends on marketing for new products and information; it depends on production, delivery, and installation to meet the promises that have been made to customers, and it depends on support to take care of the customer on an extended basis. On the other hand, every department depends on sales to locate qualified customers, establish win–win relationships, educate customers by establishing accurate expectations and roles, and fully disclose important information about delivery and support processes. Organizations that do not look at sales as a facilitator of information and a master of proper handoffs will be in for a huge shock when they encounter a competitor that does.

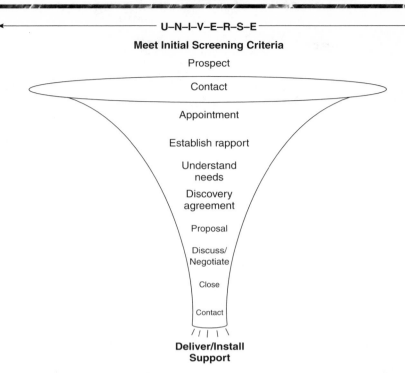

Figure 6.7   The sales process can be compared to a funnel, where the mouth may be wide at the opening, but relatively few will transition through to the bottom to become a customer.

A typical sales process, transposed on a funnel, is outlined in Figure 6.7.[12] The mouth of the funnel collects leads for the goods and services of an organization from a sizable universe of possible candidates. This universe is reduced to a much smaller size as the organization goes through the process of selecting qualified prospects and attempting to close orders and acquire new customers. The acquisition of customers, like the retention of customers, is never guaranteed; it is the result of the dynamics of processes.

The funnel can serve as a story board for the entire organization as prospects are depicted at their current location in the funnel (sales process). If they are no longer considered a prospect, they are shown outside the funnel at the point in the process they were lost. Information from the story board, such as cycle times, reasons for success and failure, closing ratios, success/failure rates at each segment, and volume per new customer are all opportunities for improvement. As the sales process becomes stable, a much higher degree of forecasting and the opportunity for revenue improvement are major benefits (see Figure 6.8).

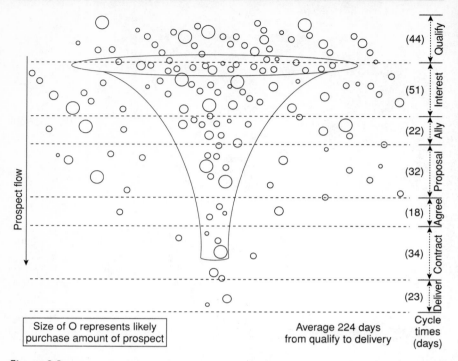

Figure 6.8 The sales funnel can be depicted on a story board to continuously show the organization the status of prospects and offer large improvement opportunities when combined with supporting information.

CUSTOMER SUPPORT

Most organizations have a function or assign personnel to carry out after-sales support. In many organizations, customer service fulfills this role. A key question to ask of any customer support function is, "Is it primarily a value-added function or is it used to correct problems?" It is likely a value-added role if it was intentionally designed as part of the product or service, part of the installation process, or is primarily a sales function. If it is used for any other purpose, it probably deals with considerable rework and waste. Even if it is primarily a value-added role, it will have huge opportunities for improvement.

Large customer support operations frequently evolve from incomplete product or service design. They are always a part of organizations that rush new products to market without stable production or installation processes or that have not properly designed and delivered proper training and other product/service support functions. In some industries, such as high-volume software providers, customer support functions are part of the ongoing product development and debugging process. In these industries, many customers (users) are willing to work with an alpha or beta product and help in its improvement. Another large segment wants a product beyond beta, but is willing to utilize customer support or on-line assistance to fill in flaws in the products or lack of documentation. This type of provider–customer relationship is expanding in many areas, as the benefits of partnering is leading to shorter cycle times and better products.

In almost every organization, customer support is a *data gathering* and *analysis* hub that can lead to many valuable improvement opportunities. In chapter 5, we saw the huge costs associated with external failure. Many customer support facilities deal with a high percentage of external failure. External failure is not limited to product or service failure.

For example, a consumer purchases a product that requires some assembly. All the necessary components are properly packed, along with a set of "technically correct" instructions. A person calls customer support for help because the instructions are "just not clear enough." That experience is an external failure. It may be easier to correct and less costly than a missing component, but it is still a failure.

Perhaps it is a failure that the supplier is willing to absorb or the customer is willing to pay in the price or the product. Perhaps, the organization may only receive a few calls, and it is less costly to handle those calls than to write the instructions at a lower level of assembly aptitude. Nevertheless, it is still a cost.

Every external failure that the provider becomes aware of, no matter how slight, should be recorded as a data element. This includes complaints, letters, surveys, and any other methodology that an organization uses to gain information from its customers. Of course, the systems for the collection of data must be extremely efficient, or the costs may outweigh the gains.

The rationale is simple. Every failure discovered is an improvement opportunity and perhaps the chance to prevent additional failure and greater costs. The gathering of data will provide information on the extent and depth of the failure, which will permit a Pareto analysis and can lead to the study, understanding, correction, and future prevention (improvement) of the type of process errors that produced the failure.

A major goal of any customer support function that spends most of its time on waste, rework, correction, or any low value adding activity should be to eliminate the need for the function and move its resources into R & D, training, production support, production or any other value added operation. The method of accomplishing this transformation is to continuously Pareto waste and rework and drive it out of the organization beginning with the highest cost of poor quality and moving to the lowest.

This requires an ongoing cross-functional effort and a high level of cooperation among departments and functions. The obstacles that stand in the way of most organizations are the barriers between departments, the lack of data captureability (which is no excuse in the Information Age), and the status differences among functions. Barriers and status are no concern when

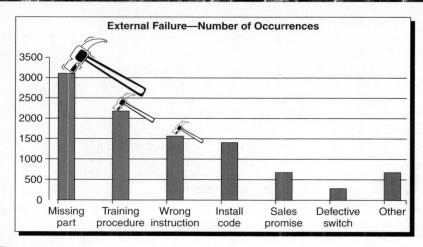

Figure 6.9 A continuous Pareto chart of categories of external failure observed or reported should lead to focusing resources to greatly reduce waste and rework.

individuals are rotated between operations and support and everyone is required to spend some time in support. The objective for the organization should be to eliminate the need for nonvalue-added support and transform it to a high value-added function. No one enjoys working in a rework or waste facility for long, unless they are involved in moving toward the goal to eliminate it.

The method to drive waste and rework out of the system is to begin with the gravest area, understand it through cost-of-quality analysis, problem solving, or the use of quality tools and begin reducing its impact and correcting its causes. When this project is underway, begin on the second highest concern in the same manner until it is severely reduced or eliminated (Figure 6.9). After just a few cycles you will see a big impact on the others, and much of your resources deployed on waste can now be used for value-added activity.

Identification of the causes of waste and rework should be a control panel item. This data will enter the organization through the customer service function, field visits, complaints and other sources.

Although the analysis may begin at a high level with general categories, it must be understood at lower levels in order to correct and eliminate. The reason for high-level reporting is to elevate its importance throughout the organization and to move it from failure to prevention. Ultimately, the solutions should be built into the product, service, inconvenience factors and perceptions in order eliminate the cause of the failure and avoid a downstream solution.

A TRANSITIONAL DECISION SUPPORT PROCESS MODEL

The control panel contains the ultimate decision support system. It also provides calculations, statistical methodology, and scenario modeling that continuously supplies high-level knowledge and wisdom. Some of the most important data elements in a control panel that merge to support decision making are goals and strategy (where going and how), current and planned projects and current productivity and capacity levels. These elements provide information on the use of current resources, future plans for their placement, and where resources can be redeployed with a minimum of disruption to the organization.

There are two data sources that greatly enhance a high level decision system. One contains all current initiatives, including operational plans and strategic endeavors that are in progress or planned for the future. An initiative must be defined by the organization. They may range from an improvement project undertaken by a work unit to the launching of a new business or the takeover of a major competitor. An executive decision process system may not be concerned with a single team project, but it may have an interest in their topics or in the cumulative effect of numerous teams or projects. In addition to providing important data for decisions, this database is used for project management, cross functional coordination, duplication avoidance and organization prioritization.

The second data source is an idea or issue database. It consists of the new ideas, opportunities, projects, suggestions, product or service changes that have not yet made their way into the organization. They may still be in a conceptual or proposed state.

At one extreme, an issues system is an on-line database that consists of several tiers of information and is managed by, or available to, different levels of an organization. At the other extreme, it is a merely a working list of ideas or proposals brainstormed or gathered by senior management. At either extreme there should be an evolving methodology to select new opportunities, abandon projects, or redeploy resources to solve problems based on their costs and benefits and how they can be integrated into existing and planned organizational strategies and tactics. The major differences between the extremes are the data available, the sophistication of the methodology, and the inclusion or exclusion of the input of employees and strategic partners in the process.

At the most sophisticated extreme, the vast majority of the issue system is utilized at the working level of the organization and is primarily used within departments, functions, work teams, and cross-functional teams. Most issues are implemented, rejected, solved, answered, or addressed at this level via electronic mail, bulletin boards or one-on-one dialogue. A few ideas will begin gathering interest that cannot be resolved at a lower level and are elevated up the organization to the appropriate management or staff area for action, review, or rejection. The very few that are strategic in nature, that offer great opportunity, or that provide a high cost saving may be sent up the organization to a senior management review team.

This high-level management team should be appointed to establish and manage the process for the review and incorporation of new ideas and projects into the organization. These should include those proposed both from the bottom of the organization to those dictated from above. Even if the decision to implement has been made, senior management should be aware of the true cost and its impact on all the other changes in the organization. The larger the impact, as defined by resource allocation or the breadth across the organization, the more the change should be challenged and second-guessed.

A simple system to bring ideas to action is illustrated in Figure 6.10. It begins with anyone inputting an idea or issue into an issue system through a computer terminal. The issue or idea is forwarded, either directly or routed by an earlier recipient, to the proper level or work area for review. The issue is then acted upon or forwarded to a higher level for consideration. The higher level either forwards it to an issue management review process or rejects the idea. The issues management process team reviews the idea in light of all other proposals and issues being considered along with current plans, projects and activities. Once the proposal (or a modified version) is approved, it is assigned to an appropriate person and moves into the organization's implementation system.

Prior to final recommendation, the team works with operational management and utilizes information from organizational plans, current and future projects, resource deployment, productivity trends, and other sources to determine the viability of the proposal. It considers the use of and impact on other resources, systems, and processes and makes a recommendation to senior management[13] on the inclusion, modification, or rejection of the proposal.

Of course, most organizations want the rare opportunities or huge return issues to be able to reach senior leadership as efficiently and expeditiously as possible. These organizations have idea sessions, open door policies, and other creative ways for ideas to move up.

These concepts require profound change in traditional organizational thinking. They must be considered in the design of the control panel and the evolution to newer organizational models (such as those outlined in chapter 7). Only when an organization is committed to continuous improvement as a competitive strategy will it modify its philosophies to allow these mechanisms to realize their potential.

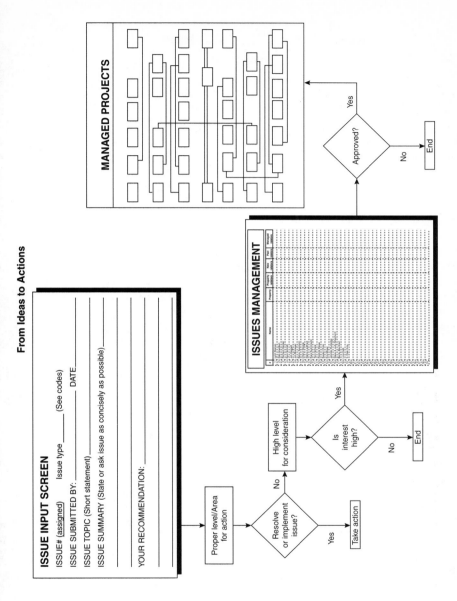

Figure 6.10 A simple process for moving ideas and issues through an organization.

155

THE FUTURE

IMPROVEMENT IN THE TWENTY-FIRST CENTURY

By now, you are probably tired of hearing that proper strategic planning is the doorway to almost every opportunity. You have important work to do; you cannot spend all your time planning. And even if you devised the perfect plan, elements will change as soon as customers, competitors, and technology change. We all know that most products and services today have a short life cycle and organizations must continually reinvent themselves in order to stay competitive.

The good news about your concerns is they have a solution. There is a methodology today that renders many of the methods of traditional strategic planning obsolete. It incorporates change on a continuous basis. It updates goals and objects and it assists in the modification of the organization to accommodate change. It is the *control panel*.

A control panel integrates many facets and dimensions of an organization. It provides the ability to look at priority, movement, acceleration, and correlation among a vast number of factors. The activity of these elements, combined with leadership judgment, and organizational vision and values provide the needed requisites to direct improvement efforts.

As the Information Age grows, strategic planning will be an ongoing process where new data, information, and knowledge continuously enters the organization and merges with the results of current strategy and tactics. Although a huge percentage of this data may result in tactical adjustments, strategic implications abound.

The art of opportunity selection or the ultimate deployment of resources may never be reduced to a science or be capable of automation, but it will become very close. Most of today's prioritization and selection matrices are two dimensional even though they may include a high number of factors. In the future, as control panels and the synthesizing of data grows, multidimensional decision matrices will be common. They will be able to comprehend how a single change, or a series of modifications, impact a system and the variables of that system, or a hypothetically modified system, with a high degree of precision and accuracy.

This is significantly beyond what is possible today, because most organizations neither capture sufficient source data nor have the systems to correlate and statistically understand the interdependence of high numbers of variables. However, there are pioneers who are pursuing both.

CONTINUOUS VALUE IMPROVEMENT— IT REALLY IS EVERYONE'S JOB

In chapter 1, leadership was defined as *taking the responsibility for and performing the action necessary to plan for and achieve desired results*. The desired results of any long term organization must be an improvement over current results; it is built into the vision. Otherwise, the organization will not survive; the market will not allow it.

In a competitive world, productivity and value are the final measures; they are the result of continuous improvement. Improvement is designed and implemented by people. Each person, separate and collectively, must use the best, most efficient tools to improve the most important elements of value that is added to the stakeholders of the organization. The search is endless; as soon as one improvement is achieved, new opportunities appear.

KEY POINTS   CONTINUOUS VALUE IMPROVEMENT

- Improvement is natural to humans.
- Improvement is both strategic and tactical.
- Although humans have a natural tendency to improve, many of the tools and techniques for improvement must be learned. These tools and techniques are also improving, along with improvement processes.
- For improvement to realize a strategic advantage, it must be prioritized and integrated across the organization.
- Two improvement models are PDCA Cycle and problem solving. They are compatible and both search for understanding of cause-and-effect.
- The selection of what to improve and to what performance level is more critical than the application of the tools and techniques. Both of these depend on information.
- Two valuable tools for selecting critical improvement opportunities from the sales process are the won–lost report and the funnel report.
- Processes that include correction, rework, and waste are always prime opportunities for improvement. Two areas that usually offer great opportunity to discover correction are the installation process and customer support.
- The greatest source of improvement comes from the creativity of people. Innovation enters the organization through ideas. An organization needs a process to discover and implement ideas.
- In the Information Age, innovation must be implemented at the lowest appropriate level. A system should be built to route high-value creativity to the right location, including executive leadership when it requires high-level involvement.
- The Pareto process should be used to continuously prioritize the processes, projects, and opportunities in an organization. This minimizes confusion, unproductive duplication, and the creep of undesired strategy.

NOTES

1. Alvin Toffler, *Future Shock* (New York: Bantam Books, 1970), p. 485.

2. These include such topics as problem solving, basic quality tools (brainstorming, Pareto, fishbone diagram, check sheets, flowcharting, nominal group techniques, run charts, statistical process control, stratification, scatter diagrams, process capability, force field analysis, histograms, etc.), management tools (affinity diagram, interrelationship digraph, tree diagram, prioritization matrices, matrix diagram, process decision program chart and PERT/CPM charts), quality function deployment, activity based costing, cost of quality, voice of the customer, mistake proofing, QC circles, Taguchi loss functions and many more.

3. Tetsuichi Asaka, General Editor and Kazuo Ozeki, Editor, *Handbook of Quality Tools: The Japanese Approach* (Cambridge, Mass.: Productivity Press, 1990), pp. 149–158. Also refer to almost any source on quality tools.

4. Deming, *Out of the Crisis* (Massachusetts Institute of Technology, Center for Advanced Engineering Study, Cambridge, Mass.), p. 88.

5. There are a couple of slight variations in widespread use today. One is to replace *Check* with *Study*, as it is not enough to merely check results but they must be studied for adjustment, if needed. Another variation is to replace *Act* with *Adjust*. These changes are slight, and all work well.

6. Peter M. Senge, *The Fifth Discipline: The Art and Practice of the Learning Organization* (New York: Doubleday/Currency, 1990), pp. 5–11.

7. See note 6, p. 6.

8. See note 6, p. 7.

9. See note 6, p. 9.

10. See note 6, p. 10.

11. Robert B. Miller and Stephen E. Heiman, with Tad Tuleja, *Strategic Selling* (Berkeley, Calif.: Warner Books, 1985).

12. Although the concept comes from *Strategic Selling*, the model in Figure 6.6 is a variation. Strategic Selling provides techniques that support three separate parts of the Sales Funnel. They are: Qualify, Cover the Bases, and Close.

13. Depending on the size and complexity of the organization, the management team should include members of the executive committee, or senior executives as well as members of operations, planning, information, and other functions. In smaller organizations, senior management may perform this role themselves.

Chapter 7

RESULTS THROUGH WORKING TOGETHER

> *This, in turn, means teamwork among line workers and a simple but comprehensive information display system that makes it possible for everyone in the plant to respond quickly to problems and to understand the plant's overall situation. In old-fashioned mass production plants, managers jealously guard information about conditions in the plant, thinking this knowledge is the key to their power. In a lean plant, such as Takaoka, all information—daily production targets, cars produced so far that day, equipment breakdowns, personnel shortages, overtime requirements, and so forth—are displayed on andom boards (lighted electronic displays) that are visible from every work station. Every time anything goes wrong anywhere in the plant, any employee who knows how to help runs to lend a hand.*
>
> THE MACHINE THAT CHANGED THE WORLD[1]

One cannot learn leadership and teamwork from a single chapter, or 20 chapters, or even 20 books. It requires a combination of determination, persistence, desire, will, and experience. Leadership principles may seem so rudimentary and simple that they demand little attention, but, in reality, they are never fully mastered, and every individual and organization must continuously improve them to new levels. The winners in the Information Age must never overlook the fundamentals.

We may have lost sight of some basics of leadership and teamwork in the Industrial Age. In order to put things in perspective, we will journey back almost a century or so to review some of the principles upon which the Industrial Age is based.

SCIENTIFIC MANAGEMENT—THE BASIS OF THE INDUSTRIAL AGE

The Industrial Revolution began in Great Britain in the middle of the eighteenth century and took a firm hold in the United States after the Civil War. The early foundations of modern management principles were laid by Robert Owen (1771–1858) of Scotland and Charles Babbage (1792–1871) of England. Frederick W. Taylor (1856–1915), the "father of scientific management", Frank (1868–1924) and Lillian (1878–1972) Gilbreth, Henry L. Gantt (1861–1919) and Henri Fayol (1841–1925) outlined much of the theory and principles of current management at the dawn of the twentieth century. This period, from around 1900 to 1930, has been called the "second industrial revolution,"[2] as it provided breakthrough gains in productivity and documentation of a scientific approach to management.

The work of these pioneers propelled the Industrial Age through most of the twentieth century. The improvements in productivity created by scientific management were astounding. There is wide acceptance that these early leaders pioneered the tremendous gains by the United States that led to victory in World War II and dominance in global commerce throughout most of the second half of the century. Many of the important improvement tools used today were founded by the early pioneers. These include the Gantt Chart by Henry Gantt, the process flow chart by Frank Gilbreth, and time and motion study by Frederick Taylor (later enhanced by Gilbreth). Collectively, their contribution is still the basis for much of the way management runs organizations today. Although a portion of their principles and theories may be sound throughout the next millennium, some are outdated today and others will disappear as more organizations enter the Information Age.

The world of the early 1900s was considerably different from today. Although there are countless contrasts, three factors are particularly relevant: education, technology, and information. We will look at some of the models of the second industrial revolution and review them in light of the progress made in the past 75 to 100 years. This is important because they still exert a heavy impact on our organizations.

INDUSTRIAL AGE ASSUMPTIONS

Most of the second industrial revolution authors had these three beliefs in common.[3]

1. They emphasized production to the point of minimizing the value of persons.

2. They were heavily influenced by Adam Smith; particularly in his theory that employees are almost exclusively motivated by economic rewards.
3. They were constantly searching for the *one best*, or ideal, way.

These three common beliefs must be challenged today. The first belief, that production is a higher value than the human, has no place now. In 1900, there was an increasing work force due to high immigration, and most jobs were being reduced to easily learned skills through scientific management. Almost a hundred years later, we have proven that an educated and innovative work force (the learning organization) creates superior production and provides competitive advantage.

Today's employees, although they desire higher financial incentives, are highly motivated by other factors. Adam Smith's theory was probably not accurate even at the beginning of the second industrial revolution.[4]

The third belief, that there is one best way, was briefly addressed in chapter 5. This belief may have made more sense a hundred years ago than today. Then, since much of the work was manually performed and repeated, it could be easily studied and great improvements made. This led to a search for the ideal. Today, many manual tasks are automated and the search is to improve the automated process. In spite of the phenomenal gains made through continuous improvement, many people still look for the one right answer instead of an evolution of knowledge and continuous improvement.

INDUSTRIAL AGE PRINCIPLES AND THEORIES

These are some of the principles and theories outlined by the early thinkers.

- Workers are afraid to work fast because their pay would be lowered or they would be laid off if they finished their tasks too quickly. This led to a "differential rate system" that paid workers based on production standards and their individual production.[5] (Taylor)
- "There is one best way to do a job and that way should be discovered and put into operation."[6] (Taylor)
- A revolution must occur in both workers and management minds regarding increased productivity. The primary issue was the division of surplus (profits) created by improved productivity. Management and labor should not quarrel about how the surplus should be divided, but should unite about increasing the size of the surplus.[7] (Taylor)
- People are basically lazy by nature. Informal workgroups should be broken up and rewards for individual performance should be emphasized. Once scientific management is established, there is no need for labor unions.[8] (Taylor)
- The planning of work and the doing of work should be separate (performed by different individuals).[9] (Taylor)

- Executives should "manage by exception" by avoiding the study of routine operations where everything goes as expected, but look closely into areas producing exceptionally good or bad results.[10] (Taylor)
- Time and motion studies of workers will raise morale, because of their "obvious physical benefits" and because they show management's concern for the worker."[11] (Gilbreths)
- An employee's work performance should be rated and displayed publicly. Workers and management should be paid a base pay, plus a daily production bonus determined by performance against standards.[12] (Gantt)
- "The more people specialize, the more efficiently they can perform their work."[13] (Fayol)

Many of these principles and theories have been questioned in the past 70 years, but some are still dominant today, and all are still applied somewhere. Deming's 14 points[14] challenged most of these principles, and Juran declared in his final speech to the 1994 Annual Quality Congress that, "In my view, replacing the Taylor system is an idea whose time has come."[15]

Probably the two most profound points from these principles and theories are (1) the separation of planning and doing and (2) the "revolution" that must occur in the minds of both management and labor. The pendulum of planning and execution seems to be swinging back toward a combination and away from separation, but it may not be happening "quickly enough" to maintain or improve an organization's competitive value position. More and more organizations involve line managers and workers in process engineering and process redesign. As the work force becomes even more educated and more empowered and demands a greater say in its future, the pendulum will continue its swing toward consolidation of planning and doing. As this happens, both job satisfaction and productivity should increase.

Taylor's vision for a revolution in both workers and management minds has not yet occurred; at least, a meeting of the minds has not happened. The issue continues today and probably creates more consternation than any other among the hierarchical levels of an organization. In recent years the differences have been widened with the advent of massive downsizing and the demise of the traditional career.

At first glance, the idea behind, or the need for a *mental revolution* may seem nonsensical. Although the basis for Taylor's logic may have been flawed, management and workers must both want to achieve high productivity in order for the organization to be successful. In all probability, this "mental revolution" will be won one organization at a time, until a critical mass forces more lasting and widespread change.

LEADERSHIP AND TEAMWORK—THE BASIS OF THE INFORMATION AGE

At the turn of the twentieth century, America was moving quickly from agriculture to manufacturing. The average education level was low. Jobs and the labor supply were abundant. At the dawn of the twenty-first century, much of the manufacturing economy has shifted to developing countries while much of the labor force has moved into service and information based work.

The dynamics of speed, the velocity of change and the enormous growth of variables that the average person encounters lead to greater and greater complexity. It is complexity that is driving the need to change our models of leadership.

In an environment of large-scale customization, high technology, short cycle times, diverse customer requirements, vast consumer knowledge, overnight obsolescence and global competition, an increasing percentage of processes are beyond the ability of a single individual to master. As this continues to grow, the traditional role of the supervisor and manager becomes an impossible task. How can an individual know all the different jobs, schedule people and tasks, train, coordinate with higher management, evaluate, and lead the improvement effort required?

The Industrial Age is grounded in control and power. The individual is not trusted to perform work without direct supervision. Supervisors are closely watched by managers and managers are, in turn, closely scrutinized by executives. The Information Age is seeing the emergence of the entrepreneur and huge increases in the power of the customer. These two forces, along with the necessity to change as information challenges capital, are forcing a solution to the mental revolution dilemma and launching a new paradigm of leadership and teamwork.

THE MENTAL REVOLUTION IN THE INFORMATION AGE

The more an organization clarifies, communicates, and carries out its mission, vision, and values, the easier it is to attract people who share similar beliefs and desires. Since the desire to achieve is an attitude, every organization has the opportunity to design attitude into the fabric of the organization. In a competitive environment, some will do this better than others and will gain the benefits.

We have learned that pay has limited value as a motivator, but there are other things that tend to encourage, inspire, and activate people. These include being part of a team, contributing to meaningful achievement, sharing in rewards, having an influence, or voice over one's own future, having a sense of being treated fairly, being recognized for results achieved, adding value to others' lives, being communicated with, helping the environment, and feeling important. The opposites or absences of these tend to create discomfort, a knot in the stomach, or depolarization with others. Most of these are human factors and apply to all categories of stakeholders in an organization.

So, the meeting of minds may not be a harmonious understanding between management and labor, it may be the creation of an environment where basic and higher level needs are addressed in a manner that leads to greater satisfaction. Instead of a voice of the customer directed only at customers, the mental revolution may well be won by better understanding all stakeholders and continually building an organization that moves toward optimally meeting their needs.

It may seem a little far-fetched, but look at the competitive advantages of such an organization. A customer focused organization concentrates on meeting the needs of customers. Customers are "motivated" to purchase the goods and services that they know and perceive are the best value for the price they pay. Every working day employees (including management) pay a dear price (real and perceived) for the salaries, benefits, and feelings (real and perceived) they obtain. The same applies to suppliers, shareholders, and the governments we support. A people-focused organization better understands the needs of all constituents and builds and improves systems and processes to better meet them.

As employees become entrepreneurs, or more entrepreneurial, the mental revolution does not depend on a perceived equitable split between worker and manager. It rewards everyone for their contribution based on the value they produce. When enlightened employees and customers gain the information necessary to continually understand the dynamics of value, it will no longer be management's / prerogative to determine everyone's share of productivity improvement. At that point, market forces will dictate the split and Taylor's mental revolution will disappear.

Even though Taylor may have been off the mark on how the revolution of the mind may be resolved, he apparently realized the important role it plays in productivity.

THE LEADER

The primary function of the Industrial Age manager is to decide what work must be done to meet the requirements of higher management and allocate various pieces to subordinates. The primary function of an Information Age leader is to integrate value-creating process with other processes, people, and information in order to deliver value to customers. The most common relationship between the traditional "superior" and the "subordinate" was one of employer/employee. The leader of the future will primarily be a *partner* with suppliers and customers. Whether an individual is employed by the organization or works as an independent contractor, an outsourcing organization, or a free-lance entrepreneur has little relevance.

The value-added chain where each link continually improves the value it adds by integrating with the whole is a much more effective and efficient producer than an organization structure where information must go up for a decision and back down for implementation. The traditional manager issued orders and always had the power of discipline or termination over the worker. The leader performs the role of mastering increasingly complex connections, while bringing greater order to value-producing processes.

The leader is connected to a team, or a number of teams. Leadership is simple in concept. *The first business of leadership is to provide purpose.* This is followed by building the means and then deploying the means to achieve the purpose.

No matter what type of organizational structure, the key to delivering performance is leadership. There are no substitutes for basic leadership, nor are there a few plain and simple techniques to follow that ensure one is able to be an effective leader. In reality, everyone possesses leadership characteristics and everyone can improve their leadership effectiveness.

However, most organizations do not allocate adequate resources in developing leaders. Our educational institutions do not focus on leadership. A person can graduate from leading business schools with advanced degrees and only cover one or two chapters in basic leadership, generally with little or no practical exercise connected with it. With a few exceptions, people all over the world are promoted into their first supervisory or management position without formal training on leadership. After promotion, a small percentage receive a few days of classroom instruction with some simulated exercises and some direction from higher management; many receive no formal education.

As one moves up the ranks, even less education is available. Very little is offered within the organization, but some advanced education is available through executive education programs from some of the top business schools. Although these programs are excellent, they reach a very small percentage of our nation's organizational leadership at the middle or higher management levels.

This must improve. The body of knowledge on basic leadership exists and is sound. We do not need to invent or discover a new set of leadership skills for the Information Age, we just need to tweak our models and adjust our application. Then, we need to train our leaders on the application of leadership in the Information Age. For more discussion on leadership and an example of where leadership development prevails, see Appendix D.

TEAM ENVIRONMENT

Teamwork in the traditional sense was based on allegiance to the unit or its manager/supervisor; teamwork in the Information Age is based on shared vision, collaboration, cooperation, and continuous learning. The leader is a part of the team, not a disjointed, or separate function.

Considerable information and knowledge are available on teams from small self-directed teams to utilizing teams in a giant corporation. Some sources are excellent,[16] many are good, and many confuse or mislead as much as they assist. The excellent ones tend to focus on lessons learned, generalized principles, flexible guides, integration, evolution, training and important issues to address. The poor ones tend to offer inflexible models (one right way), rigid beliefs, quick solutions, and endless checklists.

There are a number of different types and uses of teams.[17] The Information Age organization uses teams in a variety of ways from projects to product development to work teams. Although the fundamental team skills used by the different types of teams are similar, their purposes are different. The basic team is the work team, which is connected to higher level work teams or cross-functional teams.

In addition to mastering different types and uses of teams, the organization must learn when and when not to use teams. Teams are used most effectively on improvement, highly complex situations, and integrated solutions. They are inefficient when used on low level or routine problems, tasks that can be automated, or tasks that do not gain from synergy. Teams are learning systems that lead to improvement and increased productivity; they are best utilized in this manner.

In the traditional organizational hierarchy, as defined by Fayol,[18] every work unit has a supervisor, every supervisor, in turn, has a supervisor or manager, and every manager reports to someone higher, and so on. A supervisor oversees operations, plans and schedules work, evaluates performance, hires and fires individuals, performs or coordinates training, and is the conduit for information entering and leaving the unit.

In a team-based organization, the role of the traditional supervisor is mostly performed by the team; therefore, there is little need for a supervisor.[19] The roles of the supervisor and manager tend to merge into more of a coaching role and functions as a boundary manager[20] among teams, other boundary managers, and higher managers.

The huge jump from a traditional to a team structure should be gradual and well planned. The downside costs of an abrupt organization-wide change can be devastating. Unlike the commanding of resources to conduct activity, high performance teams cannot be ordered; they must be built and there must be allowance for evolution and growth. The team progression plan must be openly communicated, followed by a blending of training with application. Supporting characteristics such as performance evaluation, pay administration, problem resolution, training, career growth, and planning should also be transitional by communicating interim approaches with flexibility for adjustment as knowledge is gained.

The movement from a structured hierarchy to a team-based organization is natural for most individuals, but almost impossible for others. The most an organization can do for its employee and management force is to communicate fairly, provide training, and give everyone a chance to demonstrate their performance and cooperation under a changing environ-ment. As an organization moves into the Information Age, they do not have much choice, they must change.

The bottom level of the organization has the least compromising role of all, and the change is tough. Middle managers feel the most threatened because they accurately predict a disastrous disappearance of much of their current role. However, the toughest shift is experienced by senior manage-ment. They have to change the most, and they have to lead the organization through a massive modification that many will resist and that may likely adversely impact short-term performance. All of these tensions are reduced if the organization plans well in advance and gives sufficient time for a more natural transformation. Unfortunately, most organizations either wait too long or jump in unprepared for the heavy commitment and price that must be paid before significant gains can be realized.

The evolution for some organizations may be very quick; and for oth-ers it might take years. Size, the competitive environment, the degree of movement into the Information Age, the age and experience of the work force, and the desire to change will strongly influence the transition.

TEAM METRICS

A central theme of integrated leadership is to always keep the target in mind. This is essential in moving toward a more team-oriented organiza-tion. This means maintaining a focus on the *objectives* of the organization while learning and improving the performance of teams. The team objec-tives are not to become a team, or even function as a team; the team objec-tives are to carry out the mission of the team and achieve its objectives.

One of the largest failures of organizations in launching a team initia-tive is to establish the wrong objectives and use the wrong metrics. For some reason, organizations begin by being too easy on teams; they want to make sure no mistakes are made or the team does not bite off more than it can chew. Everyone wants to see some early successes so "we can set a good example" and prove that "teamwork is good" and can be used in this organization.

The effective metrics of a team system cannot be driven by such mea-sures as:

- Number of ideas implemented
- Number of team meetings
- Quality of agendas
- Number of meetings missed
- Dollars saved by the implementation of an idea[21]

The biggest problem with elevating these types of measures is they send the wrong message. Yes, it is important that a team have meetings and that people attend, and someone may record and use the information for improvement, but it is not important enough to be a team metric, and it should not be consolidated on anyone's control panel.

The topic of appropriate metrics will be covered in the next two chapters. However, it is important early in the team process to maintain a focus on the reason teams exist and not to confuse the purposes of teams with their implementation, their acceptance, the speed of their progress, or any of the metrics that can be applied. *The purpose of teams is to provide value to customers at a rate that exceeds competitors.*

Teams have been around a long time and are used in all industries around the globe to produce results that are superior to performance levels produced by a traditional hierarchical management structure. Any organization that needs to prove the value of teams has the wrong objective in mind. If teams are not viable in an organization, there is one culprit, and that is management. Leadership always determines whether a team system succeeds or fails in any organization. In the Information Age, when a traditional organization competes with another organization with a strong, focused team structure, all parties will discover the power of teams.

TEAM INTEGRATION

Since teams are organizations, the principles of integrated leadership apply: a foundation must be established; the team must align with the foundation (vertical alignment); the VOC must be understood and converted to actionable standards; the team must align with its suppliers and customers, and so on.

These points are pertinent whether the team is one of many teams in an organization or it stands alone as the organization. In reality, there are many more teams consisting of a small number of people that come together for a special purpose, including small businesses, neighborhood groups and small clubs than exist in large organizations. In groups of a few individuals, the entire organization may only be one team.

The first and most important step, once a team is established, or even proposed, is to determine its mission, or purpose. It answers the question, "What is the primary reason the team exists?" If it is a process team or work team, the reason generally will be to provide a value-added product or service to customers. A project team, special improvement team, or product development team usually is formed for a shorter duration and will have a clearly defined purpose to achieve in a targeted period.

Once the purpose is clear a team outlines its charter and ground rules and establishes goals and objectives. Frequently, the charter, mission, and general goals are provided to the team from the higher organization, but the team must state them in a form that it can understand and achieve and communicate with the higher organization for agreement. In the absence of direction, the team formulates these items and works with higher authority for support.

As an organization becomes more team focused, leadership must ensure that the missions, visions, and objectives of teams are compatible and integrated to assure targeted results. The organization's control panel should include the means of guaranteeing unity among emerging teams, traditionally organized parts of the organization, and external partners.

Not only does this system avoid unnecessary duplication of effort and the negative emotions associated with it, it offers an ongoing method of prioritization and a means of measurement. The control panel indicator is similar to the customer–supplier maps covered in chapter 4, where each unit/team's mission is stated in a box with lines connecting to its major customers. Possible conflicting or duplicating missions can be easily identified and explored and modified if needed.

BEYOND TEAMS

This heading may be a little misleading. Many organizations are struggling to build teams in traditionally hierarchical structures. Usually, their first approach is to design teams using hierarchical concepts including teams reporting to teams and so on up the pyramid. They also structure teams for a rather long duration, under the assumption that it takes a fairly lengthy period to properly build a high-performance team.

In reality, a high-performance team can be assembled relatively quickly if its members have good team skills and its leader has both good team and leadership skills. This has been demonstrated again and again by professional sports teams where players are continuously exchanged and by high stress-related teams, such as emergency recovery teams and special mission teams in the military.

The long-term approach is to focus on building team skills in people at all levels. With a solid base of employees or members with these skills, teams can be quickly formed and productive. Without the skills, flexibility and speed are limited by the need to build them first. So *beyond teams* does not equate to beyond teamwork; it refers to organizational structures that evolve from hierarchies and team structures. The new structure depends on a higher common purpose, a high level of integration, understanding cause-and-effect, and an efficient system of metrics.

THE BRAIN AS A MODEL

Mr. I. J. Grandes del Mayo, of Quality Enhancement Seminars, proposes that the team structure emerging today will eventually fall victim to and be replaced by organizations that pattern their interdynamics after the human brain.[22] He believes the job of the future can be compared to a neuron, which functions both as a gatherer and an interconnected processor of information. In the nervous system, neurons are independent, but they do not act alone.

In order to build a robust organization that continually adjusts to its environment, a few conditions must exist in each individual. These ensure that cooperation and competency requirements are met, and that the individuals have starring roles in cyberspace and the virtual organization.

- Their aim must align with the organization's.
- They must be guided by theory.
- They must possess the ability to acquire sufficient knowledge and information for action.
- They must have a firmly held and internalized value system that includes a high degree of ethics.
- They must have the capability to easily forge cooperative relations with each other.

Although this type of organization depends on many of the principles of teamwork, it does not require the startup time of building a team, nor is it delayed by the consensus-type decision-making process that is characteristic of today's teams. On the other hand, it does require a well-developed distributed networked control panel, communications system, and a continuous learning process.

NETWORKS

Another term to define an alternative form of organization is *networks*. An implication for the future was voiced in 1993 by John Arquilla and David Ronfeldt of International Policy Department RAND.[23]

> *From a traditional standpoint, a military is an institution that fields armed forces. The form that all institutions normally take is the hierarchy, and militaries in particular depend heavily on hierarchy. Yet, the information revolution is bound to erode hierarchies and redraw the boundaries around which institutions and their offices are normally built. Moreover, the information revolution favors organizational network designs. . . .*
>
> *The Mongols, a classic example of an ancient force that fought according to cyberwar principles, were organized more like a network than a hierarchy. More recently, a relatively minor military power that defeated a great modern power—the combined forces of North Vietnam and the Viet Cong—operated in many respects more like a network than an institution; it even extended political-support networks abroad. In both cases, the Mongols and the Vietnamese, their defeated opponents were large institutions whose forces were designed to fight set-piece attritional battles.*
>
> *The lesson: Institutions can be defeated by networks, and it may take networks to counter networks. The future may belong to whoever masters the network form.*[24]

THE CHAORDIC ORGANIZATION

Two huge examples of the network form are the Internet and VISA International. VISA was born out of the failure of a single institution or hierarchical organization to operate the many diverse dynamics of a global undertaking that was losing hundreds of millions of dollars annually by the late 1960s. The remarkable story of how VISA was transformed from a franchised operation to a network of more than 23,000 institutions is told by its founder, Dee W. Hock, in a 1995 article, "The Chaordic Organization: Out of Control and Into Order."[25]

Chaord is a constructed word from the first three letters from chaos and order and is used to describe:

> . . . *any self-organizing, adaptive, nonlinear, complex system, whether physical, biological, or social, the behavior of which exhibits characteristics of both order and chaos or loosely translated to business terminology, cooperation and competition.*[26]

The principles that provided direction in the early evolution of VISA seem to set a tone for the future formation of networked organizations:[27]

- It must be equitably owned by all participants.
- Power and function must be distributive to the maximum degree.
- Governance must be distributive.
- It must be infinitely malleable, yet extremely durable.
- It must embrace diversity and change.

Today, VISA is the largest single block of consumer purchasing power in the global economy.[28] Additional portrayal and results of the VISA story include the following remarkable characteristics:

> *In the legal sense, VISA is a non-stock, for-profit, membership corporation. In another sense, it is an inside-out holding company in that it does not hold but is held by its functioning parts. The 23,000 financial institutions that create its products are, at one and the same time, its owners, its members, its customers, its subjects, and its superiors. It exists as an integral part of the most highly regulated of industries, yet is not subject to any regulatory authority.*
>
> *Yet, it cannot be bought, traded, raided, or sold, since ownership is held in the form of perpetual, non-transferable membership rights.*
>
> *VISA espoused no political, economic, social, or legal theory, thus transcending language, custom, politics, and culture to successfully connect institutions and peoples of every persuasion. It has gone through a number of wars and revolutions, the belligerents continuing to share common ownership and never ceasing reciprocal acceptance of cards, even though they were killing one another.*

> It has multiple boards of directors within a single legal entity, none of which can be considered superior or inferior, as each has irrevocable authority and autonomy over geographic or functional areas.
>
> Its products are the most universally used and recognized in the world, yet the organization is so transparent that its ultimate customers, most of its affiliates, and some of its members do not know how it exists or functions. At the same time, the core of the enterprise has no knowledge of or authority over a vast number of the constituent parts. No part knows the whole, the whole does not know all the parts and none has any need to. The entirety, like all chaords—including those you call body, brain. and biosphere—is largely self-regulating.[29]

The Internet is similar to VISA in many organizational aspects, yet it is even more accessible and potentially much more encompassing. In all probability, the Internet could not exist without a chaordic approach. Ultimately, this type of base may prove superior to all others in the improvement of highly complex systems.

CONTROL PANEL APPLICATION

The control panel is a tool for leaders and teams. The movement of an organization toward its vision and mission and its long-term performance in adding value in competitive markets are the ultimate measures of leadership and its effective use of teams. In the final analysis, the top control panel indicators are based on results, and results are the top measure of leadership.

Along the way, control panel indicators assist leadership in its journey. If an indicator does not provide value, or is unlikely to provide value in the future, it should be removed and resources directed elsewhere. Occasionally, all indicators should be reviewed for appropriateness and value and only those with the highest return should be continuously monitored. Of course, sudden change can influence a shift of indicators and cause new ones to emerge.

There are a few background data elements that should be maintained on data bases that are accessible on executive control panels and are major indicators at lower levels in the organization. An example is a skill/knowledge evaluation table that shows, at a glance, the current competency and training levels of all personnel on the skills and knowledge that are needed to perform the job or assigned role (see Figure 7.1). It is an important indicator of unit and organizational competency and allows planning to fill gaps, outline development plans, staff properly, and cross train.

Other indicators that reflect leadership, other than achieved results, are covered elsewhere, and include project management, won–lost reports, value trends on the VOC, and COQ trends.

In the final analysis, leadership and teamwork are skills that are heavily influenced by attitude and personal drive. *They are not the result; they create the result.*

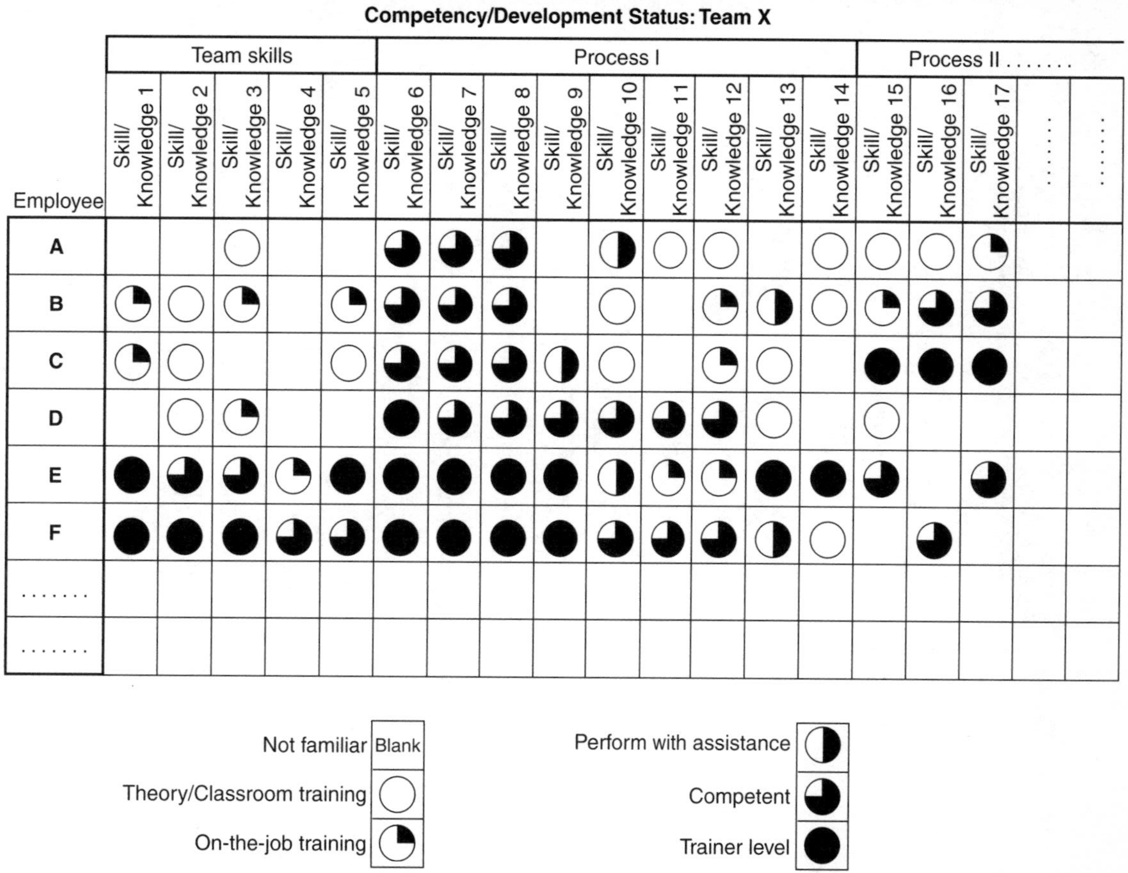

Figure 7.1 A matrix showing each team or unit member's current developmental or competency status is a simple indicator of unit competency, depth, developmental needs, and training priorities.

173

KEY POINTS   RESULTS THROUGH WORKING TOGETHER

- Two key fundamental skills that are critical to success in the Information Age are leadership and teamwork.
- There is a huge gap between the Industrial Age and the Information Age; many of the principles that emerged in the Industrial Age do not apply in the Information Age.
- Three principles that are inappropriate for the Information Age are: (1) a person is merely a production unit that is motivated almost exclusively by economic reward; (2) There is one best way to do every job; and (3) planning and execution should be separate.
- One principle that Taylor believed would solve itself was that a "mental revolution" would occur in the minds of workers and management where there would be no issue on how to divide production gains. This still has not been resolved to everyone's satisfaction and it will maintain some division until it is resolved.
- The job of supervisor and manager is changing dramatically as the increasing volume of information and knowledge render their traditional roles ineffective and demand greater and greater teamwork and participation to manage its complexity.
- Tomorrow's leaders require more traditional leadership tools as they can not depend on information as a source of control. Traditional approaches require focus, caring for the individual and continuous learning and improvement.
- Teamwork, like leadership, is an acquired skill that organizations need to foster and build systems to accommodate. As teamwork matures in organizations and individuals, new organizational structures that are patterned after neural and biological systems will emerge. Traditional structures and management hierarchies cannot compete with these systems.
- There are no known specific high-level control panel indicators that measure leadership. The control panel concept itself is a leadership tool design to achieve results and win against competition. When this happens, leadership is successful; when it does not, leadership fails.

NOTES

1. Womack and Others, *The Machine That Changed the World* (Rawson Associates, Macmillan Publishing Company), p. 99.

2. Ernest Dale, Ph.D., *Management: Theory and Practice*, 4th ed. (New York: McGraw-Hill, 1978), p. 70.

3. J. Clifton Williams, Andrew J. DuBrin and Henry L. Sisk, *Management and Organization*, 5th ed. (Cincinnati: South-Western Publishing, 1985), p. 29.

4. It is doubtful that employees were totally motivated by economic gain even early in the twentieth century. This assumption was probably not challenged by the early pioneers.

5. James A. F. Stoner and Charles Wankel, *Management*, 3rd ed. (Englewood Cliffs, N. J.: Prentice-Hall, 1986), p. 29. Taylor's methods increased production to such an extent that workers began to resist his techniques being adopted at their companies based on layoffs at the organizations that used his techniques. This resulted in a congressional investigation of his philosophies in 1912, p. 30.

6. Samual C. Certo, *Principles of Modern Management: Functions and Systems* (Dubuque, Iowa: Wm. C. Brown Publishers, 1986), p. 30.

7. See note 3, p. 31.

8. See note 3, p. 31.

9. See note 2, p. 73.

10. See note 2, p. 73.

11. See note 5, p. 31.

12. See note 5, p. 31.

13. See note 5, p. 35.

14. Deming, *Out of the Crisis* (Massachusetts Institute of Technology Center for Advanced Engineering Study), pp. 18–96.

15. Joseph M. Juran, "The Upcoming Century of Quality," *Quality Progress*, 27, no. 8 (August 1994): pp. 29–37. I had the good fortune to be invited by Chuck Aubrey of the Juran Institute to join him, Dr. Juran, and Brad Stratton, the Editor of *Quality Press*, for breakfast immediately prior to Dr. Juran's presentation. I was very impressed with Dr. Juran's passion for change that he sees as necessary to transition from scientific management to a more "team based" approach.

16. A recommended book for the larger issues is: James H. Shonk, *Team Based Organizations: Developing a Successful Team Environment* (Homewood, Ill.: Business One Irwin, 1992). For day-to-day operations of teams, I prefer material from the Miller Consulting Group in Atlanta, Joiner Associates Inc. in Madison, Wisconsin, the Juran Institute in Wilton, Connecticut, and Zenger Miller of San Jose, California.

17. Peter R. Scholtes, "Teams in the Age of Systems," *Quality Progress* 28, no. 12 (December 1995), pp. 51–58. This is an excellent article outlining many of the challenges of teams in the Information Age and seven different types of teams.

18. See note 2, pp. 98–103, for an excellent review of the many influences Henri Fayol had on the structure of today's organization.

19. Shonk, *Team Based Organizations* (Business One Irwin), p. 6, points out an organization that went from an employee-supervisor ration from 7:1 to 37:1 after implementing a team focus.

20. See note 19, pp. 133–39.

21. Many may argue this point. Under certain scrutiny this may be an appropriate metric. I have seen a number of teams who focused on cost savings reduce costs in an early process just to see more costs added in later processes. One organization added up all their team cost savings for a year to more than $6 million: unfortunately, their overall costs rose more than $3 million for the year. It is impossible to reconcile or even understand without a good cost of quality system. Yet, it gives the illusion that something good is being achieved. It is a dangerous, misleading, and worthless measure. On the other hand, if a team has an objective to reduce costs by x, while maintaining a certain level and quality of output and without adversely impacting the overall COQ, it may be an appropriate measure.

22. This concept was proposed by I. J. Grandes del Mayo of Quality Enhancement Seminars. Inc. in a presentation, "The Brain as a Model for the Organization of the Future," to the Orange Empire Section (Orange County, California) of the American Society for Quality Control, on November 12, 1996, at the Holiday Inn, Irvine, California.

23. John Arquilla and David Ronfeldt, "Cyberwar is Coming," *Comparative Strategy*, vol. 12, no. 2, pp. 141–65. The quotes came from the Internet version, which was copyrighted in 1993 by Taylor & Francis, 1101 Vermont Avenue, NW #200, Washington, DC 20005.

24. See note 23, p. 6. (From Internet version).

25. Dee W. Hock, The Chaordic Organization: Out of Control and Into Order," *World Business Academy Perspectives*, vol. 9, no 1, 1995, pp. 5–18.

26. See note 25, p. 6.

27. See note 25, p. 13.

28. See note 25, p. 13.

29. See note 25, p. 13–14.

Chapter 8

YOU GET WHAT YOU MEASURE

> *In 1991, for the first time ever, companies spent more money on computing and communications gear than the combined monies spent on industrial, mining, farm, and construction equipment.*
>
> *There has been more information produced in the last 30 years than during the previous 5,000.*
>
> *Let's say you're going to a party, so you pull out some pocket change and buy a little greeting card that plays "Happy Birthday" when it's opened. After the party, someone tosses the card into the trash, throwing away more computer power than existed in the entire world before 1950.*
>
> THE EMPLOYEE HANDBOOK OF NEW WORK HABITS
> FOR A RADICALLY CHANGING WORLD[1]

Chapter 8 covers the human systems aspects of organizations, but adds a dimension of quantification and structure. The leader must ensure that the human systems are properly staffed and all individuals have the proper skills, knowledge, and motivation to perform the jobs that blend together to create and perform the necessary tasks within the processes that produce desired results.

As humans, we seek favorable recognition and attempt to avoid punishment. We enjoy being positively appreciated, and we do what we can to elude being in disfavor. This trait is the basis for early childhood training and discipline and assists not only in instilling values but in safety and well being.

Later, we find out that success and failure are frequently measured. We earn grades in school; we have income levels; we live in certain zip codes; we must attain a certain SAT score to attend a good university; we eat a certain level of calories and percentage of fat and have certain body fat ratios. All of these, and countless others, can be converted to good or bad.

As we study business or begin work, we find that a new set of measures provides judgment on organizations and the people in them. The organizational metrics are basically financial measures or ratios such as growth rates, earnings per share, stock price per earnings and hundreds of others. However, most people are evaluated on mysterious five-point scales, subjective ratings, production rates, and performance against quotas. Most of the remainder are not provided feedback on their performance, and a very few always know the score.

THE PERFORMANCE REVIEW SYSTEM

In 1978, I was a division personnel manager for one of America's largest insurance companies. One of my assignments was to review and approve semiannual performance evaluations before they were covered with the employee or manager. They had to be carefully screened for accuracy and compliance with the increasing number of federal and state requirements on affirmative action, discrimination, and fairness.

In more than two years in this position, only rarely did I see one that struck me as being indicative of a person's performance. Most were extremely subjective, written a day or two before they were due, contained very few measures that the person had any control over, and were heavily weighted by the evaluator's most recent experience with the individual. Most management personnel and employees disliked the system and considered it a necessary evil.

Since that time, working with a number of organizations, I have spent considerable time on performance systems. I rarely see one that is any better than the one at the insurance company, and many are worse. In some organizations, large numbers of people have not been reviewed for years, if ever.

Employees at all levels of corporate America, our volunteer organizations, and government are screaming for a better system of performance feedback. Fortunately, a few organizations are moving in a positive direction in meeting their demands.

Here are the major concerns with the current system:

1. It contains considerable subjectivity; in many cases the employee does not know the performance level desired and the supervisor/evaluator has considerable discretion in selecting a ranking/rating.
2. The system is designed to maintain control over people and budgets, not process and results. I have observed several situations

where management is warned in advance of future downsizing and told to "get their rankings in line to keep those they want."

3. Usually, whether communicated or not, the system is a ranking system where each employee is evaluated against other employees. This may work against teamwork and maximization of unit output.

4. It generally focuses more on activity and behavior rather than results. If it does include results, it usually demands performance in one or two outputs that do not include quality or value or the results are dependent on factors outside of the employee's control or even influence.

5. Most systems claim to be participative but that is misleading because the person being rated usually has little say in what is being evaluated and frequently the evaluation is completed, reviewed by higher management and approved prior to the employee seeing it. At that point, it is too late to bring in additional data, or the system strongly discourages it.

6. The levels above the person doing the performance review frequently have strong opinions regarding the performance of those being evaluated. Even though the higher level may be some distance from the day-to-day operations and not a party to previous supervisor–employee discussions, they frequently heavily influence the ranking of employees. (Those doing the ranking always are aware of who, in turn evaluates them).

7. Once or twice a year is too infrequent to evaluate anyone; particularly if they work in an unstable system that goes through frequent change. Some organizations go through the motions of performance review and ignore what is outlined in past reviews because they know their priorities will change as management chases the latest opportunity.

8. The current system has been around for quite awhile. Since most of the current leaders have succeeded within the system, many are reluctant to change.

In reality, the current system is not a measurement system; it is a subjective assessment system that supports a scientific management perspective. The current performance review system works well with scientific management, offers management considerable flexibility, and maintains control. For more views on the current system, read Dr. Deming's, *Out of the Crisis.*[2] Deming raises more issues than he provides answers, but conventional wisdom usually requires challenge before alternatives are discovered.

There are many forms of performance review offered by authors, managers, and consultants. No one system works for every organization and every situation. Like the control panel, performance evaluation must fit the foundation, vision, and strategy of the organization.

THE WRONG MEASURES

If we begin with the target in mind and work backward to what it takes to reach the target, we begin to see some clues on a way to approach a performance system. In chapter 1, we saw an example of an operations executive who was expected to improve her performance during the upcoming year. One of the top objectives on her performance evaluation plan was to visit 30 branch offices during the year. She actually visited 50; will this result in improved performance over the course of the next year?

No one doubts that a football team must practice over and over again to function well as a team and coordinate their strategy both mentally and physically. If you practice more times than your opponent, will you win? If you have more years of experience, will you perform better than someone with less years of experience? If you attend a seminar on Quality Function Deployment can you bring knowledge into your organization that will develop new products at half the costs in half the time? What if you attend two seminars, or three, or three seminars plus a conference? These questions are unanswerable. Yet, a large percentage of individual performance plans use this type of deductive reasoning that certain activity leads to a desired result.

One of the extreme examples of performance planning is a large organization that uses a "top ten" approach. Each year, in November, the CEO provides a list of the top ten items that the organization should focus on during the next year. In cascading order, each executive compiles a "top ten" list, and so on down to the supervisor level. Those at the bottom of the organization have five or six of the lists tacked to bulletin boards, walls, cubicles, break rooms, and electronic message displays. None of the lists contain a quantification, explanation, or description. They are a list of projects, activities, studies, and identified problem areas. When performance review time comes around, everyone is working on topics from "top ten" lists. The most popular measurement is, "how many of the 20–30 unique items on someone's list am I working on?"

It really does not matter how many times a football team practices, if they do not have talented players with desire, skills, physical ability, strategy, tactics, basics, a sound recruitment program, support, and the hundreds of variables that add up to a winning team. They will not hit the important measures. If they only practice five plays over and over again, they should be able to execute those five plays very well, but they will not have much of an arsenal.

Anytime an activity measure is used without a connection to a result, it is the wrong measure, because it communicates a message that the activity is more important than the result. Although this may be true in some pursuits, it serves a cross purpose when the ultimate target is the achievement of a vision based on delivering value to stakeholders.

There is no limit to what can be measured. The cause-and-effect trail can always be traced back to a point beyond human understanding or a level of acceptability. The key is selecting the right measures and the most efficient measures to elevate in importance so desired results are obtained.

THE RIGHT MEASURES

There are two sources of the top measures of every department, every unit, team, or individual. The first are those goals that are derived from strategic and operational plans. The second are the requirements or standards that each level must achieve to meet the needs of its customers. The goals from both sources must be compatible, and they are the ultimate measures of every unit or division in the organization. These must be crystal clear, well defined, and always measurable. These are the *right* performance measures from the top of the organization down to the lowest unit, or team level.

Although the right measures are performance outputs that are based on primary unit goals, they, in turn, generate or are dependent on other measures. For example, a work team may have a performance goal to produce X units per day at a quality level of Y. Internally, this production level requires a certain staffing level of trained personnel. Therefore, two measures that are important to the team are proficiency level and attendance. These have little importance to the customer, as long as the performance levels are met, but they are essential measures for the team to be able to achieve higher performance.

The right measures connect with the primary goals of the unit, and the pertinent measures that assist in the attainment of the value adding and continuous improvement goals.

INTEGRATION OF MEASURES

Some important considerations for selecting a targeted measure are:

- Does it measure, or provide an *accurate* indication of what we want to achieve?
- Is it the best measure to provide this information?
- Is it linked with a causal chain that leads toward the desired result?
- Are supporting or linking measures necessary and in place to ensure undesired consequences are not obtained.

Usually, there is no one right or best measure. Some believe the only important measure for a business is profit. That may be true for a theoretical small, simple business that lasts only a few hours, but it is far from being the only important measure for an organization with vision. The measurement of profit is time sensitive, historical, imprecise, and usually inaccurate. A business can have high profits at one point in time and squander them or be out of business for failure to adequately compete by the next reporting period. That is the basis of a control panel. There is no one measure that can guide the journey; it requires the right blend of the right targeted measures.

A popular measure in most organizations is revenue. In its simplest form revenue is a combination of volume and price. Sales volume frequently comes from two main sources: current customers and new customers. Current customers who continue to purchase are called retained or repeat customers; those who do not are called lost customers. Potential new business comes from markets; a market may contain both desired customers and undesired customers. Desired customers are labeled qualified, or target, prospects.

Many industries use a sales force to directly reach target prospects and point out the benefits of using the firm's product or service. Sales successes are called closings and failures are called rejections. Sales volume from new sales is a function of closing rate, number of prospects contacted, numbers of units per order, and the price per unit. If an individual called on 25 prospects for the month, closed 40 percent of them at an average of 5 units at $1,000, the new sales volume for that individual would be $50,000 (25 × .40 × 5 × $1,000). What is the most important measure?

There is not enough information to answer this question. There are too many unknown variables. An important question is, what is an optimal number for this particular sales agent to see in a month with the agent's current level of competency? Twenty-five may be too many to be able to qualify the prospect, gather information, and adequately disclose the actual value (costs and benefits) of the product/service, or it may be too few. If certain factors are overlooked at this part of the sales process, it may have serious impact later on profitability, satisfaction, and retention rates; which, in turn, may influence the definition of targeted prospects and the sales process.

There is a causal relationship among sales competency, number of sales calls, closing rates, sales volume, pricing factors, and many other factors, that correlate with customer profitability. If we look at profitability, by customer, as a more encompassing goal, we bring in many factors that are outside the sales process. These depend largely on how efficient the organization is, how well it understands customer needs, and how it treats customers on a continuous basis.

As the dynamics are better understood, more meaningful ideal customer profiles develop, and the sales process becomes more stable, key measures will change. For example, an organization with little knowledge may give its sales force measures, or quotas exclusively for sales revenue. Although the organization may issue qualification guidelines such as being a good credit risk, little else matters other than revenue. As the organization gains knowledge, the goal may shift to sales revenue based on increasing the average revenue per sale. Later, as knowledge, process stability, and competency increase, the measures may extend to closing rates, cycle times, and number of calls.

RELATIONSHIP BETWEEN ACTIVITY AND RESULTS

If you wanted to see a coin tossed into the air land on heads 250 times, it is easy to predict approximately how many times you would have to toss it into the air in order to achieve the desired result. If you wanted to successfully close 10 sales, how many prospects would you have to call on? If you want to win the Malcolm Baldrige National Quality Award, how many internal assessments do you have to complete? If you want to produce new, improved products in half the time, at half the price, how many QFD seminars do you have to attend?

It is easy to predict the outcome of a series of coin tosses based on the laws of probability. In a stable sales process, prediction of sales becomes fairly accurate. In other circumstances, it may be impossible (how many sales calls does it take to sell 10 orders of ice cubes to Eskimos at $15 per pound?). The winning of the Malcolm Baldrige Award may not be attained, no matter how many internal assessments are performed, and attendance at a seminar may have no impact on new product introduction.

Scientific management was built on the premise that all work could be studied and broken down into fundamental steps that could be taught to almost anyone. It could not envision the Information Age, a world of mass customization or lean production. Frederick Taylor was not aware[3] of the cumulative impact that variation has on the quality and productivity of manufactured products (and services). The primary element of value that scientific management addressed was production, and it assumed management would find the best way to design the work to maximize quality. Unfortunately, quality was left to the work measurement personnel and those involved in inspection and correction.

Consequently, the focus of the second Industrial Age was on the activity of production, not on the quality or value of results produced. Initially, production standards were designed as the quantity of output that an individual should perform in a day and a rate of pay was set to compensate for that level of production. Those who did not perform to this standard were reassigned, or fired. Later, organizations started compensating for additional production and they paid based on a "piece rate." Again, quality was not an issue as long as the activity was performed as designed and taught.

Although times have changed considerably since the dawn of scientific management, many of its skeletons are still around. A substantial percentage of employees are still measured on activity and production quotas, along with a proliferation of activity that is not connected with results. For some, goals are based on such criteria. More alarming still is the increasing trend of providing numerical goals that are arbitrarily set without a stable process designed to produce the result. The third concern is the continuous changing of priorities and goals based on such things as the latest rumor, speculation, fear, uncertainty, doubt, competitive factors, or conjecture.

JOBS

So far, we have concentrated on processes as the mechanism that produces products and services that customers receive. Although many processes are automated, most are not. The processes that are not automated are performed by individuals or teams of individuals. Both those that are and are not auto-mated required design and support from other humans. The physical and mental effort that a single individual expends in performing within processes or supporting processes is called a job.

Jobs may or may not align with processes. Some individuals carry out their entire job within a single process; others shift across or support numerous processes. The primary job of traditional management is plan-ning, staffing, organizing, directing, and controlling both jobs and processes. Every individual in the organization has a job to perform. Some are well defined and others vary dramatically as they chase or are subject to the latest crisis, whim, or opportunity.

There is a difference between processes and jobs. A process consists of steps that are performed to change the state or condition of a physical prod-uct, information, knowledge, or service to a different state (an input to an output). These elements can be assigned to people and become the build-ing blocks of jobs. In some cases a job may be defined as pieces of the building blocks, and in others a job may be defined as elements of several building blocks. A job is ultimately defined by where a person spends phys-ical and mental effort performing an activity that may or may not relate to processes either internal or external to an organization.

In many cases, jobs are defined by processes; and, in others, processes are defined by jobs. In a climate of reengineering,[4] large numbers of merg-ers and takeovers, and downsizing, jobs are continuously being redefined without much apparent consideration for their ultimate impact on value or people in the longer term.

If an automated process is improved by a superior system that replaces an inferior one, no one complains (with the possible exception of the com-petition). However, when a superior producing system displaces people, things are different. Another characteristic of the economic boom that fol-lowed World War II, was the ability and willingness of organizations to pro-vide long term employment, generous benefit packages and numerous career opportunities. Many people believed as long as they performed their job as defined, they were entitled to the rewards. When global competition began rewriting the rules, things changed. Today, jobs are becoming the smaller steps of large processes that change as competitive factors force pro-ductivity improvement. The right of long-term employment is being severely challenged as more industries try to compete by being more effi-cient and effective. This entitlement may diminish in the Information Age.

Today, a job is moving away from being an established right that results from hard work, honest effort, and dedicated service to becoming a series of value adding steps in an organization's larger process. This is not necessarily negative. It is merely the result of a passage from medium productivity to higher productivity and an increasing shift of traditional wealth creation from capital and labor to information. The positive news is that opportunity may be greater than ever imagined under Industrial Age thinking.

Jobs as Value-Added Services

Every individual has tremendous value-adding capability. Some have more in certain areas, but less in other areas. An individual in the changing world can best ensure their marketability by periodically assessing their current and potential skills and competencies with their market attractiveness and their individual goals. In a smaller sense the individual is an organization with a mission, vision, and plans. The largest difference between adding value as an organization and as an individual is one of scope.

An individual can be an entrepreneur where the primary customer is a defined marketplace or can be an employee or independent contractor where the primary customer is a specific organization. In either case, the VOC must be well understood and the individual must align with both the customer and suppliers. In the beginning stages, the key suppliers may be educational institutions, personal advisers and data sources such as job banks, newspapers, and on-line information.

In addition to specialized skills and knowledge, there are general areas that are emerging as having high value added characteristics. They include teamwork, communication, human relations, problem solving, data analysis, leadership, organization, and integration. In the Information Age, these will be required skills for all positions with high growth potential.

Organizations recognize the value of commitment and long-term relationships, and these will not disappear. Organizations are growth oriented, and will continue to seek individuals to help grow the organization. However, they will also look for ways to be more flexible and adaptable.

Another emerging trend is *outsourcing*, which, like *reengineering*, has numerous meanings and applications. In the more optimistic sense, outsourcing allows a much clearer focus on a core business by reducing distractions on less value added or support processes. This, in turn, creates opportunities for additional focus or specialization by the outsourcing organization. For example, having to constantly redefine and maintain a large information system may dilute an insurance company's attention on providing value to its customers. But outsourcing much of the systems work to a strategic partner organization whose sole purpose is to design, develop, and maintain world-class systems may permit both organizations to expend their maximum efforts toward what they do best.

In the long run, this offers greater opportunity, job fulfillment, and longer term employment to everyone. A person working for the systems outsourcing organization (assuming there is an excellent alignment and integration of processes), will be able to do more productive work with less inconvenience than that same person would be able to do by working with an organization whose mission has a different focus.

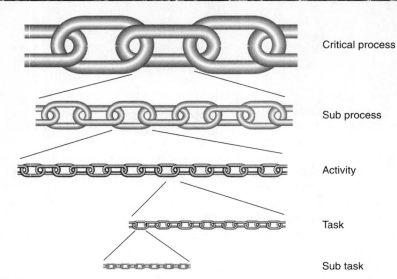

Figure 8.1   Processes can be viewed at a number of levels, from the most critical that is defined by a few major phases down to the sub task level and below.

Aligning People, Processes, and Jobs

All processes are defined by smaller processes that go essentially *ad infinitum* down to the nerve synapse level and below to the basic properties of atoms. In defining and studying jobs, processes are generally outlined down to the task or basic skill level. Listed here are a few definitions used to describe the various levels from critical processes to the sub task level. They are illustrated in Figure 8.1.

- A *process,* in an organizational environment, is a series of steps that transform a product or service from one state to a higher value-added state.
- A *key business process (or critical process)* is usually a cross functional collection of steps that utilizes a substantial amount of resources (people, energy, equipment, knowledge, materials, information) to add value to a product or service that is very important to customers.
- A *subprocess* is one of several (usually 3–8) major divisions of a key business process. Each is a logical collection of activities that, together, add up to the sub process. A subprocess may be the actual transformation steps of adding value or the support or monitoring of adding value.

- An *activity* is a logical collection of tasks that, together, form a system to transform, monitor, or support outputs to inputs at a level below subprocesses.
- A *task* is usually the lowest level that can be measured in the transformation of outputs to inputs.
- A *subtask* is any level below the task level and is usually stated in terms of steps, procedures, checklist items or application of knowledge or skill.

From a view at the top of the organization, the priority is to align processes with other processes to ensure that requirements are met and maximum value is provided to customers. As one descends to the working level, processes must be broken down into subprocesses, which are then delineated into activities, tasks, and perhaps even steps. The assignment of people to perform the activities, tasks and steps is the beginning of defining jobs.

Whether the organization is team based or traditionally organized, the alignment of people with processes must eventually answer the question, "Who does what, when, how, and to what performance level?" The first question that must be answered is the performance level, then the process can be designed and improved to meet that level. The *what, when,* and *how* are all answered by the process, and the *who* is answered in several ways. If people are currently assigned, they may be the *who;* if not, it is a matter of selecting the right skills and competencies to perform the requirements, or making the best out of current resources while others are found or existing ones are developed.

As people are assigned responsibilities, jobs are defined. Some individuals may have one primary function or a series of steps they are responsible to perform; others may have a large number of diverse results they are responsible to achieve. *A job is defined by the responsibilities a person has, as well as the performance level that is desired for each responsibility. In reality, jobs are not always aligned with processes; they are defined by a combination of those pieces of processes that a person is responsible to perform.*

A lack of alignment between jobs and processes leads to much confusion and frequently to important tasks being poorly performed or not completed. One of the largest challenges is priority and accountability. In many service operations including service support areas for manufacturing organizations, this fuzzy overlap between jobs and processes contributes heavily to a high cost of quality and less than desired results. Areas with a high supervisor/management turnover rate are very susceptible to high waste, since people are assigned jobs based on the confusion brought on by continual firefighting. When this spiral occurs there is little documentation of assignments. Priorities are disordered, and everyone turns to the supervisor for direction. The supervisor who can maintain some form of order is promoted and the spiral spins again. The way out of the spiral is to define and document the process; then, staff it with trained and qualified personnel who can work within the process to produce desired results and work together to improve it.

These elements can be assigned to people and become the building blocks of jobs. In some cases a job may be defined by one of the building blocks and in others a job may be defined as elements of several building blocks.

Processes are designed and built to meet predetermined objectives or specifications by connecting a level of input(s) with value adding resources to produce desired output(s). When processes are reduced down to the small activity, tasks and step levels, they generally involve people or people working with equipment or information processors. Just like the larger critical processes of the organization, these are also processes. They must be integrated and capable of improvement. They also utilize value-adding resources to transform inputs into higher value outputs. These variables can be tracked and measured.

JOB DESCRIPTIONS—THE PAST AND PRESENT

Traditionally, jobs have been defined by job descriptions. Job descriptions usually outline the formal reporting structure, the salary range, and the important duties and responsibilities of the job. The writing of job descriptions generally include the involvement with or endorsement by third parties such as human resource specialists, compensation experts, and work study personnel. These experts attempt to assure consistency, fairness, and independent review that perhaps a job incumbent or supervisor cannot provide.

The problem with the prevailing view of job descriptions is that they very seldom provide an accurate, up-to-date portrait of what a person does or needs to do on the job. At best, they represent an incomplete picture, at a point in the past, of what an incumbent did. Most job descriptions are too general and written to cover too long a period of time to offer much assistance in job performance. Unfortunately, they are usually the only formal documentation of a job or position.

JOB PROFILES—THE FUTURE

Every person needs an accurate, up-to-date representation of the job he or she is expected to perform. It cannot be merely a fuzzy or theoretical concept or a list of expectations and goals, nor can it be an inflexible and endless collection of checklists and manuals. A job profile should be approached from an *integrated leadership* perspective. It should have a mission, values, goals, and objectives, and possibly a vision that flow from and integrate into those of the unit and the larger organization. The final stage of the *catchball* approach to strategic and tactical deployment of an organization's plans must descend to the individual. Someone has to do the work, and the person who does the work must know what to do and how to do it.

Industrial Age thinking attempted to reduce jobs to a series of robotic and repetitive tasks. Operating and procedure manuals and job descriptions provided the necessary documentation to assure that the "one best way" was followed. This approach was tied into technology. Much time and effort were spent finding the one best way and a major objective was to extend its utility as long as possible. Operating manuals and catalogs of job descriptions were major undertakings that employed a large number of people. Changes were discouraged unless they had a high immediate return. Continuous improvement was not encouraged to the masses of employees. The support system could not keep up.

Information Age approaches are not encumbered by change. Today, one can change an on-line manual in real time with little effort. These changes can be immediately communicated, along with training when necessary, for quick implementation. Knowledgeable individuals who function as a team using a PDCA approach can validate and approve changes very quickly. An informed team is much quicker and makes better decisions than any form of bureaucracy in a hierarchical structure.

The ability to quickly validate and document improved systems and processes leads to monumental flexibility with jobs. In the mid-1980s, I was impressed with the wide diversity of skills and knowledge levels of the Japanese worker. It was driven by the constant rotation and movement of people throughout the line and support areas. A worker with some tenure had worked in an extensive spectrum of positions and had a "hands-on" view of the entire critical process as well as some of the supporting processes.

The benefits of a horizontally competent and experienced work force are obvious; not only does it provide depth, it offers flexibility and greatly reduces the cycle time of change. Additionally, it offers variety and great opportunity if an organization both understands the benefits and compensates individuals for their increasing value. An organization that places considerably higher value on vertical movement in a hierarchical structure will not improve at the level of an organization that knows how to motivate people and compensate them for their increasing knowledge and skills in delivering value to markets and customers.

Since a job can be defined by participation in and contribution to processes, and processes are documented and measured, jobs can be easily documented and measured. Consequently, the skills and knowledge levels for jobs can be assessed to define competency, people can be assessed against competency criteria, and necessary training and validation can occur.

A job profile is a collage of a limited number of assignments with purposes, objectives, and goals supported by process maps, flow charts, measures, descriptions, integration and communication points, skill and knowledge requirements, resource references, training material, and leadership assistance that are sufficient to understand the job. A job profile essentially eliminates the need for periodic performance review because performance feedback is ongoing.

JOBS IN TRANSITION

Many individuals complete their formal education and enter the work force in an entry-level position that hopefully matches their aspirations with their current skills and knowledge levels. Others take the first open position they can obtain. From there, most people balance their future hopes with available or perceived opportunities. The most desirable track has been up the vertical organization where each jump brings greater prestige and monetary rewards. The primary scorecard is based on these two factors.

What happens when the ball game changes? Many organizations are flattening their structure and downsizing their employee force and people are choosing to or having to accept less than they previously would. Are job opportunities diminishing? Unless there is an unforeseen global disaster, the answer has to be no. Competitive forces are driving this change. As the world moves from the Cold War to more democracies and freer trade, a shift must occur that will particularly impact organizations that had inherent competitive advantages before. Efficiencies and effectiveness must be improved for organizations to prosper.

The shifting of jobs is just beginning, and few organizations have given much attention to it other than through downsizing and layoffs. During the transition, jobs will be much more clearly defined through an expanding use of job profiles. The knowledge gained through this transformation will clearly show that managerial (not leadership) jobs of the Industrial Age have diminishing value in the Information Age.

In some respects, job characteristics will move back toward the days of the craft worker where an apprentice learned the job from a journeyman (or journeywoman) who assured all needed skills and knowledge were mastered before the person would be hired or paid as a competent worker. Tomorrow's apprentice will be nurtured by a team, or a very special coach/trainer, who assures that the necessary skills and knowledge are mastered.

Why will these changes happen? For the same reasons change is permeating the auto and high technology industries; a traditional organization cannot compete with a team-based, learning organization that integrates leadership and has a winning vision and a control panel to assure it accomplishes its goals.

THE SEARCH FOR OBJECTIVE MEASURES

A unit or team has performance goals. Collectively, these goals should be met or exceeded. These usually consist of goals based on production, quality, cycle time, deadlines, or implementation completion. Goals should be stated in a physical measurement where possible, not be a subjective assessment. For example, a goal of 100 percent satisfaction is certainly an admirable pursuit, and most managers would be delighted if their units satisfied their customers 100 percent of the time, but it is not the best way to state a goal.

There are five reasons why satisfaction alone is not the best measure. First, a customer can be satisfied with a product or service and still move to a competitor. Second, satisfaction is difficult to determine without asking the customer continuously, or after every transaction. Third, satisfaction can change quickly. Fourth, a response to a question on satisfaction depends to a large degree on how the question is worded and how much probing is included. Fifth, more objective and proactive measures can be used.

If we ask for satisfaction, we will find that it is usually based on subjective criteria. However, criteria that drive subjective assessment can be studied, prioritized, and understood. This is the principle behind VOC. The more the methodology that leads to satisfaction is understood, the more objective it becomes. As it becomes objective, it becomes measurable. Once it is measurable, objective goals can be set and stable processes can be built to deliver those measures that lead to satisfaction (or other subjective criteria).

For example, if we insist on customer satisfaction as the goal and we achieve it, we may assume we should not change things because our processes are meeting the requirements we set for them. However, we may ask ourselves, "What can we improve that will make our customers even more satisfied?" In order to answer that question, we should involve customers and make improvements in areas that will lead to more customer satisfaction. We quickly discover that each area that we want to improve is more objective than the broad area of customer satisfaction. In reality, we are pursuing more objective measures. Why not be more efficient and discover up front what drives satisfaction, how well we and competitors deliver in each area, and measure the most important ones? We can then continuously correlate these measures with satisfaction and adjust as required. We can build processes to meet requirements and measure the performance of systems and people in objective areas. It is more difficult in subjective areas where many variables are involved. The subjective areas must be pursued and clarified to understand what should be measured, but they are not as well suited for performance measurement as objective measures.

JOB METRICS

If you get what you measure, what are the important job measures? Individual performance measures are derived from the same metrics as the primary measures of the organization. These become the source of performance goals for the individual. Most individuals usually have two types of goals; one is based on performance and the other is based on competency. In reality, both focus on the same applied results, not just activity.

COMPETENCY

Competency is the ability to perform at a level that will lead to desired results. Many jobs demand a competency level that exceeds the normal skills and knowledge used on a typical work day. Many examples are found in safety issues, such as a police officer who is assigned to traffic duty. Most of the officer's job may be to ensure that a certain speed limit is followed or a certain area's parking requirements are enforced. At the same time, that officer must have high competency skills to deal with higher levels of crime and life-threatening emergencies and to prioritize the conflicting needs of citizens. Many of these skills may not be required during an extended assignment, but the potential for their application is continuous.

A large part of an airline crew's job is knowing how to react when there is an emergency. People working in customer support need to know how to deal with angry or threatening customers. High-profile executives must know how to handle media confrontation. Pumpers and roustabouts in the petrochemical industry need to know how to deal with potential and actual leaks and fires. Competency includes not just the ability, skills, and knowledge to perform a job, but the means of updating and continuously improving proficiency to perform under evolving circumstances, regulations, and safety concerns.

Competency cannot be taken for granted; it must be periodically assessed, developed, improved and measured through testing and observation. This is an ongoing role of the team, manager, or supervisor.

PERFORMANCE

Unit or team performance measures always come from above and from the customer. In many cases they are expressed in terms of standards, requirements, objectives, or goals. The top priority of a team or unit manager is to assure that the mission and unit objectives are met today and the means of meeting them will be available in the future. This requires a process to determine how work will be divided based on current and future competency needs.

Always in a team environment, and generally in a supervised unit, each member has three distinct roles: trainee, trainer, and producer. Those who are untrained and beginning their assignment are trainees; those who are competent train the trainees. Everyone engages in degrees of production.

Performance is a combination of meeting unit goals and assuring future capacity to meet future goals. A unit or team that barely meets today's goals by always working everyone on their single-best production area and waiting for tomorrow to take care of itself, is a failure. The leadership that allows that should receive failing marks. On the other hand, the unit that falls short of a single weekly goal, but is well poised for the future by rotating jobs and developing its personnel, is meeting its responsibility. The team that makes its goals, develops its personnel, and continually improves is a winner. It should be rewarded handsomely.

The organization that tracks only weekly production on its units' scorecards will not compete long with one that also looks ahead and has a control panel that assures competency as well as production and other measures of value.

Unit performance should be measured, reported, and compensated based on improving trends to deliver value measured through output and increasing capacity. Production, improvement, individual competency attainment, and results of training others should be the goals and performance measures of individuals. Only a competent team, a very special coach, or a hands-on, knowledgeable supervisor can assign duties, goals, and objectives, as well as assess performance at the level that is required. The traditional Industrial Age supervisor who spends days in management meetings and putting out fires is incapable of such an assignment—it has become impossible.

TRAINING

Recently, I was involved with a large organization in reviewing their training program. They had *benchmarked*, or compared their training process with, a few successful organizations and discovered that these organizations spent about 5 percent of their payroll costs on training. Unfortunately, in spite of a quite expensive undertaking, the organization failed to gather information on whether the 5 percent figure was based on gross or net payroll, whether the salary, benefits and support costs of people being trained were included in the costs of training, and how the costs of the various training departments were allocated.

In reality, these figures were superfluous anyway, because they used the wrong criteria and logic. There were strong opinions in the organization that if the training budget were increased to 5 percent of some figure, the organization would have its training in line with top-performing organization and be on its way to *world class* (which, by the way, was not defined either). In their endeavor to improve training, they offered a university-type array of classes that included innovation, communication, personal career management, process mapping, teamwork, and a variety of topics that emulated many of the courses offered by those organizations in the benchmark study. They touted their university, and many felt proud they had made quite an achievement. Unfortunately, performance had not improved and costs were high.

In addition to overlooking the actual costs associated with training, they failed to benchmark the systems and processes of the organizations that drive the training needs of the high performance organization. This is a classical failure of benchmarking, and why it generally is misused. The organization that brought me in to assist did not have a problem with training;

their current training was adequate for their current systems, poorly inte-grated process, and unfocused leadership. Training, no matter what amount was invested, could only help their performance to a limited extent, unless it was directed at senior management on ways to focus the organization and integrate systems to deliver higher value.

This is typically the case in an Industrial Age organization; they view training as a solution to something. Anytime someone says, "We need more training," "We have a training problem," or "We will perform as soon as we are trained," there is a lack of integration and focus. *Training is not a solution; competent people working in stable and value-producing processes is the solution.* Training is part of a means to gain competency, which assures performance. Competency is based on the needs of a system or process to meet targeted results. Training should always be used to help fill defined gaps between what is needed and what is currently being delivered. In many organiza-tions it is a high cost of poor quality.

Continuous learning is necessary in the Information Age because of the rate of change. Learning and training are not synonymous. In Industrial Age organizations, training is an event that people attend where they may or may not learn something that is useful. Unless jobs are defined using a job profile or similar approach, and they have a high degree of measurability using competency and performance, it is impossible to correlate training with learning and, ultimately, performance. If it cannot be correlated, then valueless measures such as dollars spent, time in training, number of courses completed and number of course offered are the only means of quantification. They give the illusion that something is being done because it is measured even if they are the wrong measures.

CONNECTING CONTROL PANELS

Every individual, every unit, and every division of an organization needs a control panel to maintain focus, gather and understand data, and assess progress along planned paths on the way to attainment of goals and visions. The control panel of a single individual is relatively simple com-pared to the control panel of a global organization but the basic principles are identical.

To some degree, the organizational control panel is a consolidation of the lower-level control panels, and the lower-level control panels are based on the direction received from the top of the organization. This allows redun-dancy for backup purposes and the need to spread information, knowledge, and wisdom across the organization. However, avoid unnecessary duplica-tion of effort and that communication of information is directed on a tar-geted "need to know basis." Different levels of every organization need dif-ferent information in different formats. Top management's needs are more than a summary of lower-level needs, and lower levels do not need a more detailed version of senior management's requirements.

The Industrial Age organization's primary means of communication is the staff meeting, supplemented by bulletins and memos (whether printed on paper or delivered via electronic distribution), and its primary method of integration is financial measurement. At the highest levels of the large organizations, staff meetings are called board meetings, executive committee meetings, and endless other terms. When decisions are made or edicts are issued at these meetings, those involved are expected to return to their areas of responsibility and carry out their part and communicate appropriately with their direct subordinates. This method cascades down through the organization as each level receives their interpretation and communicates to their sphere of influence.

In the Information Age, the amount of observed data is immense and growing at exponential rates. Those at the front lines of the organization working directly with customers, continuously observing competitors and connecting with external suppliers see endless data points. Those functions that support them are challenged by the same barrage of data. Communication and decisions must be made much more efficiently than the staff meeting mentality allows. Communication must be distributed and received through interconnected control panels, and many more decisions must be made through automated processes.

At some point in history, the leaders of the earliest organizations probably based decisions on direct observation of all data points. In the future, decisions will be based on the collective wisdom generated from billions and trillions of data points. Although the processing systems to convert data to information, knowledge and perhaps even wisdom will continue to improve at unimaginable rates, it may be a lengthy period before they evolve to the point where they become the sole decision maker. In the meanwhile, the organizational control panel will be the processor of the aggregated data and information that is synthesized at the lower ends of the organization, combined with those collected from outside sources and the accumulated wisdom of organizational leadership.

KEY POINTS YOU GET WHAT YOU MEASURE

- The human system is an inherent part of organizational processes and must have competent leadership in order to optimize performance.
- Most performance evaluation systems do not objectively assess performance results against clear, appropriate, and understood objectives.

- The right measures for the human systems should have as their base the attainment of the foundation goals of the organization; these should all be integrated to avoid conflict and assure compatibility.
- A job should be very clearly defined, measured, aligned, and assessed as a subcomponent of value adding or support processes.
- A job is independent of employment status; it profiles what needs to be done.
- Every individual should have a job profile that clearly communicates everything that is needed to work at a competent level.
- Skill and knowledge gaps should continuously be identified and training should be ongoing to assure competency and performance that meet goals and objectives.

NOTES

1. Price Pritchett, *The Employee Handbook of New Work Habits For A Radically Changing World: 13 Ground Rules for Job Success in the Information Age* (Dallas: Pritchett & Associates, Inc., 1994).

2. See Deming's *Out of the Crisis*, cited in chapters 1, 2, and 3 (the 14 points and deadly sins). It provides many of Deming's concerns with the overall approach, as well as measures and evaluations. His red bead experiment shows clearly how variation impacts performance.

3. Frederick Taylor died in 1915 before Walter Shewhart showed that productivity improves as variation is reduced.

4. Refer to Michael Hammer and James Champy, *Reengineering the Corporation: A Manifesto for Business Revolution* (New York: Harper Business, 1993), pp. 31–36, for the original definition of reengineering. The authors provide an excellent methodology to approach designing and defining jobs, from improved higher value-producing processes. However, their ideas are often not practiced as many organizations label every reorganization as reengineering. In most cases, reorganizations are based on pressures to reduce costs without much thought given to process improvement or the "what you get" side of value.

Chapter 9

CONTROL PANEL THROUGH INTEGRATING METRICS

> . . . *throughout history, soldiers, sailors, Marines,*
> *and airmen have learned one extremely valuable*
> *lesson relative to engagement with an opposing force.*
> *That is, if you can analyze, act and access faster than*
> *your opponent—you will win.*
>
> GENERAL RONALD R. FOGELMAN,
> U.S. AIR FORCE CHIEF OF STAFF[1]

As far as producing long-term performance, there is no substitute for leadership; it is everything. Great leadership is on a continual quest for wisdom and knowledge, which are the greatest of the leadership tools. The more diverse, the more widespread, the more accurate, the more creative, and the more profound the sources that lead to wisdom, the greater the potential for performance.

A common theme throughout this book is that there is no "one right way." The same is true for a system to assist in bringing knowledge and wisdom to leaders. We are only at the entrance to the Information Age. We are at a primitive state, perhaps analogous to where Johann Gutenberg was in 1456 in Mainz when he first produced the Bible using movable type; or, Ben Franklin, in 1751, when he experimented with electricity; or George Boole, around 1850, when he was formulating his thoughts on symbolic logic, which later formed the basis of the modern computer.

In any event, we are clearly moving into the Information Age. The day will come when we have billions of times more data and information than we have today, and we will have the computer systems to process it. By that point, will we have the integrated human systems to optimize it and create the wealth that it offers all humankind, or will we be overwhelmed by its immensity and clog up the decision processes that are necessary to gain its productive potential?

To a large degree, the answer depends on how we design tomorrow's control panels.

THE BIG QUESTION IS WHAT

For most of human history, where to expend one's energy was a fairly simple decision. The majority was spent on gathering food or other activities directly related to sustaining life. This included taking from others or defending from others through individual and organized means, including war. The most common analogy in economical terms is the balance between guns and butter, where a society must choose the mix because of the doctrine of scarcity of resources.

The issues facing civilized society today are many times more complex. The choices are much more interwoven. For example, as a society, we can improve life expectancy by choosing healthier lifestyles, medical care, and education, and by restricting factors that tend to decrease longevity. If we make a collective decision to increase our average longevity, we also have to modify other factors to accommodate the change, such as retirement funding, health care delivery, and hundreds of smaller issues.

There are very few isolated decisions in the Information Age. As control panels connect, a mutual dependency is created. The higher-level control panels provide their guidance to lower-level panels, which then consolidate at the higher levels to provide the greater wisdom and help guide the decision-making process. This bidirectional cascading of direction and information can be used up and down connected control panels ranging from a small, single business to a national, or international government.[2]

The primary purpose of the organizational control panel is to provide wisdom to continually improve the answer to the question, "*What* does the organization need to do to achieve its vision and mission?," or, perhaps, better stated, "*What* is the best thing to do or course to take?" The panel helps improve performance and solve problems, but those are secondary to the selection of a course of action. In other words, a control panel first and most importantly helps find the right thing, then assists in doing the *right thing, the right way.*

THE BASIS OF CURRENT CONTROL PANELS

All organizational control panels today are derived from the Industrial Age. The Information Age control panels have not been designed. The most common control panel used throughout the world by most organizations continues to be based almost exclusively on financial measures and ratios.

We can begin by looking at a fairly common goal of financial management.

The goal of financial management is to maximize the value of the firm as measured by the price of its stock.[3]

At first glance, this looks like an excellent definition. As a shareholder, I definitely want a chief financial officer and a management team that maximizes the price of the stock, at least on the day that I am going to sell. The problem with the goal of financial management is that it tends to equate value with price. In a free enterprise system where everyone has equal access to the information needed to assess value, this makes sense. However, these conditions do not remotely exist at this early stage in the Information Age.

Today, even the largest organizations experience huge stock price fluctuations over the course of a year or even shorter periods. Prices are driven minute-by-minute by quarterly earnings, economic conditions, political moves, interest rates, news, and a variety of factors that may or may not affect real value. Organizations can dilute the value of outstanding shares by issuing more shares, or they can accelerate or postpone earnings. Most importantly, all stakeholders of an organization are not equal, either in voice or in their access to information.

Most organizations do not have publicly traded stock, and all suborganizations (divisions, departments, units, teams) of large organizations cannot be accurately measured by the price of stock. Most of our control panels are based on financial measures, yet our best defined barometer of financial management does not apply to most organizations. Financial measures will continue to be an important metric of the control panel of the future, but they will not have the exclusivity that they had during the Industrial Age.

MOVING TOWARD TOMORROW'S CONTROL PANEL

All organizations use nonfinancial metrics to supplement and help predict financial measures. Many elevate these to higher status by reporting them at management and board meetings. Rarely are nonfinancial measures reported, however, to investors or even communicated through annual reports or news releases.

The financial measures reported are almost always historical.[4] Historical financial results can have a lag time of months and even years. In the linear world of the Industrial Age, historical trends are fair predictors of the future. They could be compared to driving through the desert on a straight road in excellent conditions. In the Information Age, relying on past trends may be more analogous to driving down a mountain road at night in a driving rainstorm with the headlights out, looking only through the rear view mirror.

Ten years ago, I worked with a team of quality and marketing personnel who found high correlation between current customer satisfaction levels and future profitability (several months lag time) at the small branch level. Later, in some research in the United Kingdom, we learned that we could predict loyalty to a large degree of accuracy by measuring the top-end level of satisfaction. We also found strong positive correlation between supplier, customer, and employee satisfaction.

This research led to the pursuit of what drives satisfaction. Seeking this route took us squarely into the voice of the customer. The VOC was much easier to understand in the Industrial Age than it will be in the Information Age. Tomorrow's control panel will readily see the close connection between the clarity of the VOC, value added to all stakeholders, and its impact on financial results.

A FEW EXAMPLES OF CHANGING CONTROL PANELS

Many of the progressive organizations that are experimenting with prototypes of Information Age control panels are reluctant to share the knowledge they have gained and the continuing strategy they are pursuing in better understanding the vast and interconnected variables that drive and influence their performance in a fast-paced world.

I have been fortunate to work with several organizations in the design and preliminary development of their control panels and have observed several others from both first hand and observer perspectives. Since control panels are always at a *work in progress* status, there are no common models yet established that are available for study and copy. Since every organization is unique with different vision, goals and strategies, and unmatched talent, every control panel will be distinct, but their purpose, linkages, and application will have common elements.

AT&T UNIVERSAL CARD SERVICES (UCS)[5]

One of the most successful applications of a control panel that has been communicated is the data and tracking system developed and used by AT&T Universal Card Services (UCS) at the time of its winning a 1992 Malcolm Baldrige National Quality Award. UCS had the good fortune, and the challenge, to build a metric system from the ground level up as it launched its business in early 1990. By 1992, UCS had grown from no customers to more than 16 million, which increased to more than 22 million by 1995.

UCS based its mission on the values of *"customer delight, continuous improvement, sense of urgency, commitment, trust and integrity, mutual respect and teamwork"*[6] by providing customer centered service. The process model they incorporated was called PDMI, for Plan, Do, Measure, Improve. They early on believed the key to the focus of improvement is the continuous flow through of new information.

In addition to numerous key measures of operational data, UCS established *listening posts* to observe data and opinion flow that was fed continuously and reported monthly to the executive team. This data led to eight key attributes, or *satisfiers* (which were divided into 79+ subattributes), of what customers say they want. This process offered the beginnings of an ongoing voice of the customer. This data, as well as other information, was gathered from 3,000 phone calls per month made by UCS to customers.

UCS also measured 108 quality indicators on a daily basis. These factors were used to generate "ten most wanted" quality improvement lists for each part of the organization from the entire UCS down to each individual unit. In addition to focused and measurable improvement, this system facilitated a suggestion program that provided 30 times the rate of the industry average.

The values of employees, customers, and improvement were reduced to measurable indices and separate measures that assure all moved toward goals, and there was no doubt in expectations and performance levels. Employee satisfaction, turnover, training received, and rewards and recognition were a few of the measures that were continuously tracked in addition to production levels.

UCS had a well structured and communicated strategic plan that was based on a mission, vision, values, and goals as well as a control panel that measured and continually generated information and knowledge to the organization. This system of metrics contributed highly to UCS's high growth, profitability and customer satisfaction.

FEDERAL EXPRESS

The foundation for the emerging control panel for Federal Express can best be understood by some of their own quotes.

> We believe that if we place our People first, they, in turn, will deliver the impeccable Service demanded by our customers. Profit will follow.[7]

> FedEx means more than just delivering packages. Our delivery commitment to our customers is 100% satisfaction, 100% of the time.[8]

> One thing FedEx has learned in 23 years as the express distribution leader: Customers don't necessarily care how a shipment gets where it's going, they just care that it does, quickly, on time and with full information availability.[9]

Federal Express sets a high standard of satisfaction and continually measures its performance against its employees' and customers' requirements. It sets an expectation with its customer that a package will be delivered at the destination by a specified time and day. FedEx uses a Service Quality Index (SQI) to measure its worldwide performance on a daily basis and its scores are posted every morning to all employees via electronic means.

The various components on the SQI may evolve as customers change but they clearly focus on what is currently important to customers in priority order. For example, a lost or damaged package may be weighted ten times as severely as a delivery that is an hour late, or twice that of a package that is a day late. The index may vary in the number and weighting of measures, depending on the current voice of the customer and the emphasis of FedEx in improving each.

A recent FedEx annual report[10] hints at a number of metrics that are important to the organization. It does not require much imagination to link many of these factors to financial results and increased value added and wealth creation if an organization focuses on the customer and continually measures the impact of operating cost reductions and quality of internal processes on overall efficiency and effectiveness.[11]

- The world's air cargo market will grow at a compounded rate of nearly 7 percent and the international express segment at 18 percent over the next 20 years.[12]
- FedEx links 211 countries and territories, which represent 99 percent of the world's gross domestic product; 90 percent of the world's GDP are linked by next-business-day or two-business-day service.[13]
- In Fiscal Year 1996:[14]
  ⇒ *Express Package* has average daily package volume of 2,437,662, with average pounds per package of 6.4
  ⇒ *Airfreight* has average daily pounds of 2,144,225
  ⇒ *Operating weekdays*—256
  ⇒ *Aircraft fleet*—557
  ⇒ *Vehicle fleet*—36,900
  ⇒ *Average number of full-time employees*—99,999
- Reduction in number of long-haul trucking contractors used from 80 to 9.[15]
- Number of Web site visits: 1,400,000 million per month; number of self-generated tracking requests through Web site: 360,000; number of customers using FedEx's shipping automation tools: 350,000; number of daily electronic transmissions: 45,000,000.[16]
- Number of drop box locations: 34,700; retail outlets: 7,000; world service centers: 1,400.[17]
- Number of Zip Codes served by *FedEx International First* (customs-cleared, door-to-door delivery from foreign countries and Puerto Rico by 8 a.m.): Over 5,000; Number of countries served: 17.[18]

UTILITY COMPANY

As an organization moves from a monopoly into a less regulated environment where it encounters direct competition for the first time, it must adjust its control panel to navigate some choppy waters. In the highly regulated environment, a major customer and one whose requirements had to be met was the regulatory governmental agency. The largest sale usually was the justification of higher expenses to pay for increasing costs and past decisions.

In the competitive environment, many additional customers' needs must be met, and they can be both diverse and demanding. Prior to beginning adjustments for deregulation, the organization's control panel primarily consisted of financial and energy-related measures, as well as overall customer satisfaction, by broad segmentation.

At the end of a year of gathering data and benchmarking organizations both in and outside of the utility industry, a project team of internal management selected the following metrics in addition to key financial measures to become the nucleus of an executive control panel.

- *Customer Loyalty*—defined as the percent a customer spends with the utility provider compared with the total amount they spend on all energy and energy type products that the provider supplies directly or through a strategic partner.
- *Customer Retention*—defined as the number of customers (and the revenue represented) remaining with the provider throughout a period of time.
- *Customer Complaints*—displayed by source, major cause, and trends shown in Pareto charts.
- *Customer Index*—initially, a study to determine a blended weighted average of satisfaction, loyalty, retention, market share change, and complaint metrics that best indicate a measurement of the organization's understanding of voice of the customer.
- *Perceived Customer Value and Actual Customer Value*—these are explained in chapter 3.
- *Relative Market Share*—the amount of market share the provider has in relation to other competitors in chosen market segments as measured by revenues, BTUs, and number of customers.
- *Process Productivity*—An overall performance is indexed using a weighted scale based on criticality of processes (Most of these measures are based on cycle times, defect rates, deadline compliance and production.)
- *Won–Lost Report*—similar to the format proposed in chapter 5; also includes a "Won-Lost Graph" by competitor and a Pareto analysis showing the reasons for loss.
- *Employee Satisfaction*—initially, this would be surveyed information to assist in determining correlated measures for satisfaction. Later, more leading measures will be developed and indexed.
- *Alignment Index*—the Alignment Index measures performance results against high level goals, while providing metrics that indicate the organization's movement toward its vision and its adherence to values.

NONPROFIT SECTOR—JOINT VENTURE:
SILICON VALLEY NETWORK

An example of a control panel from a nonprofit organization comes from the San Jose, California, area.

Joint Venture is a dynamic new model of regional rejuvenation. Our vision is to build a community collaborating to compete globally. We bring people together from business, government, education and the community to act on regional issues affecting economic vitality and quality of life.[19]

Silicon Valley is defined as an area south of San Francisco, including all of Santa Clara County and parts of San Mateo, Alameda, and Santa Cruz counties. Its population exceeds 2 million people. Although the vision began just over three years ago, it provides an excellent study of integrated leadership and a changing control panel concept. It also goes well beyond a single organization and demonstrates the need for strategic partnering among diverse organizations in order to effectively improve some of the root causes that drive long-term community and social environments.

The indicators on their control panel evolve and improve as more knowledge is gained. They are based on the following criteria:

- They are bellwethers that reflect fundamentals of long-term community health.
- They can be understood and accepted by the community.
- They have interest and appeal for the media.
- They are statistically measurable on a frequent basis.[20]

Listed here are some indicators on the most recent control panel, most of which are supplemented by additional measures:

Economic Indicators

- Job Quantity
  - ⇒ Gains/losses
  - ⇒ Gains/losses by employment cluster
  - ⇒ Growth rate of single employee businesses
- Job Quality
  - ⇒ Identified segment growth by job category (software)
  - ⇒ Average real wages
  - ⇒ Average wages by industry cluster
  - ⇒ Movement of women and minorities toward high-end occupations
- Business Vitality
  - ⇒ Exports sales from key zip codes
  - ⇒ Value added per worker
  - ⇒ Venture capital investment levels
  - ⇒ Number of initial public offerings (IPOs)
  - ⇒ Percent of revenue spent on research and development (R & D)

⇒   Commercial vacancy rates
⇒   Business confidence

Quality-of-Life Indicators

- Education
  ⇒   High school dropout rate
  ⇒   Student mastery level of basic skills
  ⇒   Percentage of schools connected to the Internet
- Environment
  ⇒   Number of days air exceeds ozone standards
  ⇒   Weight of toxic chemical releases
  ⇒   Tons of solid waste disposed
  ⇒   Housing affordability index
- Infrastructure
  ⇒   Average daily vehicle hours of delays on freeways
  ⇒   Public transit ridership
  ⇒   Per capita income versus per capita giving
- Children and Youth
  ⇒   Percent of low-birth weight infants
  ⇒   Number of children and seniors living in poverty
  ⇒   Child support payment rate
  ⇒   Youth crime/overall crime

As Silicon Valley's control panel continues to mature and provide increasingly meaningful metrics, there is no doubt the area will become an even greater global competitive force.

SOFTWARE

A small company who had pioneered much of the technology and the linking of processes among providers (primarily hospitals) and third-party payers (primarily insurance companies, government and self-insured employers) for paperless claims processing in the healthcare industry faced huge growth challenges in the early 1990s. Their greatest value-added product is the creation and maintenance of electronic criteria used to format payment decisions to providers on behalf of users or recipients of medical services. These claims must be paid in compliance with the many regulations and laws of federal and state regulators.

The system connected hundreds of billing systems at hospitals located around the country with a central clearing house that was additionally linked with more than 100 payers. Software must be constantly updated and loaded on all these systems in order to maintain accuracy and integrity.

In addition to growth in this core business, the firm's strategic plans called for expansion in new areas and acquisitions of related businesses. Shown in the illustration in Figure 9.1 are the major indicators on the executive team's control panel.

Executive Control Panel: Vision, Critical Success Factor Categories and Indicators

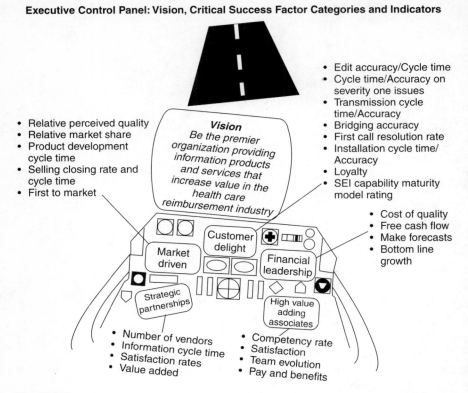

- Relative perceived quality
- Relative market share
- Product development cycle time
- Selling closing rate and cycle time
- First to market

Vision
Be the premier organization providing information products and services that increase value in the health care reimbursement industry

- Edit accuracy/Cycle time
- Cycle time/Accuracy on severity one issues
- Transmission cycle time/Accuracy
- Bridging accuracy
- First call resolution rate
- Installation cycle time/ Accuracy
- Loyalty
- SEI capability maturity model rating

- Cost of quality
- Free cash flow
- Make forecasts
- Bottom line growth

Market driven

Customer delight

Financial leadership

Strategic partnerships

High value adding associates

- Number of vendors
- Information cycle time
- Satisfaction rates
- Value added

- Competency rate
- Satisfaction
- Team evolution
- Pay and benefits

Figure 9.1 A software firm's control panel is based on 25 indicators falling under five critical success factor categories.

One of the unique indicators on the software organization's control panel is the SEI CMM rating. This is a five-level rating system developed by the Software Engineering Institute (SEI) "to provide a framework for software development organizations to achieve continuous improvement of their development processes in a controlled and predictable manner."[21] Many control panels contain difficult and hard-to-attain standards that attest to a high level of quality, stable processes, or indicators of productivity. Other examples are industry certifications, ISO (International Organization for Standardization) 9000 series, the Malcolm Baldrige National Quality Award, and other high-level recognition for excellence achievement.

MILITARY

The military–industrial complex, even after the dramatic shifting of its mission after the demise of the Cold War, is still the largest organized force on the globe. It is clearly a traditional hierarchy but it is quickly moving toward alternative forms. The military probably have the most developed control panels and the most sophisticated and linked network of sensors yet devised.

From the dawn of recorded history through the American Civil War (1860–1865) military command and control (C2)[22] on the battlefield centered around a commander personally observing (and often participating in) the battle and being linked with fighting troops through a network of runners and signals following a designated chain of command. With the advent of satellites, less than 100 years after the Civil War, it became possible for the commander-in-chief, president of the United States, to communicate live with a platoon leader engaged in a firefight in Vietnam.[23]

After the Vietnam War, all the branches of the armed forces fell under a standardized command, control, and communications system (C3) initially called the World Wide Military Command and Control System (WWMCCS).[24] By the early 1990s standardization of C3 needs extended to include coalition multinational forces that will be used increasingly to deal with international conflict such as the Persian Gulf War. The responsibility for the enhanced role falls on the Global Command and Control System (GCCS) whose mission is:

> The Global Command and Control System is an automated information system designed to support deliberate and crisis planning with the use of an integrated set of analytical tools and the flexible data transfer capabilities. GCCS will become the single C4I (command, control, communications, computers and intelligence) system to support the warfighter from foxhole to command post.[25]

The military is beginning to connect and research other opportunities to bring additional networked systems into the GCCS system. Some of those opportunities mentioned by Emmett Paige Jr., assistant secretary of defense for Command, Control, Communications and Intelligence, in prepared text at the Armed Forces Staff College, on July 30, 1996, in Norfolk, Virginia, include:[26]

- Defense Information System Agency (DISA)
- Advanced Research Projects Agency
- Defense Airborne Reconnaissance Office
- National Reconnaissance Office
- National Security Agency
- Central Imagery Office

During the above speech, Mr. Paige outlined an important breakthrough in the procurement of innovation by the military in its systems:

> Industry can be a critical resource by taking advantage of the new procurement atmosphere emerging in DoD (Department of Defense). Capitalizing on the rapid advances emerging from the commercial sector, service acquisition entities are seeking to introduce off-the-shelf innovations into their communications command and control arenas. The DoD has given its blessing by

encouraging the use of commercial technologies instead of systems built to strict military specifications. This thrust to go commercial owes as much to technological advances as it does to budgetary limitations.[27]

This comment reflects the painful lesson large businesses learned during the last decade, that systems that meet local needs such as stand alone personal computers not only provide high value added solutions at that level but they can be connected to larger systems for even higher value adding potential. As part of a vast network, they not only can receive and use data from other systems but they can also serve as sensors and data points for the host and other connected systems.

During the Cold War, America invested a high percentage of its resources into the military and defense related activity such as the space program. The military had the funds and could attract the talent to remain at the forefront of technology. The dawn of the Information Age is vastly changing the formula. The rate of information exchange prohibits long lead times in most areas of technology, and the commercial value of information and innovative technology competes with the missions of defense.

The reader is encouraged to pursue information available on the Internet regarding the rapid evolution of the C4I movement in the military. Its value is not so much in the solutions it offers as the issues it raises that apply strongly to both commercial and private organizations.

The military has one huge advantage over the nonmilitary sector in the development and evolution of control panels—it has focused on them longer and with more zeal. Most private organizations and even many aspects of government have been content with a financial control panel as its chief set of metrics. Although the military had to have a keen awareness of and attention to financial measures, the mission always came first. The military will continue to utilize existing knowledge and new concepts to excel in its mission just as many other organizations will excel in theirs. The difference will be more sharing of information, more strategic partnerships to pursue those large breakthroughs that are beyond the limits of one organization and the continual benefits of improved technology in cycle time reductions and information processing and interchange.

CONTROL PANEL CONCEPTS

A control panel is mission- and vision-based. The vision should be set for a definite period of time, and the mission should incorporate a means of perpetuation.

PLANNING

Most organizations realize as they near the Information Age that a traditional approach to long-term strategic planning is no longer adequate to deal with the speed and complexity they encounter. Senior management can no longer take a few days away to meet at a remote site and guess what changes will occur and how they can use them to a strategic advantage. They know that within a few days after their return, some new opportunity or insight will change the basis of their latest plans.

Strategic planning of the future will revolve around a control panel, and it will be a continuous or frequently managed process. Scheduling planning around a certain date each year will be obsolete. Organizations may set aside time for reflection on their values, mission, and vision and there will be time for celebration or reaction to change, but planning will become an ongoing function.

UNIQUENESS

Every control panel must be as unique as every organization, because the control panel is the ultimate statement of the organization. The control panel is used to gather and analyze the information that the organization uses to make decisions and deploy resources. It, therefore, reflects the values and priorities of the organization.

The control panel is as old as the concept of organizations and has always existed. For much of civilization, it has been mostly in the mind of one, or a small number of individuals. Since the purpose of a control panel is to create the evolved knowledge necessary to lead an organization to its vision, it must bring together the consolidated efforts and creativity of a number of minds.

SENSOR BASED

Only with the advent of sophisticated and remote sensors connected to highly efficient electronic computers has the control panel begun to strongly augment human judgment, which has been based on our five primary types of sensors since our beginning. We have used remote natural and intelligently created mechanical sensors for millenniums, ranging from tracking food sources to understanding the changing seasons to flying aircraft. However, when sensors themselves are data processors and their output becomes input to even larger data processors, and so on, the human mind needs help.

No control panel can be better than the information it receives. It receives information from sensors that may take many forms, ranging from external data bases to manually observed data. Sensors must be placed in strategic locations that cover the informational needs of senior management to oversee the operation of the organization. They must be reliable, they must be accurate, they must be representative, and they should be designed to evolve and adapt. Additionally, in some systems, they should have a high degree of redundancy and distribution.

CONTINUOUS CORRELATION, STATISTICAL PROCESS CONTROL, AND USE OF ADVANCED ANALYSIS TECHNIQUES

Subject to the principles of statistics, any set of data can be mathematically compared to another set to determine how much of their variation is explained by the strength of their linear relationship and how much is attributed to chance. The relationship is generally expressed as a "coefficient of correlation," usually expressed by the letter r, which ranges between +1 and –1. The higher the positive value, the higher the direct relationship; the lower the negative value, the higher the inverse relationship.

For example, if two sets of data return a coefficient of correlation, r equal to –0.9, the degree of relationship is calculated by squaring the coefficient of correlation; r^2 equals 0.81. In this case, the linear relationship between the two sets of data can be said to be explained 81 percent ($100r^2$) by their relationship and 19 percent by chance. Since the coefficient of correlation is negative, the relationship is inverse, so as one variable increases, the other decreases.

There are a couple of extremely important warning signs when using correlation analysis in addition to statistical sampling and confidence levels.

First, it is often overlooked that r measures only the strength of linear relationships; second, a strong correlation does not necessarily imply a cause–effect relationship.[28]

There is every reason to suspect that many future relationships will not be linear and that future leaders will need to investigate and measure the relationships among all their measures. The important point is to recognize interrelationships and the information they provide.

In spite of caution, continuous correlation analysis among control panel indicators and their supporting data is one of the most powerful metrics on a control panel. If one begins with a theoretical assumption that everything that takes place in an organization relates to the ultimate performance of the organization (however it is measured); then there are unlimited opportunities for correlation analysis. However, the principle of Pareto begins the search for the most likely or highest correlated factors; then, as these are uncovered, they should be correlated with their drivers, and so on.

Other factors that highly influence correlation readings are lag times, conflicting variables, and what is measured. With time and commitment these can be understood and their influence adjusted. As stated earlier, I was involved in a study to help determine some of the key predictors of profitability at the branch level of a large financial institution. We looked at a number of factors, one of which was customer satisfaction. Initially, we saw a medium-level coefficient of correlation of about 0.55. However, when we adjusted the data with about a five month lag, the coefficient rose significantly. Further research revealed that the largest increase in positive correlation could be attributed to branches where the branch manager was appointed within the previous two years. In branches where the manager was tenured for three years or more, satisfaction strongly correlated with profitability (with or without a lag); in branches where the manager was appointed for less than three years, correlation among satisfaction and profitability increased with tenure.

These control panel indicators led to other studies and the addition of other indicators such as demographic factors, training and education, branch composition, and the influence of the organizational structure above the branch manager level. In the short term, correlation can be misleading, misunderstood, and greatly misused. However, in the long term, with persistent and consistent application, many sins and errors are reduced and great knowledge can be revealed. Correlation, properly used, is probably the most valuable tool of a control panel.

Eventually, the use of correlation will be deluged by evolving artificial intelligence (AI), expert systems, or knowledge-based systems that use statistics, logic, data, and a knowledge base to make decisions and provide recommendations. As both the development and use of control panels progress with improved AI techniques, a new era of automatic integration will emerge. This may be the management breakthrough of some distant era.

All control panel indicators that measure process output such as production, quality, and value, should be shown, or have the capability of being displayed on run charts using statistical process control (SPC) methodology. SPC offers the capability to distinguish natural variation from excessive variation, or "out of control" indications. This allows the leader to avoid tampering with areas that may initially appear abnormal but fall under the natural variation of processes that are in control. SPC is an extremely valuable tool, and its principles should be built into control panel design and understood by all leaders.[29]

An organization that pioneers these techniques into its control panels for study and discussion purposes while it learns may have a huge advantage over those who wait.

FREQUENT USE

Some indicators of a control panel should be continuously displayed and used daily to lead the organization. Others should be displayed on demand and most should feature "drill down" or "zoom in" capability. The ability to pull in both internal and external data and information should be a feature of every control panel.

A team leader or a person whose function is to oversee operations may spend a substantial part of the job on a control panel. Senior management's time working with a control panel will vary, depending on situational needs, their involvement in firefighting, their personal work habits, their management style, their comfort with computers and progress into the Information Age, their industry, and their organization's priorities.

As the Information Age progresses, use of the control panel in assisting decisions at all levels will increase. Future leaders will be so well indoctrinated in both the technology and its applications that they will never stray far from their control panel. The day will come when basic leadership without the assistance of a control panel may be taught only as a backup under extreme emergency conditions.

In the meantime, many of today's leaders must make the transition from a dependency on specialized staff to the honing of leadership skills needed to coordinate and facilitate information and decision processes with a team. Although a small percentage of leaders have made the transition, most have a long trip ahead. Tomorrow's leaders will not have the luxury of time to appoint committees and bring in specialists on routine decisions. They must understand the multidimensions of integrated information and quickly work with team dynamics to make decisions.

Major leaps forward can be made by setting up an interactive control panel and beginning to use it with the leadership team to create the disciplines and knowledge needed to transition to the future. Initially, a control panel may be used in parallel with traditional methods, but soon its benefits will become apparent.

CONTROL PANEL ISSUES

Often, there are many technical and cost-related issues involved in the building and evolution of control panels. In a traditional Industrial Age organization these issues may evoke tremendous emotion and result in turf battles that are settled only with the use of power. For many organizations, this is the natural price of change.

Other organizations find relatively simple solutions with little emotional pain. The chief benefit of designing and building information control panels is survival and likely prosperity in the Information Age. The highest cost associated with control panels is their delay or postponement where the ultimate cost is organizational failure.

TEAMWORK AND VISION

Control panels are not built by going to users and accumulating a list of needs or future "wish lists." They are not built by technicians with the latest grasp on technology or by financial gurus with new methods of tracing costs. They are built by a cross-functional team of many disciplines with a full understanding and appreciation of the dynamics that impact and drive the organization's vision. These dynamics include value metrics, the emerging voice of the customer, the value-adding characteristics of current and improving processes, and the mind of the integrated leader.

CENTRALIZATION VERSUS DECENTRALIZATION

As organizations evolve cascading visions, missions, plans, and metrics and staff their ranks with competent integrated leaders, they move toward increasing decentralization. They become a distributed network composed of distributed networks, where each element is separate but linked electronically. If the organization becomes vulnerable in an area, the other parts of the organization immediately know and can either support or assist in overcoming the problem. As one part recognizes great opportunity, the other parts can adjust or immediately communicate concerns or even higher value alternative courses.

Under distributed systems more data are collected and used by more diverse functions. This leads to greater understanding through more solid documentation and sharing of lessons learned and the minimization of duplicated efforts.

Decentralization is an evolutionary concept, and not one that can be merely proclaimed by an Industrial Age leader. An organization must start with its current structure and engineer the architecture that will allow greater distribution. This approach is well beyond the current application of reengineering, since it blends many more dimensions than linear processes.

SECURITY

This issue is well beyond the scope of much comment in this book. The real question is how does Organization A minimize Organization B's (or Individual B's) ability to achieve strategic advantage over A or create loss to A through the acquisition of knowledge or information from A? This issue continually faces the military as their command and control centers become much more essential and valuable. The reader is advised to pursue this issue through partnership networks with the military, such as those offered on the Internet.

The future will undoubtedly provide solutions beyond current thinking. However, in the meantime, as organizations become flatter and eliminate the need for middle managers as decision makers by pushing decisions to lower levels, knowledge is more dispersed and more difficult to obtain. As more neural type networks form, the ability to capture and duplicate knowledge may become even more difficult.

EXTERNAL VERSUS INTERNAL KNOWLEDGE

Today, even the military cannot maintain control of all its information or data systems. It has concluded that it must work hand-in-hand with the private commercial sector in moving information technology forward. This dependency becomes even stronger for smaller organizations.

Entire industries are emerging based on the collection and sale of information. These industries, in turn, proliferate layers of value-added resellers of information. This trend only increases the choices that organizations have in the acquisition of information, while perhaps reducing or replacing some of the former value-adding processes of an organization.

This blending propensity of information requires control panel indicators to continuously monitor and manage the changing value of information that the organization processes into the products and services it generates. The new metrics required for financial analysis and eventual performance depend on how the value of information is understood and applied.

USING THE CONTROL PANEL

The primary use of a control panel is to help direct resources and activity. Since every organization is unique—every control panel is different and all leaders establish their own styles—the use of a control panel cannot be outlined by a checklist or an established routine. A control panel must assist in determining how to best use it as a navigation tool to the future. Although the control panel has major indicators pointing toward a long-term horizon, many day-to-day instruments need attention and adjustment.

Every person, every team, and every organization performs activities. For some, the majority of their activity may be thinking or planning; for others, it may be leading others or managing resources; and, for many, it is performing within defined processes. The constant theme throughout this book is that in order to optimize the results of activity, one needs an objective and the means of measuring against that objective, along with some means of adjustment when required. In an organization, the additional element of integration is paramount. The control panel is the tool that combines all these factors and assists in answering the question, "What is the most meaningful thing I (we) can do today?"

PERFORMANCE MONITORING

A leader should always be aware of the progress of the organization toward goals and objectives, as well as trends and exceptions to standard expectations or requirements. Performance and exception indicators should stand out on the control panel and be monitored in a Pareto fashion. These indicators are already on most leaders' control panels, whether they are communicated through a morning briefing, a computer screen, a few written reports and graphs, or direct observation.

Closely linked to the key indicators should be a small number of support indicators that provide a first-tier response to the question, "*Why* does a performance indicator read the way it does?" In the Information Age control panel, the leader should be able to "drill down" to gain more knowledge on any reading and probe for greater understanding.

The primary sensors used to provide performance information are located at key process output locations. This data must be periodically combined with cost and voice of the customer (which includes market and competitor information) data in order to assess value and market movement.

ACTIVITY MONITORING

Certain activities should be continuously monitored by a leader to assure plans are carried out. The leader should be careful not to tamper with processes or to *micro* manage based on a narrow perspective. The most important activities to monitor are projects or critical tasks that have not yet begun to produce measurable or credible results. Once results are measured, they fall under performance monitoring.

Projects and critical activities should be managed using automated project management systems (or software) that provide a continuous accounting of resources and continual update of timelines and critical paths. The leader should be continually aware of progress from both a resource and timeline standpoint, as they both impact future organizational performance and require adjustments.

Even more critical than assurance that plans are met or adjustments are made is the knowledge of resource allocation and use. The leader knows that resources are generally linked, and if a disproportionate amount is deployed to assist one project, something else will suffer. It may be another project or task, or it may be organizational performance. It is better to understand the cost of redeploying priorities and resources up front than to be surprised later on.

There is no excuse for a leader to reduce the effectiveness or success of one project or activity to help another one without the knowledge of all parties of its impact. There is no excuse for later blaming project management or individuals on shortcomings or failure when the leader made a decision without disclosure or input.

Recently, a very successful local chain of coffeehouses undertook a project to install a new financial accounting system. This new system conflicted with its management reporting system to a degree that local managers could not track and meet operating standards. The two systems and the implementation project were not properly integrated. The decision to launch the new system without understanding the impact on the current system proved disastrous.

The control panel, or a similar concept under another title, is the only methodology of incorporating overall activity with results and correlating ultimate performance with the activities that create the result. This should be a continuous function of every control panel and every leader.

GREATER UNDERSTANDING

Performance and activity monitoring are extensions of Industrial Age techniques and have occupied most of initial emphasis since the dawn of the computer. Although the Information Age will collect input from a vast number of sensors and provide real time monitoring of organization performance, it will not provide the huge gains that will be realized from the knowledge and wisdom opportunities that are created.

For the first time since the beginning of scientific management, leaders will be able to reclaim the ability to look directly at operational data and the requirements of customers independent of staff filters. They will be able to select and build a leadership team that is not preoccupied with their own personal turf, but will look at the integrated interests of the whole and be able to creatively work on its improvement.

Industrial Age executive meetings frequently take on a combative air, as there is a constant struggle for information as it resides in different areas of the organization. Probably more energy is spent on maintaining control of information, arguing about its validity, reconciling differences and pursuing it than is expended on its understanding and value. This equation is reversed in the Information Age.

When a team looks at the same information at the same time and everyone agrees on its legitimacy, it will then be able to spend its energy on productive pursuits. Unlike Industrial Age meetings, Information Age leadership teams, whether at the board level or the bottom level, will be able to optimize its time on creative, high-value added activity.

The control panel will continuously monitor and gather data and information from a large number of internal, external, and historical sources and analyze it through unlimited views. The resulting information will be presented or accessed by carefully understood Pareto techniques to display priority of areas requiring attention or offering opportunity through criteria selection techniques. It (the control panel) will correlate billions of variables into high level metrics and indicators that continually show the interrelationship of driving and lagging activity (see Figure 9.2). The availability of information is one element of the formula; this must be combined with outstanding team skills, computer knowledge (although this will change through improved generations of technology) and the ability to assimilate data into a larger perspective. The team and individual leaders will continually look at, manipulate, and analyze information in an attempt to answer these types of questions:

- What does this tell us?
- What additional information do we need?
- What new opportunities are we afforded?
- What must occur to take advantage of the opportunities?
- Knowing what we know what result is likely to occur for various actions?

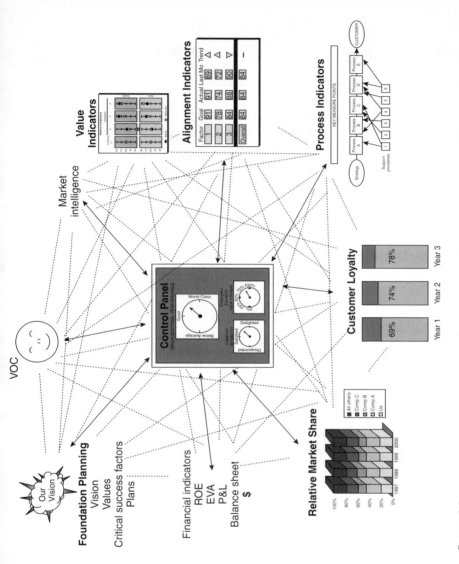

Figure 9.2 A control panel integrates key knowledge the organization needs to continuously deliver superior value to stakeholders.

The ability to quickly model scenarios combining actual data and statistical relationships based on historical, likely, projected or hypothetical variables is much of the horsepower that distinguishes Industrial Age systems from interactive, integrated, and distributed systems of the Information Age.

The next generation of organizational control panels will have essentially unlimited information available to the user. They will connect with hundreds of television networks, external databases, the Internet, supplier databases, customer databases, internal networks, and have video/telephone conferencing capability, personal management systems, communication linkups, and many features that are either on drawing boards, in the minds of pioneers, or not yet conceived. Every individual can have a computer that will function as a personal secretary, decision maker, and window to the world.

A single interactive computer screen will provide real-time data on a countless number of variables with instant analysis ability, along with libraries of stored information that exceed all the information available on earth just a few years ago. The communication capability will extend to any person, organization, or group anywhere. Decision integration will be almost instantaneous, as better planning and scenario modeling will cover almost every contingency.

PLANNING

Planning is an extension of greater understanding projected to the future. Planning is a process, like understanding, that can be continuously improved. With enhanced artificial intelligence as a tool and a partner, the process of planning will be greatly refined as it is studied and new techniques developed and applied. Soon strategic planning will change from a once in a while event to a continuous or frequent process, and tactical planning will continuously be an output of strategy.

The control panel will allow a much greater dimension of planning as it connects the organization with strategic partners and, eventually, the global community. Today, organizations plan in relative isolation as they do not want to reveal their intentions and strategies. In the future, these will be more difficult to disguise and it will become apparent that the value of cooperative planning along the entire customer-supplier chain and, perhaps in entire markets, will overshadow past concerns.

The linkages among politics, law, finance, education, government, health care, the military, commerce, and many other disciplines cannot be ignored in the Information Age. The correlation among these factors and their cause-and-effect relationships will be too transparent to hide. Wider picture planning and win–win cooperation will change forever how individual organizations function in the Information Age.

Planning will involve an expanded base of both participants and information. This is possible through the enhanced technology and improved human communication techniques of the Information Age. Although the final decision making process may involve fewer individuals, the information collection and presentation should be widespread.

Planning sessions will likely resemble the evolving military command, control, communications, computer, and intelligence center (war room) concept. Whether large numbers of individuals are gathered in a central location or spread geographically depends on new technology and the desire of the organization. In all likelihood, periodic sessions will be attended by expanded numbers because of the positive synergy and human dynamics that such a setting offers. Figure 9.3 illustrates a large multidimensional screen in front of a number of linked computers that all interact together.

Each partition and section of the large screen is a display of a computer screen that can be projected and changed on demand. A planning session for larger organizations will be facilitated by a team of professionals who are knowledgeable in the content of the information, the process of moving the sessions to targeted outcomes, and the technology involved. The success of such planning is driven by pre-planning and expertly orchestrated execution.

The output of war room planning will instantly be available for implementation and deployment. The metrics will be self-adjusting as they link to established goals and desired outcomes.

LEADERSHIP

As control panels become more widespread and as portions of organizational control panels become part of greater distributed networks, the need for competent basic leadership will grow immensely. The control panel will free leaders from their role as firefighters and focus them as strategists, creators of opportunities, and developers of human and organizational potential.

The control panel will provide more information to every leader at every level than the most powerful and informed executive had available in the Industrial Age. It will be a simple to use, intuitive, interactive system. A menu will be available that will access all information available within the organization, as well as essentially all the power of millions of databases interconnected around the globe. Unlimited news, financial data, sports, as well as entertainment will be readily available on a real time basis at the click of a button or a voice, or perhaps, even a thought command. The control panel will have continuous alerts, warnings, reminders and tools available to assist with every decision and keep the individual on track. An individual's day, week, month, and year and longer can be continuously well organized.

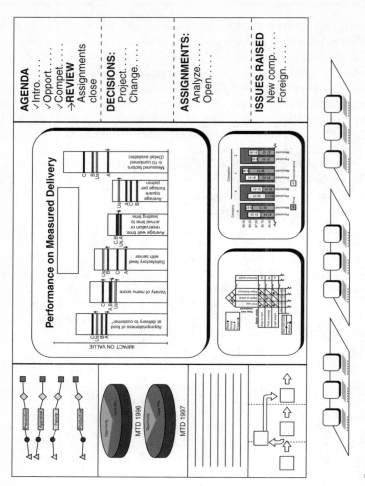

Figure 9.3 War room strategy sessions must be well planned with all the information and support necessary.

220

For the first time in more that a century, leaders will spend a preponderance of their time on creative value-adding efforts. Not only will the control panel and its extensions to the combined resources of organizations be the tool of the leader, it will also be their developer and, to some degree, their mentor. In other words tomorrow's leader will be partially a product of the control panel's evolution. The future career path of the leader will follow one's performance in mixing information with other resources and human creativity to produce and deliver high value products and services demanded by tomorrow's markets and customers. The path will be observed, tested, developed, and defined along the way through the use of performance on both real and test case studies monitored on control panels.

A PERSPECTIVE ON CONTROL PANELS
AND INTEGRATED LEADERSHIP

The control panel is a major leadership tool for the Information Age. It is the means of managing the massive amount of information available with the human dimensions that motivate customers, shareholders, employees, and stakeholders. However, it is a tool that must be designed and built with integration of information, human, and organizational systems continuously in mind. It is not an information system, it is an integration system. As such, it is a cybernetic system, it must continually grow and adapt.

Every modern aircraft has a modern control panel. Its control panel, by itself, is one aspect of a coast to coast flight. The control panel must be utilized by humans and is continuously receiving and sending data from and to other control panels. It links thousands of sensors with several major systems and thousands of subsystems in order to assist in a successful flight.

The control panel has little utility without the linkage of its sensors, systems, and human intervention. Would an F-18 cockpit mounted on an 1850s stagecoach help it navigate from Los Angeles to San Francisco in less than an hour? An Information Age control panel has little value without the foundation of sound systems, leadership, sensors, and guiding principles.

It is difficult to fully envision tomorrow's control panels, but they will be an integration of boundless information systems into human systems located in existing and evolved future organizations to meet the purposes of organizations and add value and wealth to all constituents. A control panel is one part of the formula for success. The other critical pieces include robust and high-quality automated and human production and creative systems and the means of continuous evolution and improvement. The foundation for practically all created value is the human mind. The human mind is well equipped to move from data to information to knowledge and wisdom; the control panel will become the means to provide the mind with assembled knowledge and wisdom as a higher form of data which the mind will convert to even higher forms of knowledge and wisdom.

So, the human system is the more important system. As we move into the Information Age, human systems must always be at the forefront of integration. In organizations, human endeavor is placed in value-adding processes or the support of value-adding processes. The fundamental sub-processes that power the major critical processes are labeled as *jobs*; the robustness of jobs are both individual and team competency. The coordination that synergizes the individual and provides high value added output is called *teamwork*. The force that creates it all, establishes the vision, and assures the results is called *leadership*.

This book focuses on the development of leadership that is necessary to integrate information systems into the human systems of our organizations in order to create wealth from the abundance of knowledge and wisdom available in the Information Age.

KEY POINTS   CONTROL PANEL THROUGH INTEGRATING METRICS

- We are at the primitive stages of the Information Age. We do not yet know what challenges we have. We must depend on solid, basic leadership skills to help us plot the future.
- As information explodes at a exponential rate, we must focus our attention to integrating all our systems and processes through an organizational control panel.
- Although there are a number of current examples of control panels, they must be studied and improved at a fast pace to keep abreast of the information explosion and the impact it has on our organizational systems and institutions.
- Although the military will depend more on the free enterprise system for innovation in technology, it is, and will probably continue to be for some time, the leader in control and command systems. This is because it is the only large-scale organization that currently concentrates such a high level of resources of its use as an Information Age tool.
- Strategic planning will soon be a continuous function of the control panel concept. It will no longer be a "once in a while project"; it will become an ongoing activity of management. This is driven by the fast pace of the Information Age and the opportunity for wealth creation outside of the realm of head-to-head competition.
- Every organization must have a unique control panel.

- With improved technical analysis techniques, artificial intelligence, and a sensor network that is patterned after the human body, control panels will soon automate much of the decision process and provide a multidimensional view of the organization, the market, customers, competitors and outside factors that is almost beyond today's imagination.
- In addition to high leadership competencies, organizations must continually evolve a high level of teamwork skills throughout the organization to prepare for the challenges of the Information Age. Jobs will function like intelligent and creative neurons in future organizations.

NOTES

1. Lt. Gen. John S. Fairfield, "Horizon—A Jointly Focused Vision Charting the Course for the 21st Century Air Force," *Armed Forces Journal International,* January 1996.
2. For discussion on additional possibilities with networked control panel, see chapter 10.
3. J. Fred Weston and Eugene F. Brigham, *Essentials of Managerial Finance,* 7th ed. (New York: Dryden Press, 1985), p. 6.
4. Other than the rare organizations that report financial projection or projected growth rates, which are heavily discouraged today.
5. This information is gathered from a presentation by Rob Davis, who was chief quality officer, AT&T Universal Card Services, Jacksonville, Florida, at the time of the presentation at the Third Annual Service Quality Conference, *Improve the Bottom Line by Winning and Retaining Customers,* on April 19, 1994, at the Disneyland Hotel, Anaheim, California. The Conference was sponsored by the American Society for Quality Control and its Service Industries Division.
6. Robert Davis, Susan Rosegrant, and Michael Watkins, "Managing the Link Between Measurement and Competition," *Quality Progress,* vol. 28, no. 2 (February, 1995), pp. 101–106.
7. Overhead, presented by William J. Cahill, managing director of compensation, Federal Express Corporation, *Journey Towards Quality,* at the First Annual Service Quality Conference, *Service Quality: Competitive Advantage of the 90s,* April 6–7, 1992, Hyatt Regency Chicago.
8. Federal Express Corporation, *1995 Annual Report,* p. 6.
9. Federal Express Corporation, *1996 Annual Report, The Facts,* p. 12.
10. See note 9.
11. See note 9.

12. See note 9, p. 1.

13. See note 9, p. 4.

14. See note 9.

15. See note 9.

16. See note 9.

17. See note 9.

18. See note 9.

19. Joint Venture: Silicon Valley Network, Inc.: *Index of Silicon Valley 1996: Measuring Progress Toward a 21st Century Community*, 1996, p.1. Additional information is available from Joint Venture: Silicon Valley Network, Inc., 99 Almaden Blvd., Suite 610, San Jose, CA 95113-2002; phone 1-800-573-JVSV; World Wide Web: http://www.jointventure.org.

20. See note 19, p. 2.

21. Mark St. Quintin, "Quality Models and Standards for Software," presented at the 1993 International Conference on Software Quality, *Winning in the '90s the Quality Way*, held October 4–6, 1993, at the Hyatt Regency, Lake Tahoe, Nevada, sponsored by the Software Division of the American Society for Quality Control (ASQC) and the Santa Clara Valley Software Quality Association, located in Conference Proceedings, p. 366.

22. William J. Koenig, *Weapons of World War 3* (London: Bison Books Limited, 1981), p. 31. "Command is the process of making a decision and control is the execution of that decision."

23. Col. Richard S. Friedman and Others, *Advanced Technology Warfare: A Detailed Study of the Latest Weapons and Techniques for Warfare Today and into the 21st Century* (New York: Harmony Books, 1985), p. 160.

24. See note 22, p. 32.

25. The Global Command and Control System home page on the World Wide Web, at http://spider.osfl.disa.mil.

26. Emmett Paige Jr., "Ensuring Joint Force Superiority in the Information Age," Defense Issues, vol.11, no. 82. Downloaded on the World Wide Web at http://dtic.mil/defenselink/pubs/di_index.html.

27. See note 26, p. 3.

28. John E. Freund, *Modern Elementary Statistics*, 6th ed. (Englewood Cliffs, N.J.: Prentice-Hall, 1984), p. 443.

29. For excellent discussion on SPC and tampering, see Deming, *Out of the Crises*. Although chapters 11 and 12 focus on these issues, examples can be found throughout the book.

Chapter 10

THE FUTURE

> *Value creation is the ultimate "win-win handshake" between a company and its stakeholders. . . . And Zytec's entire mission is to create value.*
>
> - *Value for our customers by delivering quality, service and value.*
> - *Value for our employees by offering a lifetime of personal growth.*
> - *Value for our shareholders by consistently producing returns on invested capital in excess of our cost of capital.*
> - *Value for our suppliers by providing long-term relationships.*
> - *Value for our communities in which we live and work by providing consistent economic growth.*
>
> —Zytec Corporation, Eden Prairie, Minnesota[1]

We can all imagine a world that is much safer, more enjoyable, and offers tremendous opportunities and freedom. Walt Disney once said, "If we can dream it, we can build it."

Using the principles of integrated leadership, an organization, of any size, can achieve practically any vision that its stakeholders and constituents collectively agree upon and commit to. The only exception is when two or more organizations are competing and there can be only one winner.[2]

In the distant past, the largest organizations with a common purpose or vision were nations or the alliance of several nations. With the advent of the League of Nations after World War I and the United Nations at the end of World War II, the foundation for a possible common global purpose was structured. The Information Age will likely see the development of longer term global visions as nations, communities, and people become more connected.

A few areas may best be positioned with a collaborated long-term global vision in order to maximize performance or speed. These include space exploration and colonization, the avoidance or minimization of massive natural catastrophes, world peace, attainment of minimal living standards for every human, preservation of nature, standards for human rights, and open trade or the optimization of commerce. In order to support global visions or to greatly improve the welfare of a nation and its people, national visions must emerge. These include topics such as politics, education, social interaction, legal/justice, crime, wealth distribution, infrastructure, health care, role of government, and collaboration/interaction with other nations.

Global and national visions must be both supported and driven by local communities. In the Information Age, a community may be defined much differently than it was previously. A community may be defined by interest, ethnicity, and beliefs or values, as well as geographic or national citizenship. The overlap of these variables requires integration that was impossible under earlier ages. These community visions will include the preservation of ideals, beliefs, and cultures, as well as formation of new ones; the prioritization of goals, objectives, and values, and the means of assuring the vision. The community will become the most collaborative of all the layers as it struggles to both preserve and improve its destiny.

PERFECT, REUSABLE, AND EVOLVING PROCESSES

One of the tools of the quality revolution is process improvement. Processes can be designed and built to higher and higher levels of accuracy, approaching perfection. Those processes that historically required human judgment can be studied and automated. The instructions, or software, for every substep can be recorded and duplicated. Better information systems and control panels placed at various levels can easily record and assist in the improvement process until desired levels of performance are obtained.

The software for these perfect processes can easily be transferred, or downloaded, to any number of systems for duplication anywhere on the globe, space, or other worlds. Any user who discovers techniques for improvement or add-on uses, or who encounters new difficulties, can immediately communicate the new knowledge to other users.

The first generation control panels are currently being built and employed around the globe by practically every type of organization. They are primary operated as monitors, recorders, and reporters of information to select levels within an organization for assistance in decision making. They are a two-way communication system, meaning that the leader will use the system for information and relay back to the various components (either human or mechanical) orders that modify the system or the results that the system produces.

Although these early control panels are a vast improvement over previous monitoring systems, they will quickly seem like Stone Age relics, as the second generation control panels close the communication loop by becoming self-monitoring and greatly reduce the need for human intervention in the adjustment process. Subsequent generations of control panels may duplicate some of the higher-level functions of the brain, such as creativity and thought. They will open up doors that are probably beyond today's comprehension, merely because the basis for the level of wisdom that can be formulated does not exist today.

Soon, we will build products and services that are essentially perfect, at least perfect for what they are intended. Everyone will have access to almost unlimited amounts of information, software, processing speed, and assistance. This will probably drastically alter our lives and our institutions and profoundly affect many of our basic beliefs.

Following are a few possible and likely changes:

- Politicians will not be elected or appointed based on their charm, promises, and special-interest sponsors. They will be qualified based on their ability to integrate and facilitate solutions to both the resolution of issues and the attainment of well-endorsed and published goals.
- Those who serve the public, including government officials, educators, managers of publicly traded companies, lawmakers and law enforcers, medical practitioners, nonprofit organizations, and the regulators who oversee commerce will soon, one by one, be compelled to higher levels of competency. The Information Age provides the means to quickly expose and replace those who use position or insider knowledge for personal gain, or are incompetent.
- Much greater efficiency in education will provide a much wider percentage of population with higher education. Increasing incentives to learn and apply greater knowledge will motivate almost everyone to take advantage of the opportunities education provides. Most of those who choose to ignore this movement will encounter an almost insurmountable barrier to economic and social well being.
- The renaissance in education, as well as improvements in social reform, can lead to unheralded reduction in crime. Much more efficiency in prevention, early detection, quick crime solving, and speedy justice will greatly reduce crimes of all types.
- The benefits to society from these social improvements, economic productivity increases, enhanced education, and instant communications can eliminate the need for much of the current centralized government functions and grant new opportunities for joint collaboration in high value-added ventures.

- The institutions and organizations that we spend our energy and resources with will provide a much higher duty of care and disclosure to its stakeholders, including owners (investors), employees, customers, and suppliers. Today, a highly disproportionate few individuals possess and control the key information that is needed to properly ascertain the true value of the organization and its return to its stakeholders.

As more extensive and reliable control panels are built, vain promises will mean little and performance will mean everything. Organizations who gained share by being first to market by selling alpha and beta products and services that they advertise as being stable and reliable will be replaced by those with the foresight, processes, and systems to deliver quality the first time. The productivity and quality gains of the Information Age will extend not only to free markets but to governments and any remaining restricted markets. Soon all markets will have to open their doors or they will not survive.

The magnificent gains of the Information Age will open up unheralded advances in education, law, international cooperation, science, exploration, medicine, human behavior, and more effective and phenomenal solutions to crime, poverty, illness, depression, age, and a number of other problems. It may not be utopia, and it will undoubtedly create new problems, but it will be able to deal effectively with many of the dilemmas we will not solve today.

THE ESSENTIALS

Although the control panel is essential to an Information Age organization, it is primarily a viewing tool or a window; it is not the bedrock upon which organizations are built. The bedrock is based on vision, mission, values, and strategy. The *ability to define and link this foundation to external markets with the help of cooperative partners in a form that provides high value products and services* is the basis of creation of Information Age wealth.

ORGANIZATION-SPECIFIC SUCCESS DRIVERS

Every organization that survives its initial startup and overcomes adversity knows its most important success drivers. These are the very few and rare qualities that promote growth and attract others to the organization. For a retail bank, it may be friendliness; for a steel company, it may customization speed; for an electronics manufacturer, it may be product introduction cycle time; for an educational television network, it may be the integration with school lesson planning; for a governmental agency, it may be minimal inconvenience to citizens; and, to a delivery service, it may be maximized integration between the needs of the shipper and the recipient. Every organization must understand these drivers and measure them at their maximum point of value. These points of value then should directly correlate to easier success measures such as market growth, sales, loyalty, satisfaction, and profit. These measures, along with their continual analysis with results, should be one of the cornerstones of every control panel.

VALUE DRIVERS AND MEASURES

The continual delivery of value is based on the fundamental understanding of value to its recipient—the customer. In the past, value was created or added primarily in a linear fashion to physical goods or to defined and observable services. In the future information and knowledge will be such a high value component of most goods and services that they may render everything else to a commodity status. Information value added can be invisible to the user; it can negate or greatly amplify existing value, it can continually and instantly be updated, and it is practically limitless.

Since traditional financial measures and indicators may be useless, or, at least, severely limited as a leading indicator of value-added information and knowledge, new methods must be discovered. Although a number of ideas and methods have been identified, many more must be discovered and applied. The customer–supplier chain of value add will take on geometrical complexity as information bases merge. The key will still be an understanding of the priority of needs and their fulfillment in the most effective and efficient manner.

The principle of synergy takes on new meaning as organizations collaborate and discover new uses of information. Competition becomes more intense as new opportunities are recognized immediately upon the advent of the latest discovery. This may lead to increased competitive cooperation as a means to enhance the wealth and well-being of society. Very emotional issues over ownership, control, and legal rights will add complexity to the metrics of value. When value is added by numbers of individuals and organizations, what are the rights of each? Our past application of intellectual property law will soon be woefully inadequate. The continual understanding and measuring of value may not only offer huge market opportunity, it will almost certainly be the means of preservation of past gains.

INTEGRATED LEADERSHIP

The role and challenges of the other aspects of integrated leadership will also expand in the future, but its principles will continue to apply. Perhaps the goal of leadership should be tweaked to expand responsibility and increase the search for better measures of value. At the beginning of the Information Age, the *purpose of leadership* should be:

> *To maximize the value and wealth-creating propensities of an organization as determined by its continuing contribution to its stakeholders and society.*

This is a bit philosophical and somewhat idealistic. Optimistically, it is a hope for the future. If we do not include elements of ethics and benefits for the good of our planet in our basic purposes and values, we may put the short-term interests of a few over the long-term survival of the future.

THE TRANSFORMATION

The transition from the Industrial Age to the Information Age will not occur overnight. Some highly competitive markets such as the overnight shipping business have competitors that have made the commitment to the change and are pioneering newer methods. Others believe the Industrial Age is here to stay and the Information Age is a figment of someone's imagination.

I believe that the change will occur quite suddenly once a few milestones have been reached. There may not be a single flash point or actuating event that triggers a critical mass. It most likely will be the result of a series of connections among governments, commerce, a few powerful institutions, and an aggregate of individuals who come to realize their dependence on each other to achieve their visions. A related alternative is the continued knowledge gained by customers that demand change. The target of that demand may be a government, global institution, or an industry. The realization of any of these scenarios (and others) could spread around the globe with lightning speed.

In any event, once customers realize their consolidated power when they have information and knowledge, the Information Age will ignite and the Industrial Age will disappear.

THE COST OF NONADHERENCE

When customers know as much or more about value and its distribution as producers and suppliers, they will require a much higher level of performance. Organizations that help effect this transformation by assuming a partnering role and develop an internal system of efficient, integrated leadership will survive and prosper. Those that do not will be replaced by those that do.

The real cost is not the survival or prosperity of single organizations, it is the terribly high cost of missed opportunity. For an example of the enormity of this cost, we can look at one program of one organization in the United States—the Internal Revenue Service's (IRS)Tax Systems Modernization (TSM) program.[3] This program is an example of the high cost associated with poorly integrated systems, the lack of an adequate control panel, and, most importantly, the lack of a sustained vision. The IRS has been planning an overhaul of its information systems since the late 1960s and has not yet come to terms with the opportunities that can be realized from a continuous and linked effort.

The cost to date of the system has exceeded $4 billion, which is small compared to the annual missed opportunity costs of $50 billion.[4] The $50 billion is the estimated amount that the IRS fails to collect annually, and this amount is repeatable every year that the agency does not achieve its goals of collecting an increased percentage of what is due. Government and private groups offer explanations of the shortcomings such as:

- *Failed to do much-needed business process redesign before it began its system development.*
- *Neglected to develop an overall systems architecture or development blueprint.*
- *Employed primitive and, at times, "chaotic" software development methodologies.*[5]

These are clearly a violation of integrated leadership principles and should be readily corrected with an integrated and shared vision and leadership.

As staggering as $50 billion per year may seem, it is minuscule compared to the real cost of poor quality and lost opportunity costs that exist around the globe today. The ultimate costs of not fixing our political and educational systems alone has to be in the trillions of dollars. The shame is that we have the knowledge, we have the technology, and we have the ability to elevate global wealth several fold, but we do not have the shared vision. We have not integrated those few driving institutions that are necessary for unheralded growth for all living species.

A JOURNEY OF VALUE

Our biggest limitations are ourselves. We restrict our thinking by imposing barriers based on our own experiences and how we see the past and present world. We are greatly restricted by our institutions, our cultural values, and our continuous quest for universal truth. Although these are probably the foundations that preserved our heritage and perhaps our survival, they must change in the future. We saw the sudden destruction of one of the world's largest communist systems at the end of the Cold War. Its speed was staggering.

As an increasing percentage of our population connects via electronic means and learns to understand and communicate at a productive level with an increasing number of organizations and individuals, profound productivity will occur. A knowledge level that once took centuries to encompass the world will take seconds. Not only will it eliminate unnecessary duplication, it will foster cooperation and immediate improvement. It will open up options that were never possible before.

To realize our individual and collective dreams, our visions must be of high value. We must produce lasting and cumulative wealth, not only to survive as a species but to attain the diverse goals that we all seek. We pay a high and dear price for life itself, and we are entitled to a return on the payment. Whether the return exceeds the payment is a matter of choice. We all, individually and collectively, possess the means to generate high returns. It is in our nature, and from that nature we have evolved the fabulous knowledge and ability to return a premium on our payments. The *how* is no longer the dominant question, we either know how or we will find the path; the larger question is *what*?

Every individual and every organization from the two-person marriage through our nations and united nations should answer the *what*. We should help each other individually, and we should all demand visions from our organizations and collective activity. Most of us are a part of a relatively few organizations or institutions. We spend a high amount of our time and energy with these few institutions. We are a stakeholder of every one and we have not only the right but the duty to understand, and perhaps help formulate, their vision. If they do not have one, it is the wrong one, or it is one that is not based on value for all stakeholders, we should help them form it, correct it, or find an alternate organization that does.

Once we clearly understand where the organization is going, we must affirm that it has the proper metrics and means to navigate the journey. The highest level metrics should show value. The rest will be both fun and fulfilling. If not, you are on the wrong train. Get off at the first stop and find the right one.

RETURN TO TAYLOR'S MENTAL REVOLUTION

A person may work faithfully for an organization for 20 years, adding value every day. That person may be partially compensated with deferred income based on stock ownership of the firm granted quarter by quarter for the entire 20 years. New management may appoint a new executive team who decides to downsize the organization and terminate the tenured employee and give what they consider is a generous settlement of a week's pay for every year employed. As a bonus, the new management offers a free tip: "Hold on to the stock, we will double its price in the next year."

By the end of the next year, the new management has been replaced (they all received a nice golden parachute for three year's pay, plus benefits), the stock price is now less than 40 percent of where it was a year earlier, and the newest wave of management is taking their positions. New management may or may not produce increased value. Where is the solution to the "mental revolution"?

With the lack of confidence and the great inequities in the United States Social Security system, many people are struggling to hold on to what little vested rights they have or to place their assets in alternative investments. Unfortunately, most investments remain a crap shoot. The timely information that an individual investor needs to make decisions in the highly volatile stock market is held by a very small number of individuals who continue to accumulate great wealth at the expense of the massive numbers of investors who have access to partial information on a delayed basis.

Consequentially, daily, there are wild swings in the global equity markets, particularly at the individual company level. The actual value of organizations do not vacillate daily in parallel with the market; it is perception based on lack of information, inaccurate information, the greed of a few individuals, and the acceptance of the system.

Again, there is poorly integrated leadership. Many decisions are made based on historical financial data and the projections of few individuals, mostly removed from the actual knowledge of the internal dynamics of the organization. Government strongly influences the markets through policies, regulation, and intervention.

The primary element that is missing for individuals to make legitimate choices is reliable information. Since governments do not formulate and gain support for long-term visions because of spoils systems, power politics, and selfishness, a few retain the power to control markets, and many other aspects that influence growth and wealth.

As information becomes more available and more individuals and organizations become more knowledgeable in the dynamics that influence and control many of the important aspects of their lives, revolutionary change can occur. This change can and should be driven within a free enterprise system. The biggest obstacle standing in the way of individual freedom today is the right to make *informed* decisions. We have become conditioned to accept our institutions and organizations because we knew as individuals that we were powerless to understand them and challenge them. With instant communications and much greater demand for information that can change quickly. The question is, will we accept our institutions as we better understand them, or will we work together to replace, improve, or modify them?

The dilemma is that Taylor's mental revolution has not yet been resolved. Taylor and the gurus of scientific management felt that it would disappear, since everyone would be happy that they gained something from increasing productivity. They were wrong because their underlying premise was wrong. The human species does not exist solely for, nor is it primarily motivated by, economics. There are stronger factors that emerge once basic needs are fulfilled.

The Information Age will resolve the mental revolution and it will probably be for vastly different reasons than the early twentieth century pioneers envisioned. It will be resolved because the individual will have much greater freedom of choice in exercising their options on where they deploy their productivity improvement efforts. Information, collective collaboration, and creativity in the free market system will find ways to share gains based on contribution, not position.

GREATER UNDERSTANDING BY THE INDIVIDUAL IN THE INFORMATION AGE

With pertinent information one is able to make better choices. With information and the means to communicate with large numbers of individuals and groups with similar needs comes power. A little power, initiative, collaboration, and motivation can lead to monumental change.

As individuals gain greater understanding into how value is added or lost, along with the means of obtaining increased knowledge on specific industries and their component products and services, they will seek improved methods of delivery. At a minimum this will create increased competition and consequently, higher value. At the other end, it will probably lead to the formation of associations and maybe coalitions of associations that will enter competitive markets.

There are a number of products and services that a substantial percentage of the population use on a frequent or ongoing basis. These range from regulated monopolies to highly competitive markets where there is a high degree of freedom of entry for new competitors. Government and other regulated monopolies will receive unprecedented pressure to change and become efficient and effective as the population gains greater and greater insight, information and knowledge into their operation and demands higher and higher standards to meet their requirement for higher value services. Many of the services formerly provided by government will either move to the private sector or survive in the public sector by meeting the changing requirements.

The most massive change will affect those institutions that produce and deliver services such as insurance, lending and deposit (such as banks, savings and loan, credit unions) health care, utilities, real estate, travel, investments and other support services. Almost all of the *large* providers of these services today have an extremely high cost of poor quality due to varying degrees of high acquisition and delivery costs, redundancy, cost and value shifting, improper incentives, lack of integration of external information and organizational inefficiency. The opportunities for current providers of these services to gain market share by adding significant value to customers through enhanced productivity is enormous. Those who believe there is plenty of time to change may regret their indecision.

The solution is simple in concept but becomes quite complex in practice because of the horrendous mess of regulations, laws, disguised information, and past precedence. The value delivered as a percentage of value that would be delivered at a zero cost of poor quality varies greatly by type of service, organization, and geographic area. The cost of inconvenience is extremely high overall, differs greatly, and is difficult to factor into the equation. The short-term key to radical reform that will provide market advantage is to simply understand the customer through VOC analysis and work on value improvement through reduction in both inconvenience and the poor cost of quality. Longer term reform requires collaboration with customers, competitors, and government.

The hidden cost of service is inconvenience, or the burden the customer endures to receive the service. Although the level of acceptance of inconvenience is driven by a number of factors, the largest is probably lack of information about its costs and how they can be minimized or avoided. What are the costs of inconvenience when a retail establishment advertises a certain product at an attractive price, entices a number of shoppers to its establishment, and runs out of the product? A real estate agent spends a day driving a family around to a number of prospective houses, only to discover there was not a proper understanding of their needs and requirements—what is the cost? What are the costs every day of millions of lines or queues at retail stores, banks, government agencies, entertainment facilities, on roadways and freeways and public quorums? At any point in time, how many people are on hold on telephone lines, or cannot be connected with someone to help with support for a product or service, receive information, apply for a service, complain about poor service, report a failure, or communicate an improvement? What are the costs when a travel provider overbooks and individuals cannot be accommodated or travel is delayed or canceled? With many of these costs exceeding the value of the service or product pursued, how long will we accept levels of poor performance?

As forums appear to voice or report these inconveniences and they are analyzed in a clear and concise manner, customers will demand change. Those that are unavoidable will be improved; those that are caused by lack of care, incompetence, intention, or inattention will be reduced and eliminated by more productive providers.

THE INDIVIDUAL REACTS

As more people realize they are paying high premiums in both price and inconvenience for the value they receive and they grasp the enormity of value that can and should be added to these services, change will follow. If existing institutions do not change or new entrants do not provide radically higher value, customers will look to alternative solutions. A likely scenario will be the formation of customer organizations who will not only gain from joining with other customers to obtain the benefits of volume purchasing but the expansion of the role of the individual beyond that of a customer to becoming an owner, supplier, and perhaps even an employee (or at least a contributor to a value added process of the organization).

When value becomes the highest metric, behavior changes. Market forces driven by customers seeks the highest level of value, and they do not care which organizational form provides it. A customer will partner with a organization as an owner, advisor, or provider of information if there is a greater return of value associated with the relationship. On the other hand, the customer is willing and may prefer to be *only* a customer.

An example is a community hospital. A small community may have invested community and individual resources into forming a small hospital to support local needs. Years later as both the community and hospital grew, the hospital may have reached a level of unacceptable inefficiency and a national hospital chain acquires it. Through cost cutting, productivity gains, and other adjustments, the hospital becomes profitable. At first, the value the hospital delivers improves. But over time, because of investment pressure, demands of stockholders and desire for profit, the quality delivered (what customers receives) declines. When profits are squeezed enough and the community understands that local resources are being shifted out of the community, it becomes unacceptable to its ultimate customer. The community will then react and, either through demand to the hospital chain or other means, it will effect change. The hospital will either improve the value delivered or will be replaced by a more efficient provider, which may very well again be a much enlightened community.

As individuals are transformed from ignorance to wisdom through information, they can make vastly superior decisions on value in most aspects of their lives. An individual seeking a marriage partner will likely know much more about both parties and perhaps will have established the foundations of a common vision and goals prior to the marriage. Their home and means of support will align with their lifestyle. Their children will likely be planned and receive a superb education. As much as possible, they will understand their choices regarding how they spend and invest their resources. Although the number of choices will be vast, so will the efficiency of making decisions. The primary criteria of most decisions will be based on value. Where value is insufficient, the individual will collaborate with others and assist in its improvement.

The future belongs to those who align their lives with this greater vision and collaborate, socialize, and work with others who do also. The final outcome is a higher quality of life for the planet.

KEY POINTS THE FUTURE

- From the global quality revolution, we have learned to continually improve processes to a level that approaches perfection as measured by intended results.
- The biggest challenge is where to deploy resources and efforts on improvement. This requires collaboration on shared and integrated visions from the global perspective downward.
- This will be achieved through increased cooperation of global governments by the pressure from its much greater informed citizens.

- Success will continue to be the result of integrated leadership at all levels.
- The transformation to the Information Age will not be a technological breakthrough, it will most likely be the achievement of a critical mass of integrated leadership driven by customer enlightenment.
- The cost of delay is staggering; it is incalculable, but greatly impacts all of Earth's citizens.
- Taylor's mental revolution will not be solved in the Industrial Age; it will be resolved only when individuals are truly aware of the benefits and options associated with their contribution to productivity improvement, both collectively and individually.
- The greatest gains in productivity in the near term will be in the service sector.
- Eventually, the individual will gain the most from the Information Age.

NOTES

1. Zytec Corporation, *1996 Annual Report,* page 2. The Annual Report arrived in my office less than two weeks before the final manuscript of The Value Journey was due to the publisher. This quote was apparent as soon as I scanned the report. Zytec offered a succinct statement of the importance of value to the mission of an organization.

2. However the consolidated visions of these competitors will propel the excellence of performance to a level that would not be achieved without the competitive factor. All things being equal, the eventual winner in a competitive event will most likely be the one with the strongest commitment and the most disciplined use of integrated leadership principles.

3. The information on the TSM program of the IRS comes from the following articles in *Computerworld,* vol. 30, no. 42 (October 14, 1996): "IRS project failures cost taxpayers $50B annually," 1–28; "Time is taxing," p. 28; "IRS: Tough to get any respect," p. 28; "40 whacks with the budget ax," p. 29; and, "Learning lessons from IRS' biggest mistakes," p. 30.

4. See "IRS project failures cost taxpayers $50B annually," p. 28. Others have estimated the amount several times higher.

5. See note 4.

Appendix A

USING THE HOUSE OF QUALITY FOR CONTROL PANEL INFORMATION

(Note: It is recommended that the reader who is unfamiliar with the voice of the customer review a primer on QFD before covering these topics.)

VOC is most commonly used in concert with QFD in the design and development of new products and services. However, this tool is greatly leveraged when it becomes the foundation for ongoing market research in an organization. Currently, many organizations primarily use market research to explore identified opportunities or justify projects or past actions. Many other organizations pump out study after study, showing observations of the market, competitors, and the organization that are fragmented and of little strategic use.

EXPANDING THE TRADITIONAL MODEL

The model used here adds a new matrix to the most accepted versions of QFD that shows the market's perception of quality, value, inconvenience, and cost outlined by competitor. This information, when overlaid with actually measured data on these same factors, offers great opportunities for marketing, positioning, and branding advantages.

An underlying reason for this limited use of market research is lack of an organization-specific model to link research with strategy. VOC does not provide a complete and comprehensive model, but it does offer a foundation for one. *Company P* uses a format derived from the house of quality to calculate actual and perceived value every six months, as shown in Figure A.1. This format has many dimensions and provides a wealth of information on customers, competitors, opportunities, and areas for focus. Figure A.2 highlights just a few of the areas of importance from the model shown in Figure A.1.

The house of quality provides powerful and actionable information on current needs that eventually drive both perceived and actual market value. Two components that are added to the traditional matrix are perceived price and inconvenience. These are part of the initial data gathering that takes place during the competitor input portion of the VOC analysis.

Although Figure A.1 is somewhat detailed, such fine points are ultimately essential in order to assess value and opportunity in a competitive environment. The actual work is generally coordinated by a cross-functional team and conducted by a number of individuals who gather data from customers and markets as collateral tasks.

As the data are consolidated and move up the organization toward the control panel, they become more informational and are depicted to emphasize importance, movement, and velocity of change. People at the top should be familiar with the process of detail collection and analysis, but will generally be dealing with higher-level information. The detail can always be traced back to the data level if needed.

Competitive decisions should be made with higher-level information and confirmed with those knowledgeable with the detail. Decisions at the detail level are generally very dangerous because the scope is too narrow. As organizations become flatter and more knowledge is available to all, better and quicker decisions will be made.

COMPARING PERCEPTION WITH ACTUAL PERFORMANCE AND PRICE

The model outlined in Figure A.2 shows the location in the house of quality of:

1. Improvement priorities for need fulfillment of organization at current time (the higher the *demand weight*, the more attention should be given to the need)
2. Importance of each solution in improvement in meeting customers' basic needs
3. Actual measured quality of current solutions (product, services, or features), scored for each competitor
4. Customers' perception of quality, value, inconvenience, and price, listed by top competitors (total cost can be calculated from data)

The only data missing are actual prices and an analysis of inconvenience costs in order to compare perception with reality. The completion of that analysis, shown in Table A.1, provides valuable insight into factors the customer uses to perceive value.

Voice of the Customer Measures: Company P—Confidential

Basic Needs	Importance	Company P	Competitor X	Competitor Y	Competitor Z	Performance target	Improvement rate	Sales point	Absolute weight	Demand weight
Basic need 1	6	8	3	4	5	6	0.8	1.5	6.8	8%
Basic need 2	3	3	5	3	6	6	2.0	1.2	7.2	9%
Basic need 3	4	6	4	6	5	6	1.0	1.2	4.8	6%
Basic need 4	4	4	6	5	4	6	1.5	1.0	6.0	7%
Basic need 5	7	7	3	7	8	7	1.0	1.5	10.5	12%
Basic need 6	4	8	2	4	5	7	0.9	1.0	3.5	4%
Basic need 7	5	3	6	7	6	7	2.3	1.2	14.0	17%
Basic need 8	8	4	5	6	5	7	1.8	1.5	21.0	25%
Basic need 9	2	5	4	2	5	6	1.2	1.0	2.4	3%
Basic need 10	4	5	6	6	6	7	1.4	1.5	8.4	10%
TOTAL									**84.6**	**100%**

(Note: Arrows indicate direction/intensity of movement during last six months.)

How Met/Measured — Basic solutions matrix (Total / %)

Basic solution	Total	%
Basic solution 1	90	4%
Basic solution 2	258	12%
Basic solution 3	81	4%
Basic solution 4	457	20%
Basic solution 5	297	13%
Basic solution 6	36	2%
Basic solution 7	369	17%
Basic solution 8	357	16%
Basic solution 9	135	6%
Basic solution 10	151	7%
Total	**2231**	**100%**

Weighted average measured quality

	BS1	BS2	BS3	BS4	BS5	BS6	BS7	BS8	BS9	BS10	Wtd avg
Company P	6	4	3	5	6	7	5	8	6	4	5.49
Competitor X	3	5	7	4	4	7	6	6	8	6	5.26
Competitor Y	4	3	4	6	6	5	7	7	5	5	5.68
Competitor Z	2	7	4	6	4	7	8	8	5	2	5.92
Plan	5	7	6	7	6	7	8	8	8	6	7.07

Perceived value summary

	Us	X	Y	Z	Target
Weighted average perceived quality (calc.)	4.85	4.72	5.61	5.51	6.68
Average perceived value (benefit/total cost)	1.00	0.96	1.10	1.07	1.20
Avg. perceived inconvenience cost/total cost	0.18	0.24	0.16	0.08	0.10
Average perceived price	7.04	6.54	7.40	7.49	

Figure A.1 The house of quality structure can be used to help monitor actual and perceived value.

241

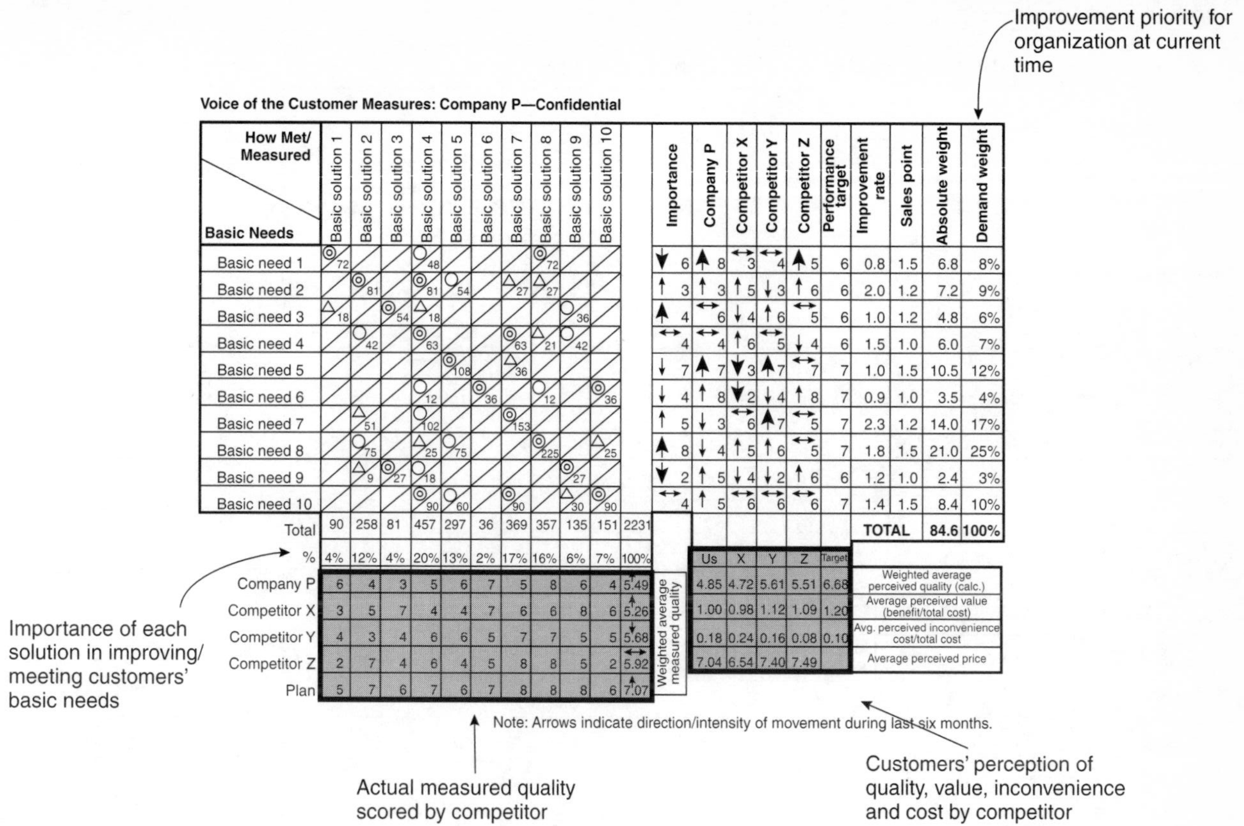

Figure A.2 The above matrices outline critical metrics of competitors in an actionable format.

242

Table A.1	Competitive price and inconvenience information are collected to supplement the house of quality in monitoring value.

Voice of the Customer Measures: Company P—Confidential
Price and Inconvenience Comparisons by Competitor

How Met/ Measured Price	Basic solution 1	Basic solution 2	Basic solution 3	Basic solution 4	Basic solution 5	Basic solution 6	Basic solution 7	Basic solution 8	Basic solution 9	Basic solution 10	Base price	Package price	Inconvenience cost (% of base price)	Inconvenience cost	Package + Inconvenience cost
Company P	0.0	2.4	0.8	5.6	0.0	2.6	0.5	4.1	0.0	0.0	6.98	8.10	9.6	0.67	8.77
Competitor X	0.0	3.6	0.5	0.0	3.0	0.7	0.3	0.0	0.4	2.0	6.34	6.88	19.6	1.243	8.12
Competitor Y	3.4	0.0	0.0	7.9	1.5	0.0	0.0	0.0	0.4	0.0	7.69	8.71	4.7	0.361	9.07
Competitor Z	0.0	0.0	0.0	0.0	0.0	0.6	0.6	1.0	0.0	0.0	7.27	7.43	14.8	1.076	8.51

Percent of base price for each solution; 0, if included in base price

The actual prices of goods and services are generally available through competitive analysis; however, creative methods frequently must be used, because of disguised packaging and pricing strategies. Inconvenience studies are a challenge, and they often require customer observation, interviewing, testing, or mystery shopping (depending on type of product or service) in order to measure results.

Table A.1 provides information on both price and the inconvenience customers experience when purchasing products and services that offer solutions to the basics needs outlined in the VOC matrix shown in Figure A.1. The table provides commonly quoted prices for the basic product or service (base price), as well as a breakdown of the price for each basic solution.[1] If a basic solution is optional, a percentage of the base price is shown.

The sum of all the basic solutions and the base price equals the package price. The measured cost of inconvenience is stated as a percentage of the base price and is added to the package price to provide the *package price* and *inconvenience cost* listed in Table A.1.

There are many methods and techniques available to understand and use the massive information collected in VOC and pricing studies. An important element that should always be considered is the accuracy, integrity, and representation of the data. In most cases, some data will be more valid and reliable than others. The analysis and reporting of information must be conducted with its integrity always kept in mind.

Only those gathering and analyzing data know its validity and weaknesses. Inherited data should always be questioned and understood before merging it with known information.

Although these characteristics are challenging, they offer great opportunity to those who dare to gather and study them. The key to realizing the potential of the opportunities is continually gaining understanding of the causal relationship between customer satisfaction and its drivers.

Table A.2 offers a relative value analysis using the VOC measures matrix, Figure A.1, and the *Price and Inconvenience Comparisons by Competitor*, Table A.1. It uses the elements of the value formula (What is received/What is paid) to offer relative comparisons between the stated value from VOC and measured values from the pricing data. Although there are dozens of ways to look at the data, this particular chart uses as much measurement as available to dissect the various factors of value.

Table A.2, rows one, two, and five contain data elements from the house of quality (Figure A.1) that show perceived quality, perceived value, and measured quality. Row 12 provides the calculation of value derived from both perceived and measured elements from data contained in Figure A.1 and Table A.1. The calculation assumes an equal weighting for both measured and perceived factors, which may vary depending on actual experience. The control panel indicator that shows the output of Table A.2 is shown in chapter 3, Figure 3.11.

Another organization with a different history and results may take a contrasted approach.

NOTE

1. Some providers will either "bundle" or separate the various features of its products and services differently from other competitors. Since some may require certain ones as part of the base price of the product or service and others separate them, it is necessary to compare them as a sum of their parts and view which ones are part of the basic package.

Table A.2 A relative value analysis shows the relationships among various value elements for different competitors.

		Relative Value Analysis	Metrics				Relative to Company P			
			P	X	Y	Z	P	X	Y	Z
PERCEIVED INFORMATION	1	**Weighted average perceived quality [from VOC]**	4.85	4.72	5.61	5.51	**1.000**	**0.973**	**1.157**	**1.137**
	2	**Stated average perceived value [from VOC]**	–	–	–	–	**1.000**	**0.960**	**1.100**	**1.070**
	3	Perceived price [from VOC]	7.04	6.54	7.40	7.49	1.000	0.929	1.051	1.064
	4	Average perceived inconvenience [% of total cost stated in VOC]	0.18	0.24	0.16	0.08	1.000	1.333	0.889	0.444
	5	Perceived inconvenience [calculated from VOC]	1.55	2.07	1.41	0.65	1.000	1.336	0.912	0.421
	6	Perceived price + perceived inconvenience (4 + 6)	8.59	8.61	8.81	8.14	1.000	1.002	1.026	0.948
MEASURED INFORMATION	7	**Weighted average measured quality [from VOC]**	5.49	5.26	5.68	5.92	**1.000**	**0.958**	**1.035**	**1.078**
	8	Base price [from market research]	6.98	6.34	7.69	7.27	1.000	0.908	1.102	1.042
	9	Measured package price [from market research]	8.10	6.88	8.71	7.43	1.000	0.849	1.075	0.917
	10	Inconvenience % [from market research]	0.10	0.20	0.05	0.15	–	–	–	–
	11	Inconvenience cost [calculated from market research]	0.67	1.24	0.36	1.08	1.000	1.854	0.539	1.606
	12	**CALCULATED VALUE** (1 + 7) / (6 + 9 + 11)**	0.60	0.60	0.63	0.69	**1.000**	**1.001**	**1.060**	**1.153**

**Calculated Value = (Actual + Perceived Quality)/(Actual and Perceived Cost + Actual and Perceived Inconvenience)

Appendix B

CURRENT ASSESSMENT TOOL, QUALITATIVE

Use the following chart to assess your progress or current standing in each factor. Use a ten-point scale ranging from 1 for "We do not address this issue," to 10 for "We perform as well as anyone, anywhere." A rating of 5 should equal "Adequate." Your rating should be based on how well you rate your current performance at the demand level of your customers when they have a substantial amount of information on the value both you and your competitors deliver.

If you do not have competitors, rate each factor on how well you must perform to deliver a high level of value to your customers or those you exist to serve as they gain increased information on your operation, product, or service. The chapter column tells you where to find information about the topic in this book.

For example, under the third factor, "Do you have a vision . . . ?", if your organization does not have a vision, your score will be 1. If you have a vision, but it is just some nice words to satisfy someone, it may have a rating of 3. If it is adequate for your long-term survival, but does not demand growth or high contribution, it should be rated a 5. If it has growth and contribution, but is short of being the best, or world class, it may be rated a 7 or 8. If your vision clearly puts you at the top of your field and has definite time targets and a degree of measurability, it is a 10.

Integrated Leadership Assessment		
Assessment Factor	**Score**	**Chapter**
Do you have a mission, and does it accurately reflect the purpose of your organization?		2
Are your values clearly stated, and does everyone in the organization know them and practice them?		2
Do you have a vision that is based on your mission and values, and is it specific, measurable, and doable, with a defined date for attainment?		2
Do you have a formal planning process that requires constant input and attention of senior leadership?		2
Does your planning include identified critical success factors, measurable goals that are specifically assigned, and targeted completion dates?		2
Do you have both current strategic and operating plans, and are these communicated throughout the organization so *everyone* knows their roles?		2
Are your plans aligned so every goal is deployed down through all the levels that are required to meet it?		2
Are your plans deployed in a manner where everyone's responsibility is clear and there is no conflict or chance of misunderstanding?		2
Are plans continually reviewed by management and are adjustments made? Is this practice done based on flow of new and specific information?		2
Does your control panel include the ongoing gathering and analysis of market, competitor, and external factors with internal information?		2
Does operations proactively adjust based on widespread use of information or does it react to every change from a narrow perspective?		2
Is your vision continuously displayed through a variety of mediums, and does everyone always know where you are in its attainment?		2
Are all major organizational goals continuously displayed and does everyone always know where you are in their attainment?		2
Are all plans and operations integrated? Do they share a common data base and are they accessible by everyone?		2
Do you know the top 10 drivers of value in the products and services your organization delivers? Are they constantly updated on your control panel?		3
Do you view your customers as partners? Do you have connecting processes, metrics, and indicators to support this relationship?		3
Do you measure the quality of what your customers receive? Do your measures include service quality, as well as product quality?		3
Do you have a high understanding of your suppliers' costs and margins of the products and services you receive from major suppliers?		3

Integrated Leadership Assessment—Continued		
Assessment Factor	**Score**	**Chapter**
Do you fully understand and measure the inconvenience or burden your customers endure with the products and services you provide?		3
Do you understand and measure your customer's perceptions of the major elements of the products and services you provide?		3
Do you understand and track the components of value, actual and perceived, that major competitors deliver to their customers?		3
Do you understand and measure your customer's perceptions of your performance against their expectations of your products and services?		3
Do you understand the needs of customers and the capabilities of competitors to the degree that you have a competitive advantage?		3
Do you continuously report the relative value and quality, both perceived and actual, you deliver compared with major competitors?		3
Do you track your competitors' strategies based on their continuous attention to the priority needs of customers in your market segments?		Appendix A
Do you compare how well you meet top customer needs compared with your competitors on a priority feature-by-feature basis?		Appendix A
Does everyone understand the value that is added along the customer chain from your suppliers' suppliers to your customers' customers?		4
Are your major customer's requirements clearly prioritized and weighted relative to each other?		4
Do all levels of your organization and every unit report their performance on how well they meet customer requirements on a frequent basis?		4
Do all personnel, at all levels, have service standards that they are accountable for, and are these reported?		4
Does the organization have a map of its critical process and support processes? Is every unit and individual included?		4
Does every unit/every individual have a current process map of their operation, including how it merges with the organization's critical process?		4
Are sensors that report key value added flow part of every unit's process map, and does this information transcend to a control panel?		4
Are key performance measures communicated to or available to key customers?		4
Does senior leadership spend most of their time on effectiveness or efficiency? Do they know how much they spend on each?		5

Integrated Leadership Assessment—Continued		
Assessment Factor	**Score**	**Chapter**
Does "group think" exist to large degree in the organization? Does it stifle or reduce the effectiveness of decisions?		5
Is strategic planning a continuous endeavor in the organization? This means it is an ongoing function, not an activity that is never completed.		5
Does the organization use activity based costing or a similar methodology to understand costs at the activity level and distinguish them from NVA costs?		5
Does the organization have a realistic estimation of its cost of quality? Does it have specific goals with specific plans to improve them?		5
Does it have a method to review the COQ at the unit level? Does it constantly identify the highest opportunities and work on them?		5
Does the organization have a strategy to become the low-cost provider? Does the definition of low cost provider include a clear level of quality?		5
Is profitability by product or service line, calculated by true costs (not allocated costs) on the organization's control panel?		5
Is unit and organizational productivity reported on the control panel, either directly or indexed?		5
Are cost of quality metrics on your control panel? Are they displayed both from a historical and targeted perspective?		5
Is improvement a strategic issue in your organization? Do you have a process of prioritizing improvement opportunities?		6
Is everyone in your organization knowledgeable in the fundamentals of improvement, and do they see improvement as part of their role?		6
Does your organization have an improvement model that everyone understands and uses? Are improvements communicated in this format?		6
Are improvement efforts coordinated throughout the organization to gain from the sharing of knowledge and avoid duplication of effort?		6
Is your organization a "learning organization" where systems thinking, personal mastery, coordination, and shared visions dominate?		6
Do you have a formal decision and implementation process that continually coordinates new activities with existing plans and operations?		6
Do you study your sales successes and failures using a won–lost analysis? Is the knowledge acquired communicated throughout the organization?		6
Is your customer support operation primarily a value-added organization or a rework and correction institution?		6

Integrated Leadership Assessment—Continued		
Assessment Factor	**Score**	**Chapter**
If it has a high percentage of waste and correction, do you have definite plans with time lines to convert it to a value-adding operation?		6
Do you have a *formal* process of bringing innovation and creativity into the organization? Is it efficient because it implements at lowest possible level?		6
Is your strategic planning process a periodic event or is it a continuous function of senior leadership using a stable process?		6
Is continuous value improvement a part of everyone's job? Is it a major part of their objectives, evaluation, and rewards and recognition?		6
What major industrial age assumption, principles, or theories are used in your organization that must change as you enter the Information Age?		7
Is there a harmonious understanding among all levels of your organization on how productivity improvements are shared?		7
How well evolved is teamwork in your organization? Is it defined as going along with the boss or as shared vision, cooperation, and collaboration?		7
Do you have a formal, ongoing leadership development process that is specific to your organization and its values and philosophies?		7
Do you have a progressive team process where everyone continually learns team and team leadership skills?		7
Are your team metrics superficial measures of activity, or are they based on valued-adding results?		7
Are all of your teams integrated, and can an individual easily move from one team to another?		7
Do your teams know their performance goals at all times, are they appropriate, and are they continuously measured?		7
Is your job performance review system primarily based on control of workers or assessment of skills and competencies for improvement?		8
Do you review individuals based on their performance in stable processes where they are properly trained and fully understand their role?		8
Are all individual measures fair, accurate, achievable, always measurable, results (not activity) oriented, and not dependent on subjective review?		8
Do individual performance goals always add up to unit goals; which, in turn, add up to organizational goals? Are there any disconnect points?		8
Does every individual have a thorough job profile that states precisely all responsibilities, all measures, and how to find answers to perform the job?		8

Integrated Leadership Assessment—Continued		
Assessment Factor	**Score**	**Chapter**
Are all processes aligned throughout the organization down to the task and subtask levels; are they integrated through appropriate metrics?		8
Are skills and competencies clearly defined and communicated for every job, and does every incumbent know what must be done to be competent?		8
Is training viewed as a solution to something, or is training defined by a gap between individuals' skills and competencies and those skills and competencies required?		8
Are communications and decisions primarily conducted through meetings, memos, and bulletins, or are they built into work and information processes?		8
Does your organization continuously answer the question, "What is the best course to take to attain our vision?"		9
Does your organization's control panel provide continuous and prioritized information on the voice of the customer by segment and product?		9
Is the control panel balanced by integrating knowledge on customers, employees, suppliers, internal and external processes, and owners?		9
Does the control panel measure the value the organization adds and its customers receive? Is it indexed, relative, or absolutely measured?		All Chapters
Does it include customer loyalty, retention, and satisfaction and correlate this data with the VOC?		9
Does it reflect movement of market opportunity and the organization's and competitors' relative share of the changing market?		9
Are productivity measures reported for all critical process steps? Are these measures acquired through the use of automated sensors?		9
Are head-to-head sales measured through competitive won-lost analysis and progression of prospects through the sales process?		9
Is alignment with the vision, mission, and values measured as well as performance against top organizational goals?		9
Does everyone in the organization always have the information they need to do their job at the time it is required?		9
Does the organization conduct its strategy planning using a "war room" where information is gathered, scenarios are challenged, and decisions are made?		9
Does your control panel perform continuous statistical analysis, including correlation figures on high-level indicators and measures?		9

Integrated Leadership Assessment—Continued		
Assessment Factor	**Score**	**Chapter**
Is the control panel used by top leadership a vital part of their everyday activity, or is it an infrequent tool for planning only?		9
How is leadership measured and evaluated? Do employees and owners see both the goals and results of senior management performance?		9
How well is your organization linked to the control panels of government, support institutions, and the voice of the citizen?		10
Has your organization fully solved Taylor's mental revolution? Are the gains from productivity improvements shared to everyone's delight?		10
How will your organization fare when customers have as much, or more, knowledge about the value your organization adds as you do?		10
Do you have your life aligned with a greater vision of the Information Age to come, and are you collaborating and working with others who also have theirs aligned and focused?		10

Appendix C

LESSONS FROM AUSTRALIA

A few years ago, I worked with local executives of a large finance company[1] in Australia to help them improve operational results. The long-term vision of the organization was growth, but there was confusion regarding strategy. Senior management was convinced that the personal loan business for finance companies had been saturated in Australia, and the only growth opportunities would be captured by banks and building societies (similar to savings and loans in America). They believed that the acquisition of competitors was the only way a large finance company could grow.

In January 1987, the first problem solving meeting was held in Melbourne and focused on how to cultivate growth opportunities. The initial meeting included senior managers, followed by sessions with middle managers and branch-level supervisors. These meetings lasted for two weeks and were followed by the appointment of a cross-functional team directed to increase growth.

Most of the discussions up to this point had occurred at high levels between Australian management and the U.S. parent company. Every executive had his or her own ideas, and no one had spent much effort involving branch employees, much less customers, for their ideas.

The company had an edict from their parent to increase receivables outstanding (total amount currently owed to the company in loans) during 1988. The amount of targeted gain was $28 million in Australian currency (A$), equivalent to approximately U.S.$24 million.

The challenge that faced the operation is outlined in the graph in Figure C.1, which shows low historical growth against a very aggressive 1988 plan, which called for a late year bulk purchase of loans from another finance company for A$14 million. Everyone knew the bulk purchase was very unlikely and was designed to allow about eight months of breathing room.

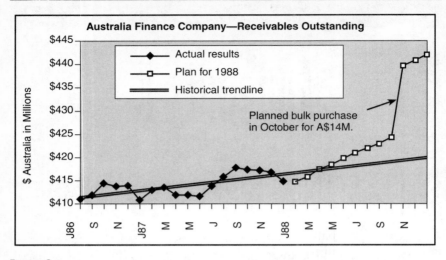

Figure C.1   The 1988 plan greatly exceeded the historical trend line.

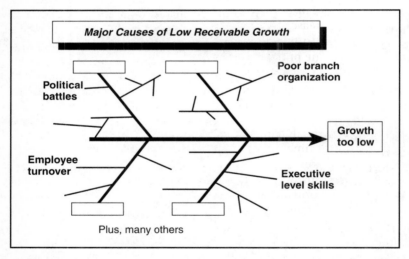

Figure C.2   These four items initially emerged as the four largest causes of low receivables growth.

The average loan was very short-term and most loans were small ($A1,500 or less), presenting a challenge to receivable growth. A large percentage of loans were paid off during the year and had to be replaced. Current market penetration was about twice that of the U.S. operations, which had created some resentment for being directed to take on such a challenge.

Several days were spent identifying and exploring hundreds of possible causes of low production. The fishbone diagram in Figure C.2 shows the major categories of causes of poor production.

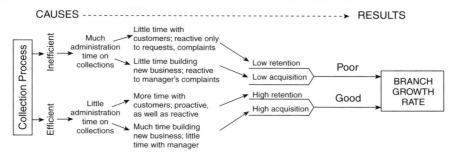

Figure C.3   The causal chain of factors influencing branch growth rates.

The political battles and executive-level skills reflected a frustration with their American parent, who, the Australians felt, did not understand the business culture of Australia. There was certainly work to be done in this area, but it seemed outside the scope of the mission. Employee turnover was a concern, because turnover is a symptom of deeper problems. Generally, turnover decreases when other causes are remedied. Nevertheless, the executives agreed to pursue the high turnover problem, which they hope would lead to some profound solutions.

The cross-functional team went to work to find out more. Correlation analysis between branches that grew and those that lost receivables showed remarkable differences. Intense research at both the branch and customer levels yielded two key findings. First, poorly performing branches did not spend much time with current customers, and, second, they spent an inordinate amount of time on administrative functions relating to collections. This causal relationship is shown in Figure C.3. Collection activity is directed at those customers with past due amounts.

The poor performance branches had no significant differences from the high performing branches in the areas of delinquency rates, bad loans, or in competency and customer service skills. However, there were significant differences in customer retention and loyalty, because poor performance branches spent much more time with collections. Conversely, successful branches were more efficient in identifying and handling delinquencies.

Additional research revealed that a few of the most successful branches used their automated branch operating system to help work their collection activity, whereas most other branches relied primarily on a manual "tub" process for both the identification and follow-up for collection management. Although the automated system had been designed with a very efficient collection system, the training and spread of knowledge necessary to effectively utilize it had not occurred. It quickly became apparent that there were better ways to manage the collection process. As soon as a few changes were made, along with outstanding leadership from the Australian management team, everything began to improve.

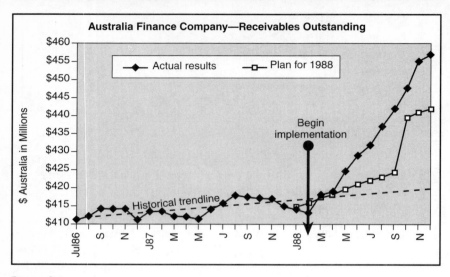

Figure C.4   As branches became more organized, better production results were realized.

The successful branches' techniques were quickly studied, automated, and disseminated across the country, producing the results shown in the graph in Figure C.4.

The company continued to work on some of the other challenges such as turnover, training, and executive skills, and political concerns diminished over time. The breakthrough results continued at a new level through the first half of 1990,[2] as shown in Figure C.5.

Two important lessons emerged from this experience:

1. In order to significantly improve or solve a situation, one must become a zealot in the pursuit of the root cause(s). Surface causes, symptoms, or high-level causes are not enough.[3]
2. In all major areas that impact organizational performance, one should always understand the voice of the customer and build or improve the necessary processes to meet their requirements.

The key to adding value begins with understanding customers. The voice of the customer is the target for the organization. It is the destination in the journey for value.

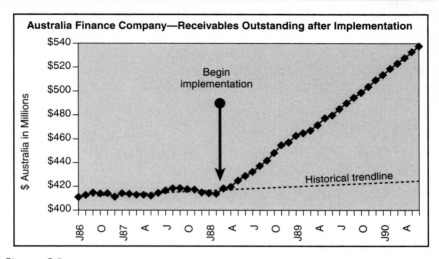

Figure C.5 Breakthrough growth improvement continued at a much steeper pace.

NOTES

1. The company is not identified, although the process and results are well documented. Much of it can be found in the submission for the 1989 Australian Quality Award, in which the company was selected as a finalist.
2. At this point, I stopped tracking results.
3. The actual root cause of the inefficient branches was a computer programming error that had been undetected for five years and resulted in delinquency being handled in a cumbersome, manual method in the branches. The better branches had discovered ways to improve the manual system.

Appendix D

STUDYING LEADERSHIP

Benchmarking is one of the most productive techniques for performance improvement when it is conducted correctly. It is a form of information or knowledge transfer. The military has been an institution for thousands of years and has continually updated its leadership models. Like all organizations, the military is having to adjust the application of its model to the Information Age as well as much higher public scrutiny than in the past. However, the basics are sound, and it is an excellent source for case study regardless of organization affiliation. Following are a few thoughts and examples of military leadership.

The military is exceptional in its leadership training, from the most basic level through its senior level. Fortunately, many private and business organizations inherit considerable leadership talent that has been developed through military service, and a few have adopted the military as a model. The military succeeds in leadership development because it has a strong focus. An example is shown by the U.S. Army's Center for Army Leadership, which exists for the following:[1]

Purpose: Improve leadership in America's Army
Vision: Develop creative, adaptive and competent leaders
Mission: Develop, integrate, and execute leadership policies, programs, doctrine, education and training across the Army

A military officer usually spends nine months or more (four years plus for the military academies) in basic leadership training and application before they are eligible to receive a command assignment. Higher level officers spend years in more advanced leadership and specialty training before they are appointed to greater responsibility.

Basic leadership is primarily a human relations skill that probably changes little over generations. It is not an exact science and it varies based on situations, stress, and the character of individuals who are followers, peers, and superiors. A person may be a great leader under certain circumstances and fail in other situations. Some leaders work well in teams and others seem to only excel in command positions. There are rare individuals who seem to excel in all types of environments.

No individual completely masters leadership. It is a performance that can be continually improved, and most individuals should update and constantly upgrade their skills. Two outstanding authors on leadership skills at the executive level are Warren Bennis and Peter Drucker. There are boundless biographies and case studies available on great leaders throughout history and men and women in leadership positions today.

At the basic level, manuals for officer candidate school (OCS) leadership courses in the military are excellent, even if you locate a dated copy. The older ones certainly have to be translated into today's politically correct language, but their principles are sound. The basic publications for the U.S. Army are *FM (Field Manual) 22-100, Military Leadership; FM 22-101, Leadership Counseling;* and *FM 22-102, Soldier Team Development.*[2] The military takes an integrated approach to training. It indoctrinates recruits into the basic values, policies, and customs in the military during basic training and continually provides both a hands on view along with a wider horizon.

Some of the values that were expected of army officers (in the mid-1980s) include: *commitment, competence, confidence, courage, candor, dedication, responsibility, loyalty, discipline,* and *selflessness.*[3] These are well defined with examples of each and they are openly discussed and challenged by new recruits in the classroom. At the end of officer's candidate school, there is little doubt or confusion associated with these terms.

At the end of World War II, the "Blue Book" was introduced at the Naval Academy. It is full of wisdom for a naval officer trainee about leadership. The following is one of its hundreds of lessons on leadership (my apologies for including a reference that was written for men, but there were no women cadets at Annapolis in 1949).

> *It has been written that every naval officer must be two things. First he must be a gentleman and, second, he must be learned in his profession. But all of the knowledge in the world will not help you if you fail to meet the standards of a gentleman. If you are uncouth in your manner, foul in your talk, boastful to your friends, inconsiderate in your relations with others; if you lie or cheat under any circumstances, or cannot lose without complaining, you are not a gentleman, and will never command the respect of others, no matter how intelligent you may be. So take stock of yourself now. You are in new surroundings, making new friends; now is the time to make a new start and to eliminate the ungentlemanly qualities from your nature. In your classmates you have several hundred critics who will be stationed with you and create your service reputation for the rest of your life. Live your life with them now so that they cannot but respect you and refer to you as a gentleman. No naval officer can afford to do otherwise. You must be a gentleman or a failure.*[4]

Although most of this advice for a leader is just as sound today as it was almost 50 years ago, it is difficult to find in most basic leadership training. The Marine Officer's Guide[5] is packed with leadership principles and wisdom for leaders in every walk of life. Below are a couple of gems from the basic book for young officers that contribute to the "esprit de corps" that is the hallmark of the Marine Corps.

> *A Marine has to be good. In the Marine Corps, your best is just the accepted minimum. It is expected, as a matter of course, that the technical performance of a single Marine or a whole Marine outfit, whether on parade or in the attack, will be outstanding.*[6]
>
> *The foundations of an individual's performance as a Marine are discipline, a sense of duty, courage, self-assurance, and cooperative thinking. . . . Establishing such foundations remains the salient objective of leadership.*[7]
>
> *In the final analysis, the essence of Marine leadership is looking out for your people. For the sake of the unit, you must be tireless, you must be imaginative, you must be willing to shoulder responsibility. Their good must be your first preoccupation. Their interest and advancement must be always on your mind. . . . If you let down one of your Marines, you are letting down the entire Corps.*[8]

Since performance depends on the competency of people, one trait of a leader is the development of people not only to carry out their duties and achieve objectives, but to continuously improve their results. The leader should always know the strengths and shortcomings of individuals as they relate to their role and always filling in gaps with education and development of skills and knowledge.

Leadership is everything. The largest distinct difference between leadership and the management approach of the Industrial Age is the value of the individual. Management reduces the human to an intelligent production unit; leadership elevates the individual to a distinct and limitless source of creativity, innovation, and value. The Information Age will provide this source of unlimited talent with the freedom to soar.

NOTES

1. Internet address: http://www-cgsc.army.mil/, November 1996.
2. Printed by the U.S. Government Printing Office, Washington, D.C.
3. United States Army Infantry School, *OCS Leadership Workbook* (Fort Benning, Ga.: U.S. Government Printing Office, Region 4, 1985), Soldierly Qualities/Professional Values, p. 2.
4. Prepared under the direction of the superintendent, naval leadership: for the instruction of midshipmen (Annapolis, Md.: U.S. Naval Institute, 1949), p. 215.

5. Kenneth W. Estes, Lieutenant Colonel, USMC, *The Marine Officer's Guide,* 5th ed. (Annapolis, Md.: Naval Institute Press, 1985).

6. See note 5, p. 2.

7. See note 5, p. 293.

8. See note 5, pp. 308–309.

Bibliography

3M. *Annual Report*, 1995.

Alberts, David S., and Richard E. Haynes. "The Realm of Information Dominance: Beyond Information War." First International Symposium on Command and Control Research and Technology (June 1995).

American Express Company, *1995 Annual Report*.

Anthes, Gary H. "IRS: Tough to get any respect." *Computerworld*, vol. 30, no. 42, October 14, 1996: 28.

———. "40 whacks with the budget ax." *Computerworld*, vol. 30, no. 42, October 14, 1996: 29.

———. "IRS project failures cost taxpayers $50B annually." *Computerworld*, vol. 30, no. 42, October 14, 1996: 1–28.

Armstrong World Industries, Inc. *Shaking the Armstrong Tree: Reshaping for Growth; Annual Report*, 1995.

Arquilla, John, and David Ronfeldt. "Cyberwar is Coming." *Comparative Strategy*, vol. 12 , no. 2: 141–65. The quotes came from the Internet version, which was copyrighted in 1993 by Taylor and Francis, 1101 Vermont Avenue. NW #200, Washington, DC 20005.

Asaka, Tetsuichi, general editor, and Kazuo Ozeki, editor. *Handbook of Quality Tools: The Japanese Approach*. Cambridge, Massachusetts: Productivity Press, 1990.

ASQC Quality Costs Committee. Jack Campanella, ed. *Principles of Quality Costs*. 2nd ed. Milwaukee: ASQC Quality Press, 1990.

AT&T. *1994 Annual Report*.

Bennis, Warren, and Michael Mishe. *The 21st Century Organization: Reinventing Through Reengineering*. San Diego: Pfeiffer & Company, 1995.

Brimson, James A. *Activity Accounting: An Activity-Based Costing Approach*. New York: John Wiley & Sons, Inc., 1991.

Buzzell, Robert D., and Bradley T. Gale. *The PIMS Principles*. New York: The Free Press, 1987.

Carlzon, Jan. *Moments of Truth*. Cambridge, Mass.: Ballinger Publishing Company, 1987.

Certo, Samual C. *Principles of Modern Management: Functions and Systems*. Dubuque, Iowa: Wm. C. Brown Publishers, 1986.

Collins, James C., and Jerry I. Porras. *Built to Last*. New York: Harper Business, 1994.

Covey, Stephen R. *The Seven Habits of Highly Effective People*. New York: Simon & Schuster, 1986.

Crosby, Philip B. *Quality is Free: The Art of Making Quality Certain.* New York: Mentor, 1980.

Dale, Ernest, Ph.D. *Management: Theory and Practice.* 4th ed. New York: McGraw-Hill, 1978.

Davis, Robert, Susan Rosegrant, and Michael Watkins, "Managing the Link Between Measurement and Competition." *Quality Progress,* vol. 28, no. 2, February 1995: 101–106.

Deming, W. Edwards. *Out of the Crisis.* Cambridge: Massachusetts Institute of Technology, Center for Advanced Engineering Study, 1989.

Drucker, Peter F. *The Frontiers of Management.* New York: Truman Talley Books/E.P. Dutton, 1986.

Eastman Chemical Company. *1995 Annual Report.*

Estes, Lieutenant Colonel Kenneth W., USMC. *The Marine Officer's Guide.* 5th ed. Annapolis, Maryland: Naval Institute Press, 1985.

Fairfield, Lt. Gen. John S. "Horizon—A Jointly Focused Vision Charting the Course for the 21st Century Air Force." *Armed Forces Journal International,* January 1996.

Federal Express Corporation. *1995 Annual Report.*

———. *1996 Annual Report, The Facts.*

Ford Motor Company. *1995 Annual Report.*

Freund, John E. *Modern Elementary Statistics,* 6th ed. Englewood Cliffs, N.J.: Prentice-Hall, 1984.

Friedman, Col. Richard S., and others. *Advanced Technology Warfare: A Detailed Study of the Latest Weapons and Techniques for Warfare Today and into the 21st Century.* New York: Harmony Books, 1985.

Gibson, James William. *The Perfect War: Technowar In Vietnam.* Boston: The Atlantic Monthly Press, 1986.

Hammer, Michael, and James Champy. *Reengineering the Corporation: A Manifesto for Business Revolution.* New York, HarperBusiness, 1993.

Harley-Davidson, Inc. *1995 Annual Report.*

———. *1996 Annual Report.*

Hewlett-Packard Company and Subsidiaries. *1995 Annual Report.*

Hock, Dee W. "The Chaordic Organization: Out of Control and Into Order." *World Business Academy Perspectives,* vol. 9, no 1: 5–18.

Horovitz, Bruce. "Value-minded consumers call the shots." *USA Today,* September, 10, 1996, Money section.

Jevons, W. Stanley, *Investigations in Currency and Finance,* Pt. 2, Cp. 4, 1884, quoted from *The Columbia Dictionary of Quotations* is licensed from Columbia University Press. Copyright © 1993 by Columbia University Press.

Joint Venture: Silicon Valley Network, Inc. *Index of Silicon Valley 1996: Measuring Progress Toward a 21st Century Community,* 1996.

Juran, Joseph M. "The Upcoming Century of Quality." *Quality Progress,* Vol. 27, no. 8, August 1994: 29–37.

———. *Juran on Quality by Design: The New Steps for Planning Quality into Goods and Services.* New York, The Free Press, 1992.

Kano, Seraku, and Tsuji Takahashi, "Attractive Quality and Must-Be Quality," 1984. Presented at Nippon QC Gakka: 12th Annual Meeting.

Kaplan, Robert S., and David P. Norton. "Putting the Balanced Scorecard to Work," *Harvard Business Review,* September–October 1993.

Kaplan, Robert S., and David P. Norton. "The Balanced Scorecard—Measures That Drive Performance." *Harvard Business Review,* January–February 1992.

Koenig, William J. *Weapons of World War.* London: Bison Books Limited, 1981.

Kotler, Philip. *Marketing Management: Analysis, Planning and Control.* Englewood Cliffs, N.J.: Prentice-Hall, 1980.

Lucent Technologies. *First Annual Report, 1996.*

Lucky, Robert W. *Silicon Dreams: Information, Man and Machine.* New York: St. Martin's Press, 1989.

Maglitta, Joseph. "Learning lessons from IRS' biggest mistakes." *Computerworld,* vol. 30, no. 42, October 14, 1996: 30.

Manes, Stephen. "Software Today: It's All Beta." *PC World,* October 1996.

Mann, Edward. "Desert War: The First Information War?" Airpower Journal (Winter 1994): 4–14.

Marsh, Stan, John W. Morgan, Satoshi Nakui, and Glen D. Hoffherr, *Facilitating and Training in Quality Function Deployment.* Methuen, Mass.: Goal/QPC, 1991.

Maslow, Abraham H. "The Theory of Human Motivation." *Psychological Review,* vol. 50, 1943: 370–96.

Miller, Robert B., and Stephen E. Heiman, with Tad Tuleja. *Strategic Selling.* Berkeley: Warner Books, 1985.

Motorola, Inc. *1995 Summary Annual Report.*

———. *1996 Summary Annual Report.*

Nordstrom, Inc. and Subsidiaries. *1995 Annual Report.*

Paige, Emmett Jr., "Ensuring Joint Force Superiority in the Information Age." Defense Issues, vol. 11, no. 82. Downloaded on the World Wide Web at http://dtic.mil/defenselink/pubs/di_index.html.

Plenert, Gerhard. *World Class Manager: Olympic Quality Performance in the New Global Economy.* Rocklin, Calif.: Prima Publishing Company, 1995.

Pritchett, Price. *The Employee Handbook of New Work Habits For A Radically Changing World: 13 Ground Rules for Job Success In the Information Age.* Dallas: Pritchett & Associates, Inc., 1994.

Reeves, Carol A., David A. Bednar, and R. Cayce Lawrence, "Back To The Beginning: What Do Customers Care About In Service Firms." Quality Management Journal, vol. 3, Issue 1, 1996: 56–72.

Rubbermaid Incorporated. *1995 Annual Report.*

Scholtes, Peter R. "Teams in the Age of Systems." *Quality Progress,* vol. 28, no. 12, December 1995: 51–58.

Senge, Peter M. *The Fifth Discipline: The Art and Practice of the Learning Organization.* New York: Doubleday/Currency, 1990.

Shewhart, Walter A. *Economic Control of Quality of Manufactured Product.* Van Nostrand, 1931: repr. ed., American Society for Quality Control, 1980; reprinted by Ceepress, The George Washington University, 1986.

Shippey, Penelope Fitzgerald, in *The Gate of Angels,* Chapter 6 (1990). The Columbia Dictionary of Quotations is licensed from Columbia University Press. Copyright © 1993 by Columbia University Press.

Shonk, James H. *Team Based Organizations: Developing a Successful Team Environment.* Homewood, Ill.: Business One Irwin, 1992.

Solectron Corporation. *1995 Annual Report.*

St. Quintin, Mark. "Quality Models and Standards for Software," presented at the 1993 International Conference on Software Quality, *Winning in the '90s the Quality Way,* held October 4–6, 1993 at the Hyatt Regency, Lake Tahoe, Nevada, sponsored by the Software Division of the American Society for Quality Control (ASQC) and the Santa Clara Valley Software Quality Association, Conference Proceedings.

Stoner, James A. F., and Charles Wankel. *Management,* 3rd ed. Englewood Cliffs, N.J.: Prentice-Hall, 1986.

Superintendent, Naval Leadership. *For the Instruction of Midshipmen.* Annapolis, Md.: U.S. Naval Institute, 1949.

Toffler, Alvin. *Future Shock.* New York: Bantam Books, 1970.

——. *Powershift: Knowledge, Wealth, and Violence At The Edge Of The 21st Century.* New York: Bantam Books, 1990.

——. *The Third Wave.* New York: Bantam Books, 1981.

Tribus, Myron. *Quality First: Selected Papers on Quality and Productivity Improvement.* 4th ed. Washington D.C.: National Institute for Engineering Management & Systems, 1992.

United States Army Infantry School. *OCS Leadership Workbook.* Fort Benning, Ga.: U.S. Government Printing Office, Region 4, 1985.

Weston, J. Fred, and Eugene F. Brigham. *Essentials of Managerial Finance,* 7th ed. New York: Dryden Press, 1985.

Williams, J. Clifton, Andrew J. DuBrin and Henry L. Sisk. *Management and Organization,* 5th ed. Cincinnati: South-Western Publishing, 1985.

Womack, James P., Daniel T. Jones and Daniel Roos. *The Machine That Changed The World.* New York: Rawson Associates, Macmillan Publishing Company, 1990.

Xerox Corporation. *1995 Annual Report.*

Zytec Corporation. *1996 Annual Report: Creating Value.*

Index

Absenteeism, 125
Accounting systems
    activity based costing (ABC), 119–20
    cost of quality (COQ), 119, 120–23
    traditional, 112–15, 132
Acquisitions, value of, 143
Activities
    defined, 187
    monitoring with control panel, 215
    recording value in COQ analysis, 128, 129
    relation to results, 182–83
Activity based costing (ABC), 119–20
Actual value, 57–58
American Express, vision statement of, 34
Anger, in customer satisfaction scale, 65
Appraisal costs, 122, 128, 129
Armstrong, value statement of, 32
Arquilla, John, 170
Artificial intelligence, 211
AT&T, vision statement of, 34
AT&T Universal Card Services, 200–201
Attitude, as a competitive advantage, 163–64
Australia, finance company study, 255–59

Babbage, Charles, 160
Baldrige Award, 3, 26
Base price, 243
Basic solutions, in monitoring value, 243
Benchmarking, 193–94, 261–63
Bennis, Warren, 32, 262
Best value, 57
Blue Book, 262–63
Bottom-up tool, 126–27
Brain, as model for organization, 169–70
Budgets, 113. See also Accounting systems

Call management systems, 104
Catchball approach, 41–42, 43, 188–89
Cause-and-effect model for improvement, 139–40
Center for Army Leadership, 261–62
Change
    barriers to, 231
    managing, 117–18
    and PDCA approach, 189

    from traditional to team-oriented
        structure, 166–67
Chaordic organization, 171–72
Charter, 51
Coefficient of correlation, 210
Collaboration, 229
Command and control systems, 207
Communication
    and vertical alignment, 42–44
    staff meeting versus control panel
        approach, 195
Community, in Information Age, 226
Competency, 192
Competency/development status, 172, 173
Competition, 21, 48
Competitive advantage, 53–54
Competitors
    measuring perceived value against,
        70–71, 239–45
    pressure to improve from, 139
    protecting information from, 213
Complaints, customer, 125, 203
Complexity, and evolution of
    management, 163
Continuous improvement, 136–38, 156–57
Continuous learning, 193–94
Control panel
    basic concepts of, 208–12
    cost metrics on, 130–32
    creating, 44–47, 105–7, 212–14
    evolution of, 198–200, 226–28
    examples of, 200–208, 239–45
    improvement tools for, 145–56
    as leadership tool, 2, 9–11, 172, 219–21
    linking with systems, 216–18, 221
    as strategic planning tool, 156, 218–19
    tracking and integrating functions of,
        169, 194–95
    using, 214–21, 239–45
Core competencies, 37
Correlation, 210
Correlation analysis, 210–11, 257
Cost drivers, 119
Cost of inconvenience, 60–61, 71–72,
    235, 243
Cost of nonconformance, 120

Cost of quality (COQ), 120–27, 132
Costs
   accounting for, 119–23
   comparing to value added, 123–25
   control panel metrics for, 130–32
   traditional approaches to, 112–15
   unnecessary, 115–17
Covey, Stephen, 5
Crime, predictions for future of, 227
Critical processes
   and cost of quality, 123–25
   defined, 88, 110, 186
   improving, 97–98, 147–50
   specifications for, 93–94, 95
Critical success factors, 36–38
Crumly, Mark, 57
Culture, effect on improvement efforts, 143
Customer chain, 83–87
Customer-driven organizations, 4–5
Customer focus, 37
Customer loyalty, 63, 203
Customer/market driven, as principle of
   integrated leadership, 2
Customers
   complaints of, 125
   computer links with, 55
   defining, 82–83
   delighting, 53–54, 65–66
   expectations of, 48, 64–68, 72–74,
      88–92, 230
   loyalty and retention of, 203, 257
   measuring VOC, 239–45
   partnership with, 54–55, 230
   pressure to improve from, 138–39,
      236–37
Customer service/support
   limitations as VOC metric, 48
   tracking problems, 91–92
   and value added, 150–52
Cycle time, 37, 90

Data
   gathering, 151, 209
   increasing use of, 216–18
   validity of, 243
Databases, in Information Age, 13
Decentralization, 213
Decision making
   based on VOC analysis, 240
   and improvement, 143–44
Decision matrices, 156
Decision support systems, 153–54
Defect rate, 104
Delegation, 116
Delight, zone of, 65–66
Demand weight, 72–74, 240
Deming, W. Edwards, 16, 76–77, 79, 140,
   162, 179
Deployment, of plans, 39, 41–42
Deregulation, 202–3
Developing nations, shift of manufacturing
   to, 163

Differential rate system, 161, 162
Disclosure, adding value by, 63–64
Dissatisfaction, zone of, 65
Distributed systems, organizations as, 213
Drill down approach, 46
Drivers, 4, 228–29
Drucker, Peter, 262
Duplication of efforts, cost of, 116–17

Eastman Chemical, vision statement of, 34
Economic indicators, as control panel
   metric, 204–5
Economic value added, 10, 59–60
Education
   of leaders, 165
   predictions for future of, 227
Effectiveness, 115–18
Efficiency, 115–23
Effort, duplication of, 116–17
Elections, predictions for future of, 227
Employees
   competencies of, 172, 173
   motivating, 161, 163–64
   performance reviews, 178–83
   satisfaction of, 203
Enlightenment, 12
Evolution of knowledge, 20–21
Exception indicators, 214
Excitement, of customers, 66
Expectations, versus performance, 64–68
Expenses, 113
Expert systems, 211
External failure, 151–52

Failure costs
   in COQ approach, 122
   identifying, 128, 129
   and improvement, 151–52
Fayol, Henri, 160, 162, 166
Federal Express
   control panel example, 201–2
   mission statement of, 30
   vision statement of, 34
Finance companies
   Australian case study, 255–59
   perceived value and, 62–63
Financial management, in control panels,
   198–99
Financial metrics, evolution of, 9–10
Fishbone diagram, 140, 256
Fitzgerald, Penelope, 53
Fogelman, Ronald R., 197
Ford
   value statement of, 32
   vision statement of, 34
Foundations
   designing, 6
   establishing, 28–30
   planning, 2 (see also Planning)
Frequent-use programs, 63

Gantt, Henry, 160
Gantt chart, 160
Gilbreth, Frank, 160, 162
Gilbreth, Lillian, 160, 162
Global Command and Control System, 207
Global vision, 226
Goals
    creating, 23–24, 38–39
    monitoring performance toward, 214–15
    objective versus subjective, 190–91
    for work teams, 167–68
Government, predictions for future of, 227
Grandes del Mayo, I. J., 169
Group think, 116
Growth, planning, 255–56

Harley-Davidson
    value statement of, 32
    vision and goals of, 35
Hewlett-Packard, mission statement of, 30
High-level customer maps, 102
Historical trends, 199
Hock, Dee W., 171
Horizontal alignment, 2, 7–8, 79–81
House of quality, 69, 74, 239–45
Human systems, 222

Idea database, 153–55
Ideas, acting on, 153–55
Implementation, of decisions, 144–45
Improvement
    barriers to, 151–52
    control panel tools for, 145–56
    models for, 139–41
    principles of, 136–39, 258
    targeting, 141–45, 240
Improvement rate, 21–23
Inconvenience
    cost of, 60–61, 71–72, 235, 243
    perceived, 243
Individuals
    adding value as, 185
    future gains for, 233–37
    and jobs, 183–84
    value of, 263
Industrial Age
    management principles of, 160–62
    predicted disappearance of, 230
Ineffectiveness, cost of, 115–17
Inefficiency, cost of, 115–17
Information
    expanding role of, 11–14, 214, 229
    protecting from competitors, 213
    sensors for gathering, 209
Information Age
    predictions for, 225–36
    role of computers in creating, 13
Information management, 37
Initiatives, on control panel, 153
Integrated leadership
    applied to teams, 168–69
    assessing, 247–53
    basic principles, 2
    future trends, 229–30
    illustrated, 3
    See also Leaders; Leadership
Integration
    of improvement efforts, 143–44
    of performance measures, 181–82
    of systems, 215
    of teams, 168–69
Internal Revenue Service, Tax Systems
        Modernization program of, 230–31
Internet, as example of chaordic
        organization, 172
Issues system, 153–55

Japanese products, improvement rate of,
        21–23
Jevons, W. Stanley, 1
Job descriptions, 188
Job profiles, 188–90
Jobs
    creating, 187–88
    critical measures for, 191–93
    defined, 183–84
    in Information Age, 222
    as value-added services, 185
    versus processes, 134, 183–84
Juran, Joseph, 32, 162

Key business process, 186
Knowledge
    evolution of, 20–21
    external versus internal, 213–14
    increasing with control panels,
        216–18, 221
    value of, 13–14
Knowledge-based systems, 211

Leaders
    education and training of, 165, 261–63
    effective, 5–6, 19, 164–65
    importance of control panels to, 211–12,
        214–22
    role of, 164–65
    use of process maps by, 98–102
Leadership
    assessing, 247–53
    challenges of, 48
    defined, 5, 222, 229–30
    effective, 5–6, 19, 117–18, 164–65
    evolution of, 219–22
    performance and, 165, 197
    planning model for, 39–41
    principles of, 2, 6–11
    of teams, 168–69, 172
    and wisdom, 197
Leadership planning/deployment model,
        39–41

League of Nations, 225
Lean production, 13
Learning organizations, 144
Listening posts, in AT&T UCS tracking system, 200
Long-term employment, threats to, 184
Long-term planning, 36
Low-cost provider, as strategy, 128–29
Loyalty, customer, 63, 67, 257
Lucent Technologies, slogan of, 31

Management by exception, 162
Manufacturing, global trends in, 163
Margin, 59, 112
Marine Officer's Guide, 263
Market-driven organizations, 4–5
Marketing, 69, 129–30
Market price, and actual value, 58
Market research, 239
Market share, 22, 203
Market value added, 10
Maslow's hierarchy of needs, 62
McCain, Gary, 67–68
Measurability, of goals, 190–91
Measures
    of customer requirements, 88–92
    of employee performance, 180–83, 191–93
    financial, 9, 198–200
    objective versus subjective, 190–91
    for teams, 167–68
    of value, 9–11, 239–45
    See also Control panels
Mental revolution, in Taylor's theory, 161, 162, 163–64, 232–33
Mergers, 143
Metrics. See Measures
Milestones, 38
Military
    control panel example, 206–8
    leadership training in, 261–63
Mische, Michael, 32
Mission, 28, 30–31
Modeling, 218
Moment of truth, 64, 77
Morale, 125
Motivation, of employees, 161, 163–64
Motorola, value statement of, 31–32
Multidimensional decision matrices, 156

National vision, 226
Networks, as models for organizations, 170
Neuron, as model for jobs, 169
Newport News Shipyard, mission statement of, 30
Nonprofit organization, control panel example, 204–5
Nordstrom, value statement of, 31

Objective/means method, 41–42, 43
Objectives
    conflicting, 42–44
    monitoring performance toward, 214–15
    for work teams, 167–68
Officer candidate school, 262
On-line links, with customers, 55
One-best-way approach, 161
Operating plans, 39, 181
Operation cycle time reports, 104
Organization charts, 81, 94–96
Organizations
    decentralization of, 213
    defining, 28–29
    illustrating functions of, 94–102
    new forms of, 169–72
Outsourcing, 185
Owen, Robert, 160

Package price, 243
Paige, Emmett Jr., 207–8
Pareto analysis, 51, 151, 152
Pareto principle, 210
Partnering, strategic, 59
People development, 37
Perception, and value, 61–64
Performance
    critical measures for, 191–93
    improving, 235, 258
    monitoring, 102–8, 214–15
    reporting, 104–8
    versus expectations, 64–68
Performance review systems
    current state of, 178–79
    designing, 181–83
    invalid, 180–81
Persian Gulf War, as example of strategic success, 18–19
Plan deployment, 39, 41–42
Plan-Do-Check-Act (PDCA) Cycle, 8, 140, 189
Planning
    and change, 118
    and deployment, 39, 41–42
    importance of, 28
    operational, 39
    process illustrated, 35–36
    separate from execution, 161, 162
    strategic, 39
    using control panels for, 156, 208–9, 218–19
Planning/deployment model, 39–41
Planning sessions, 219
Plenert, Gerhard, 33
Policies, relation to values, 32
Preferred customer programs, 63
Prevention costs, 122, 128, 129

Price
    components of, 59–60, 243
    market, 58
    and value, 16, 111–12, 243
Price/inconvenience split, 71–72
Primary customer, 83
Prioritizing
    customer needs, 88–90, 92
    improvement efforts, 142–43
Problem solving, and improvement, 141
Processes
    and costs, 112, 113, 128
    defined, 79–80, 184, 186
    improving, 147–50, 226–28
    levels of, 186–88
    value added, 79–82
    versus jobs, 134, 183–84
Process flow chart, 160
Process improvement, 226–28
Process maps
    creating, 96–102
    illustrated, 88, 93, 97, 99–101
    as improvement tools, 123–25, 147–50
Producer, in customer chain, 84
Production, in scientific management, 161,
        162, 183
Productivity, 131–32, 160–62
Productivity index, 132
Profitability, 131, 182
Profits, as performance measure, 181
Progress, assessing, 247–53
Project management systems, 215
Projects, defining, 39
Project teams, 39
Purpose, defined, 51

Quality function deployment (QFD),
        68–69, 239
Quality-of-life indicators, in control panel,
        204–5
Quantification of customer needs, 90
Questionnaire, for measuring COQ, 126–27

Reengineering, 213
Referent power of satisfaction, 67–68
Regulations, effect on control panel, 202–3
Resources, allocating, 215
Response time, 90
Responsibilities, jobs and, 187
Results, performance measures and, 180–83
Revenue, as performance measure, 182
Review, and vertical alignment, 44
Rework, 151–52
Right and wrong, versus efficient and
        effective, 117
Roll up approach, 46
Ronfeldt, David, 170
Rubbermaid
    mission statement of, 30
    value statement of, 32
    vision statement of, 33

Sales force
    performance measures for, 182
    role in improving products, 145–50
Sales process story board, 147–50
Sales reports, 145–47
Satisfaction
    customer, 64–65, 67–68
    employee, 203
    limitations as performance metric, 191
    and profitability, 199–200
Scientific management, 160–62, 183
Second Industrial Revolution, 160–61, 183
Security of information, 213
Sensors, 102–4, 209
Service Quality Index (SQI), 201–2
Services, future trends for, 234
Service standards, 104–8, 110
Shewhart, Walter, 16, 140
Shewhart Cycle, 140
Silicon Valley, control panel example, 204–5
Skill/knowledge evaluation table, 172, 173
Software companies, 150–51, 205–6
Software Engineering Institute ratings, 206
Software products, 54, 64
Solectron, mission statement of, 30
Specialization, 162
Specifications, creating, 93–94, 95
Staff meetings, 195
Stakeholders, 4
Standards, 91, 206
Statistical process control, 211
Stock market, 233
Stock price, 199
Story boards, 47
Strategic partnering, 37, 59
Strategic planning, 39, 156, 181
Strategic selling, 147–50
Strategy, improvement and, 136, 142
Strategy creep, 142
Subprocess, 186
Subtask, 187
Success, 19–20, 228–29
Supervisor, traditional responsibilities
        of, 166
Suppliers
    in critical process, 98, 99–101
    in customer chain, 84
    effect on price, 59
Support indicators, 214–15

Task, defined, 187
Tax Systems Modernization program,
        230–31
Taylor, Frederick, 160, 161–62, 232, 233
Teams
    building control panels, 212
    and continuous improvement, 137
    evolving beyond, 169
    measuring performance of, 192–93
    principles of, 165–69
    types of, 166

Teamwork, in Information Age, 222
Technology, as critical success factor, 37
3M, value statement of, 31
Time and motion study, 160, 162
Toffler, Alvin, 11, 14–15, 135
Total quality management, 58, 76–77
Training
    continuous improvement and, 136–38
    of leaders, 165, 261–63
    versus continuous learning, 193–94
Transactions, net value of, 15
Translating customer needs, 91–92
Tribus, Myron, 111
Turf battles, 216
Turnover, employee, 125, 257

Understanding, use of control panels to
        promote, 216–18
United Nations, 225
United States Army, Center for Army
        Leadership, 261–62
Unit performance, measuring, 181, 192–93
Utility company, control panel example,
        202–3

Value
    adding, 37, 55–56
    attributes and importance of, 14–16
    as basis for decisions, 237
    as criterion for product/service selection,
        1, 14
    future drivers and measures of, 229
    increasing, 37
    measuring, 57–64, 69–74, 239–40, 241
    monitoring, 239–45
    perceived, 61–64, 239–40, 241
    versus price, 199
Value added, 10, 123–25
Value-added chain, 165
Value-added processes, 79–82, 185

Value formula, 15, 57–64
Value management, 2, 8–9
Values
    for military leaders, 262
    of organizations, 28, 31–32
Vertical alignment, 2, 6–7, 41–44
Vietnam War, as example of strategic failure,
        17–18
VISA, as example of chaordic organization,
        171–72
Vision
    control panels and, 44–47, 212
    defined, 28, 29
    defining, 32–35
    displaying progress toward, 44–47
    global, 225–26
    national, 226
Voice of the customer (VOC)
    described, 4
    improvement and, 145, 258
    methodology of, 68–69, 239–44
    See also Customers

War room concept, 10, 219, 220
Waste, eliminating, 151–52
Wealth, creation of, 16–17, 228
Wisdom, 11, 12, 197, 221
Won-lost reports, 145–47
World Wide Military Command and Control
        System, 207

Xerox
    mission statement of, 31
    value statement of, 32

Zone of anger, 65
Zone of dissatisfaction, 65
Zytec Corporation, mission statement of,
        225

READER FEEDBACK

Fax to ASQ Quality Press Acquisitions: 414–272–1734

Comments and Areas for Improvement:
Value Leadership: Winning Competitive Advantage in the Information Age

Please give us your comments, feedback, and suggestions for making this book more useful. We believe in the importance of continuous improvement and in meeting your needs. Your comments will help determine what improvements can be made in all ASQ Quality Press books.

Please share your opinion by circling the number below:

Ratings of the book	Needs Work		Satisfactory		Excellent	Comments
Structure, flow, and logic	1	2	3	4	5	
Content, ideas, and information	1	2	3	4	5	
Style, clarity, ease of reading	1	2	3	4	5	
Held my interest	1	2	3	4	5	
Met my overall expectations	1	2	3	4	5	

I read the book because:

The best part of the book was:

The least satisfactory part of the book was:

Other suggestions for improvement:

General comments:

Name/Address/Phone (optional):

Thank you for your feedback. If you do not have access to a fax machine, please mail this form to: ASQ Quality Press, 611 East Wisconsin Avenue, P.O. Box 3005, Milwaukee, WI 53201–3005 Phone: 414–272–8575